Key Concepts in
Leisure Studies

Recent volumes include:

Key Concepts in Medical Sociology
Jonathan Gabe, Mike Bury and Mary Ann Elston

Fifty Key Concepts in Gender Studies
Jane Pilcher and Imelda Whelahan

Key Concepts in Social Research
Geoff Payne and Judy Payne

Forthcoming titles include:

Key Concepts in Critical Social Theory
Nick Crossley

Key Concepts in Urban Studies
M. Gottdiener and Leslie Budd

The SAGE Key Concepts series provide students with accessible and authoritative knowledge of the essential topics in a variety of disciplines. Cross-referenced throughout, the format encourages critical evaluation through understanding. Written by experienced and respected academics, the books are indispensable study aids and guides to comprehension.

DAVID HARRIS

Key Concepts in
Leisure Studies

⑤SAGE Publications
London ● Thousand Oaks ● New Delhi

SAGE Publications Ltd
1 Oliver's Yard
55 City Road
London EC1Y 1SP

SAGE Publications Inc
2455 Teller Road
Thousand Oaks, California 91320

SAGE Publications India Pvt Ltd
B-42 Panchsheel Enclave
Post Box 4109
New Delhi 110 017

British Library Cataloguing in Publication data

A catalogue record for this book is
available from the British Library

ISBN 0 7619 7057 6
ISBN 0 7619 7058 4

Library of Congress control number available

Typeset by M Rules
Printed in Great Britain by The Cromwell Press Ltd, Trowbridge, Wiltshire

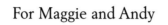
For Maggie and Andy

contents

vii

viii

acknowledgements

This book has been written in my 'free time', and I would like to thank the usual support networks: family, friends, and colleagues, including the excellent librarians at the College of St Mark and St John, Plymouth, and all the 'support staff'. The students have been a constant source of support, challenge and motivation too.

I would also like to thank Chris Rojek and Kay Bridger, Susan Dunsmore, the first-class copy editor, and the production staff at Sage for their patience, good humour and help.

ix

Selecting key concepts obviously involves making choices about what to include and how to structure the discussion. The choices in each case are likely to be controversial, and this is to be expected. Leisure studies is not a subject with agreed or fixed boundaries, but one which focuses on different topics and different concepts at different times. These topics and concepts overlap with others discussed in physical education, tourism and sport. In its broader conceptions, 'leisure' also includes activities that are analysed by media studies and the social sciences, history and economics. Indeed, according to recent commentaries, the experience of leisure and its pleasures can be detected in most human activities, including activities which go on at work. I tend to favour this broadest of definitions myself, so that studying leisure involves studying a very broad range of activities indeed; in this book, we examine activities which include eating, visiting heritage sites, playing electronic games, consuming pornography, and getting bodies tattooed or pierced. It follows that one of the challenges of studying topics like this is that sometimes a detached stance is required, one that does not involve making immediate value judgements of support or condemnation.

On a more technical level, there have been occasional discussions among academics about where the boundaries of leisure studies should lie. At one stage, for example, there was a suggestion that the subject should be virtually replaced by the characteristic arguments and topics developed in cultural studies. Some people think that a strict boundary should be maintained between leisure studies and tourism, or between leisure studies and media studies, while others would suggest the opposite. To some extent, these academic disputes reflect opinions and policies outside the academy as well. Government policy can almost force a focus on particular kinds of activities which they define and fund as 'leisure', most spectacularly in the debates in the 1980s about how we were moving towards a 'leisure society', which preferred certain kinds of socially functional leisure in order to compensate for the decline of traditional patterns of work. There is also the argument that leisure studies is a 'teaching object', to borrow a debate from cultural studies. This means that the topics of leisure studies are shaped more by the internal requirements of universities and their courses than by any

1

conceptual framework: the subject has expanded to include the more popular commercial and casual leisure activities in order to attract students and meet new vocational needs, for example. Organizational politics can also play a part as different academic departments compete for resources; leisure can be included under broader headings (the UK Government currently includes it in an academic unit with hospitality studies, sports, outdoor education and tourism), or can go it alone.

I have attempted to pursue fairly open boundaries with neighbouring social science disciplines, especially with sociology, media studies, cultural studies and sports studies. This may involve risk, in that specialist debates in those areas may be glossed or omitted. I have not focused so clearly on relevant debates about leisure that might be found in psychology, economics or management. It is beyond my expertise and scope to venture very far into these areas, and there are much better specialist books and journals. Those wanting to explore those areas more deeply might well wish to begin with the special editions of the journal *Leisure Studies*. Volume 18, No. 2 (1999) introduces some recent perspectives in economics, while Volume 17, No. 2 (1998) discusses leisure, commerce and policy.

I suspect that some readers might think of a 'key concept' as involving a fairly simple definition of a technical term. I do offer introductory definitions, but then move on to consider debates and arguments. Leisure studies does not have relatively stable concepts in the sense that mathematics does, and there is always going to be dispute and argument. However, such activity can look like an unnecessary academic game to the beginner. There are some definite benefits in suggesting different avenues and approaches to topics, though, and for considering concepts as guides for research rather than as fixed labels. The field is an expanding one, for example, and it may be necessary to consider various perceptions of emergent forms of leisure. It is often thought that policy implications follow best from simple definitions and concepts, but premature policy, based on incomplete understanding, can be ineffective or counter-productive.

Finally, I have some suggestions about how student readers specifically might want to use this book. An interactive style of learning is generally held to be more effective, even as far as books are concerned. I do not think that this means we should take 'interaction' too literally, and proceed immediately to 'in-text questions' or suggested exercises, since interaction can often involve 'inner dialogues' initiated by all sort of elements in texts, not just the ones designed to do so. However, it is important that this book offers a variety of routes to understanding. To take an obvious example, although the content is organized in terms of 'concepts', a number of substantive studies are included as well. Discussing more concrete studies and current controversies can be a useful teaching strategy, and some students prefer to work from actual studies back towards concepts or theoretical frameworks. Readers of this book should use the section outlines as a guide to content as well, therefore, or else they might not realize that, for example, the entry on adding value contains specific discussions of selling Nike trainers, that the entry on ecstasy considers dance and clubbing as well as drugs, the entry on effects analysis examines electronic games, and that on semiotics includes analysis of James Bond movies.

Finally, I am conscious that some experienced leisure studies students may well find these key concepts unusual in a particular sense. The material could appear to be less obviously practical or vocational, for example, although it could be argued that it is extremely relevant vocationally to understand the pleasures that commercial leisure can offer, or how tastes develop. Nevertheless, in order to help come to grips with this slightly unusual material, I have discussed some possible teaching and learning strategies in the section on using the book.

3

how to use this book

There are no fixed ways to teach or to learn, despite the emergence of enthusiasms for different approaches from time to time. There has been a great deal of research on teaching and learning, including some highly influential work on approaches to study (see Entwistle, 2003; Entwistle and Ramsden, 1983; Morgan, 1993). This work suggests that students should avoid what used to be called a 'surface approach', which involves putting in a lot of hard work to remember the immediate details such as names, facts and dates, specific quotes and specific examples. This can be desperately inefficient and also heartbreaking on encountering some academic work which is packed with detail of this kind. It does not even generate the kind of learning that is most likely to be effective in terms of gaining high grades, since most university assessment is based on quite different requirements, for example, that students should understand the basic principles of an argument, be able to provide a few relevant examples, put arguments in their own words, make criticisms of arguments, and forge connections between arguments that they may have encountered in different texts. I have encountered spectacular examples of students who have not realized this and who have had a very unhappy and unrewarding time at college as a result, including a student who evidently believed that it was necessary to remember 'all the dates' (which turned out to be the dates in brackets used to reference books and journals). Since just the opening paragraphs of books commonly contain many of these, I began to see why this student had suffered so much!

It is useful to practise summarizing the main principles of an argument, and beginners very often find they first need to learn what these principles might be. The 'key concepts' format of this book offers a chance to practise on relatively small sections of text. Thus one thing that students might want to do is to attempt to summarize each 'concept', focusing on the main points, identifying the main debates, illustrating the points with a few key examples, and learning to read and make notes selectively. The activity of making notes itself might be important, judging by the work offered on writing skills (Learning Development and Continuing Education Unit, 2003). Writing is itself positive and creative, and it involves skills that students will be using a lot, so it makes obvious sense to encourage people to interact with academic arguments by writing about them. Useful suggestions produced by this Unit include taking full advantage of the flexibility offered by writing, for example, giving each paragraph a sub-heading, producing an abstract, writing a question for each section, identifying keywords, re-writing a section in a more popular style, organizing critical thought by writing a question for oneself to answer such as 'I understand this argument, but . . .', and so on. Focusing on 'key concepts' should help students not to be distracted by so much else that goes on in more conventional chapters, including establishing one's reputation and engaging in the occasional scholastic display for the benefit of other scholars.

The concepts on display here are arranged in alphabetical order, and this is a strategy which misses chances to structure them deliberately for teaching purposes. A more rational order might involve placing concepts in a hierarchy, with the most abstract and general ones at the top and the more specific and limited ones at the bottom. A common teaching strategy would then begin with the more specific ones and move on to the more abstract ones. Other common ways to offer concepts in sequences involve pairing those which are in some sense opposed to each other, so that a debate can be pursued.

It is useful to remind students that they can impose their own order, according to their own preferences, including these sequences or clusters if necessary. It might be useful, for example, to consider 'postmodernism' as a concept at a higher level of generality than concepts such as 'hyperreality', and note that it is also used in more specific discussions of topics such as 'heritage', or 'Disneyfication'. This offers readers the opportunity to impose their own sequences and choose the best way to read about these concepts. You might want to read the more specific discussions first and then come to the more abstract one with a knowledge of typical 'applications', or start with the general concept and work back to see how it is 'applied', or even oscillate between the two. To take another example, concepts such as 'gender', 'race' and 'social class' can be grasped separately and then grouped together under a more general concept 'social inequality' or 'social difference' – here, the reader supplies the more general concept, which is an excellent way to interact with the text.

If my suggestions about the skills required to do well in academic assessment are correct, readers might also consider organizing their work accordingly, and try to structure debates around concepts. Which is the more important social division, for example, among the three we mentioned in the preceding paragraph? How would a general approach like postmodernism or gramscianism enable us to see how 'race', class and gender and their effects on leisure are related? What are the differences between postmodernism and gramscianism in this respect? On another tack, the entry on figurationalism uses examples such as sport and food to demonstrate its approach – are there any other areas where it might usefully be applied? Are the functionalists right to think that their approach can illuminate all the other examples – how would they attempt to grasp the work on 'the gaze', and how resistant are the problems identified in the entry on leisure policy? To take yet another sequence, I have discussed some examples of the semiotics of tourist brochures and mainstream movies, but what of the semiotics of the sports ceremony? Is it possible to take a theme such as gender, and track it through a number of other discussions, or to examine different types of methodology used and developed in different entries? The great strength of the alphabetical list is in enabling many strategies and sequences like this, and I merely hint at some possibilities in suggesting connections with other entries as we go along.

The relationships between the concepts can also be depicted pictorially, as a concept map (students might have come across more specific examples of diagrams used like this in 'mind mapping' study skills sessions). You take a cluster of concepts and try to map the relations between them, perhaps in terms of generality and specificity, or by asking which ones differ radically from each other and why. I became involved with a project to develop concept maps as a curriculum design tool while working at the Open University, and noted the superiority of the technique as against the far more common practice of setting objectives or learning outcomes for teaching sequences or books. To summarize the debate in the form of a homely analogy, the latter offer a set of signposts to help students navigate the terrain, while the former provide much more information in the form of a map. I would be very interested to see if and how readers construct their own concept maps with this book.

Finally, I have also provided some additional material on my personal website (Harris, 2003). I have long been interested in taking advantage of the facilities offered by electronic teaching, and considering what sort of electronic documents might be best developed. I have provided 'reading guides' – reviews of various books and articles I have read over the years – and I have some examples associated specifically with this book (see http://www.arasite.org/keyconc.html). I can add more as I keep reading and you can read them there in the future. These, together with some suggestions for further reading in this text itself, indicate ways to develop critical interactions with the literature more widely.

7

REFERENCES

Entwistle, N. (2003) 'Promoting Deep Learning through Teaching and Assessment: Conceptual Frameworks and Educational Contexts' [online] http://www.ed.ac.uk/etl/docs/entwistle2000.pdf.

Entwistle, N. and Ramsden, P. (1983) *Understanding Student Learning*, London: Croom Helm.

Harris, D. (2003) 'Dave Harris (and Colleagues): Essays, Papers and Courses' [online] http://www.arasite.org/.

Learning Development and Continuing Education Unit (2003) [online] http://www.thinkingwriting.qmul.ac.uk.

Morgan, A. (1993) *Improving Your Students' Learning: Reflections on the Experience of Study*, London: Kogan Page.

8

Key Concepts in Leisure Studies

Adding Leisure Values

> *The term 'adding value' refers here to a number of processes integrated together in modern production and consumption. Goods are consumed not just for their immediate use, but because they are somehow associated with additional values. This also increases their economic value.*

Section Outline: *The basic mechanisms. The Sony Walkman, Nike products and Barbie dolls as examples. Commodification and re-enchantment. The ability of consumers to add (sometimes competing) values.*

This process is usually seen as a recent development, once the economies of advanced industrial societies moved beyond supplying immediate needs, and is displayed particularly well in the case of leisure goods. The Sony Walkman, for example, appeared as one of the first commodities produced by the company to be devoted entirely to leisure. Before then, recording devices had obvious and immediate functions – to record music or speech for some later use by broadcasting companies or other businesses. The Walkman, however, had no immediate functional purpose and there was some doubt initially about who would want a portable cassette playing and recording device. Let us consider the problem slightly more abstractly at first: many of the goods around today have acquired particular qualities associated with the areas of choice, freedom, pleasure and enjoyment.

Anyone who has studied leisure will recognize these areas immediately. They are the defining values of leisure itself, at least in normal common-sense usage. Academics find it difficult to actually pin down what the characteristics of leisure are, and several entries in this book explore the many alternatives – the entry on **work–leisure** perhaps most of all. For business and for the consumer, there is no need to develop any kind of academic rigour. The common and widespread view of leisure, as an area of freedom, choice, self-expression and pleasure can be

11

developed very nicely as a source of values to add to particular goods. If you can persuade somebody that buying a miniaturized cassette player, a sophisticated mobile phone or set of expensive trainers will bring the sense of having fun and being allowed to express oneself, then leisure values have been added. It is clear that some companies, who specialize in the production of leisure goods, have attempted to do precisely this, to sell their goods with the promise that they will lead to leisure in the widest sense.

This is seen most clearly, perhaps, in advertising campaigns. Goods are displayed in a leisure context and are seen being used by people who are clearly having fun. They are often young and attractive people who display no guilt, anxiety, or reservation about using luxury items in order to enjoy themselves. Williamson (1978) explains that advertising involves a transfer of qualities between the attractive people doing leisure, and the actual goods that they are displaying in the process. All the values of fun, freedom, and self-expression become associated with the miniaturized cassette player, the glass of lager, the new Ford Ka, or whatever the product happens to be. Advertisements also need to strip away the less pleasant characteristics of those goods, which is why we almost never see any goods actually being produced – production carries meanings that relate to hard work, hierarchy, dour business practices, low wages, and pollution. The leisure goods in advertisements just appear as if by magic.

It is for this reason that advertising and promotional work have become fully integrated into the production of some highly successful leisure goods. Background social and economic changes have made this possible, notably the globalization of production. Leisure goods might well be physically assembled in low-wage areas of the world, but those symbolic activities that add the most value are usually located in the more affluent areas of Japan, Europe, or the USA. For this reason it is often well worth exploring the production dimensions of leisure goods, despite the clever attempts to conceal production from the eyes of the public, as in the work we discuss in the section on **McDonaldization**. It is also possible to encounter analyses of production mechanisms when discussing goods produced in Japan in particular: the cluster of economic and social processes that have led to highly successful production is sometimes known as 'Japanization', and has been widely imitated elsewhere (see Amin, 1994).

For highly successful products, such as the Walkman or Nike trainers, the process of adding value actually starts with production. Japanese electronic goods are famous for their quality, and the business of adding quality begins right at the heart of the production process: all members

12

of the workforce get a chance to discuss quality and how to improve it, and a constant surveillance system checks on the work being produced. In their analysis of the success of the Walkman, Du Gay et al. (1997) also show how the engineers themselves were informed of the marketing and consumer end of the operation, and were expected to build these aspects into the original design. In one example, it became apparent that users of the early Walkman wanted to listen to cassettes entirely on their own, and not, as the manufacturers had originally thought, as couples. The socket that permitted two sets of headphones to be connected to the machine was rapidly replaced, while advertising emphasized the pleasures of being in a private soundscape in a busy world.

In another example, the company noticed that young people were listening to cassettes while exercising, as part of the health and fitness craze that began in the 1980s. In response, they offered anti-roll technology so that customers could listen while they jogged. The WM-F5 version was even waterproofed for people who preferred swimming (see Walkman Museum, 2003). As the original Walkman became common, various specialist models were developed in order to market to niches (including the solar-powered WM-F107 – Walkman Museum, 2003), and also to facilitate the process of 'distanciation' (discussed in the entry on social class). People display leisure goods in order to signal similarities and differences, social proximity and distance: a beautiful new miniaturized Walkman can indicate that we belong to an affluent social group that welcomes responsible technological change. Although there have been warnings about ill-effects (see Hearing Walkman, 2003), Sony has largely avoided the adverse publicity of Nike and Barbie, which we consider below.

It is this ability to follow through the whole cycle of production, advertising and consumption that Du Gay et al. say explains the great success of Sony in its expansion into the leisure area. Du Gay et al. use the term 'articulation' to explain the ways in which the company managed to connect the different stages together into a coherent programme: this particular term carries some additional theoretical baggage, as we show in the entry on **articulation** itself.

There are many other examples of more conventional rational business practice to add to this cultural work, including Sony's decision to position itself as a global company, not a particularly Japanese one, by changing its name and expanding into the American economic system. For those interested in discussions of the tremendous amount of business activity involved in successful leisure production, Sheff's (1993) analysis of Nintendo offers a very detailed account of the mergers, rivalries, ways of

13

dealing with competition, and global positioning undertaken in the rapid rise of this company.

To take another example of adding value, the spectacular success of the Nike Company has been charted by Goldman and Papson (1998). To summarize drastically, it is based upon recognition of the leisure uses of athletic sportswear, which opened up a huge market, much larger than would be provided if only athletes and sports peole were considered. No-one now needs to be a runner or a tennis player to be able to buy high status trainers or sportswear. The heroic, sporting, and fantasy-based values associated with sport have become located in the clothing that is worn. That clothing in turn can be bought by anyone who can afford it, and the company geared up to produce goods effectively and cheaply, and to distribute them efficiently on a global scale. For Goldman and Papson, the same kind of circuit is established between production, distribution and consumption as with Sony, involving the co-ordination of activities across the world.

Goldman and Papson also analyse the particular effectiveness of Nike advertising. As is well known, Nike signed up famous sports people to sponsor their products in a fairly obvious way: the charisma and popularity of a Dennis Rodman or a Tiger Woods could be transferred, in that magical and irrational world of the advertisement, to the products. Fans would buy the goods in order to reinforce their imaginary and fantastic identifications with those celebrities. Perhaps some fans even thought, in a way that would not survive rational consideration, that Nike trainers or baseball caps would help them to play better as well. Nike advertising worked hard to establish their logo and slogan more generally. Both were suitably vague, 'empty signifiers', which permitted a wide range of applications. Young people in the streets could feel empowered by the injunction to 'Just Do It!', and any student of leisure studies can easily see the connection with the spontaneity and self-expression that are supposed to characterize any leisure activity.

Goldman and Papson (1998) also indicate that the Company employed advertising that developed an applied understanding of **semiotics** and of the ways in which their advertisements were being read. A relatively sophisticated urban audience, well used to exaggerated claims of advertising, were perhaps already beginning to develop that weariness and cynicism that some cultural commentators have noticed (we discuss some of them in the entry on **hyperreality**). As a result, a different strategy was devised, which openly rejected the simple selling strategies of the earlier ones – thus the US basketball star Charles Barkely apparently announced that he had no intention whatsoever of being 'a role model' for people watching the advertisement, and that parents should be responsible for raising their own children. Other advertisements featured social critics such as William Burroughs or stars such as Dennis Hopper reprising his role as an obsessed madman. These advertisements 'engage viewers in a tongue-in-cheek form of hero worship for a media-literate audience' (ibid.: 82). They connect to the growing cynicism in US culture which 'aligns [Nike] with viewers and against the powers that be' (ibid.: 90). This flatters viewers and helps build up the company's image as sincere, trustworthy, and realistic, encouraging a more rational identification by dispensing with the more obvious and hackneyed hard-sell agenda.

It is interesting to note the latest turns in Nike advertising that have not followed this strategy, but seem to be aimed at niche marketing. There is the chance to individualize your own trainers, for example (see Nike iD, 2003), or to buy ultra-lightweight trainers with a very short life (the suggestion being that you would use these to do serious competitive sports and not just to pose around town). Nike was among the first sportswear companies to market to women specifically as well (see Helstein, 2003).

The case of Nike can also be used to show the limits of even the most successful advertising and value adding processes. There has been considerable criticism of Nike's policy of using low-wage workers to produce highly priced leisure goods (Oxfam Community Aid Abroad, 2004). Nike trainers have been implicated in a series of consumer tragedies, real or mythical, involving people being killed for their trainers, or schoolchildren being persecuted and bullied because they were not able to afford the 'correct' brand. Consumers have resisted the strategy of providing endless novelty and variety. Nike have found themselves engaged in 'sign wars', therefore, in Goldman and Papson's phrase, as have other global companies such as McDonald's or Disney. This must have ambivalent results as far as those companies are concerned: campaigners obviously hope to be able to affect sales and bring about reform, but there is an old adage in business that 'there is no such thing as bad publicity', and in the case of the Barkley advertisement, 'The ad's creators relished the letters of protest it generated' (Goldman and Papson, 1998: 85). It is also doubtful whether those companies sell much in the first place to members of those social groups who are campaigning against them. Certainly, all the companies involved have been able to launch subsequent waves of marketing and promotion which appear to take on board the criticisms and to improve their products as a result.

Analysis of the marketing strategies of Barbie dolls indicates a similar awareness (Rogers, 1999). The producers (Mattel) have generated their own strategy of releasing 'news' about Barbie, such as the launch of new versions or the celebration of anniversaries. They also make news by apparently responding to criticism (with ethnic Barbie, or slimmed-down and breast-reduced versions). Rogers gives an example of a campaign that caused controversy when Mattel released 'Share a Smile Becky, Barbie's friend in a wheelchair' (Rogers, 1999: 99): the resultant wide publicity, not all of it positive, 'positioned Barbie in much the way . . . [that] . . . Elvis . . . [is]. . . positioned', as a brand with universal recognition. The company can even add the pleasures of collecting and completing that are associated with 'serious leisure' (which we discuss in the entry on **escape**): 'collectors account for a substantial and growing percentage of Barbie doll sales' (ibid.: 100) (and see Barbie Bazaar, 2003).

Rogers is highly critical of what Barbie represents as an image of women, and suggests that this image does have effects on children's play and on the current cult of permanent thinness. As an example of feminist reactions to this image, involving a feminist campaign which swapped the voice boxes of Barbie and Ken, see Barbie Liberation Organization (2003). Rogers is also aware that the fantasies which involve Barbie are powerful and multiple. Barbie can offer 'something to many types of consumers' (1999: 148), and, indeed, Mattel picks up on this flexibility in their representation of Barbie as empowering: 'Girls Can Do Anything: Barbie Can Go Anywhere and Be Anything' as Rogers puts it (ibid.: 150). Here, the producers have once more designed in enough ambiguity or 'emptiness' for the consumers to attach their 'own' values to the goods.

The same strategies are found throughout the leisure business. Theme parks 'add value' to their visitors in mixtures of ways (see **Disneyfication**), as does **visitor interpretation** for the heritage industry. It is clear that many critics are alarmed by these processes (sometimes referred to as 'commodification' or 'commoditization', which implies a marxist critique of the capitalist mechanisms driving the whole cycle). It is easy to see why – if even fantasies and the other pleasures are no longer associated with 'free time' or 'self-expression' but with consuming goods, then there are no sources of resistance or refusal left, and we all come to depend on the system. Cook (2001) has pursued this concern with children's leisure goods in particular.

We follow this more 'political' argument in several entries too, but it is worth pointing out that there are other critical approaches which do not involve marxist commitments. Some major new work has been undertaken using the Weberian concept of 'disenchantment' (see Ritzer, 1999), discussing a wide variety of examples, including 'themed'

Adding Leisure Values

environments. We discuss some implications in the work on **McDonaldization** and **shopping**; briefly, Ritzer argues that the rationalization of the social world is universal, involving the transformation of leisure as well as work. One consequence is growing consumer resistance to the cold and inhuman nature of this process, so that they become 'disenchanted' as the world loses its subjectivity and its mystery. Leisure organizations in particular respond by adding values back in, so to speak, as 're-enchantment'. Shopping malls take on the air of 'cathedrals of consumption', and become places for recreational shopping, or baseball stadia add elements of heritage or nostalgia (see Ritzer and Stillman, 2001).

This is still pretty manipulative, of course, but there could be yet another wave of consumer disenchantment with these added values too. Overall, the creation of meaning and the addition of values to experience may not just be confined to the specialists employed by big companies – after the shifts in culture that we might call **postmodernist**, many more resources are available for us all to do it.

FURTHER READING

You can follow up any of the readings summarized here, such as Goldman and Papson (1998), Ritzer (1999), or Rogers (1999), or research the consumer controversies on some of the associated websites such as Just Stop It! (2003) or Barbie Liberation Organization (2003).

REFERENCES

Amin, A. (ed.) (1994) *Post-Fordism: A Reader*, Oxford: Basil Blackwell.
Barbie Bazaar (2003) [online] http://www.barbiebazaar.com/
Barbie Liberation Organization (2003) [online] http://www.struggle.net/barbie.php
Cook, D. (2001) 'Exchange Value as Pedagogy in Children's Leisure: Moral Panics in Children's Culture at Century's End', *Leisure Sciences*, 23: 81–98.
Du Gay, P., Hall, S., James, L., Mackay, H. and Negus, K. (1997) *Doing Cultural Studies: The Story of the Sony Walkman*, London: Sage in association with the Open University Press.
Goldman, R. and Papson, S. (1998) *Nike Culture*, London: Sage.
Gottdiener, M. (1995) *Postmodern Semiotics: Material Culture and the Formations of Postmodern Life*, Cambridge, MA.: Blackwell.
Hearing Walkman (2003) [online] http://www.youth/hearit/org/page.dsp?forside= yes&area=853
Helstein, M. (2003) 'That's Who I Want To Be: The Politics and Production of Desire Within Nike Advertising to Women', *Journal of Sport and Social Issues*, 27 (3): 276–92.
'Just Stop It! (2003) [online] http://www.geocities.com/Athens/Acropolis/5232/

Keyconcepts

Nike iD (2003) [online] http://freestyle.nike.com/id-shop/exit/english/exit.html
Oxfam Community Aid Abroad (2004) [online] http://www.caa.org.au/campaigns/nike/
Ritzer, G. (1999) *Enchanting a Disenchanted World: Revolutionizing the Means of Consumption*, Thousand Oaks, CA: Pine Forge Press.
Ritzer, G. and Stillman, T. (2001) 'The Postmodern Ballpark as a Leisure Setting: Enchantment and Simulated De- McDonaldization', *Leisure Sciences*, 23: 99–113.
Rogers, M. (1999) *Barbie Culture*, London: Sage.
Sheff, D. (1993) *Game Over: Nintendo's Battle to Dominate an Industry*, London: Hodder and Stoughton Ltd.
Walkman Museum (2003) [online] http://pocketcalculatorshow.com/walkman/museum/html.
Williamson, D. (1978) 'Language and Sexual Difference', *Screen*, 28 (1): 10–25.

Articulation

A process by which concepts, meanings, interpretations, or practices get joined together into politically and culturally meaningful sequences or structures. Sequences take place over time, while structures refer to elements joined together across space, as it were. A particular way of joining together such elements for gramscian analysis.

18

Section Outline: *General mechanisms of cultural articulation from semiotics. Particular* **gramscian** *(CCCS, Stuart Hall) arguments on modern marxist analyses of youth cultures and political ideologies. Problems and incoherencies.*

This kind of joining together is a crucial way in which human beings make sense of their world. In brief, any new event is joined together with more familiar events in order to make sense of the new. A number of different perspectives in sociology and psychology have pursued this basic insight in a number of ways.

Some approaches in sociology study human consciousness and how it manifests itself in action. Human action depends on people attaching meanings to what they do, and so it becomes important to examine how these meanings are articulated together. In one approach, humans possess a unique capacity to combine and compare present events in consciousness with those of the past (we discuss this further in the entry on **fantasy**). Thus I come to understand my experiences as a visitor to Disney by drawing upon my previous experiences as a tourist and a traveller. Gottdiener (1995) has developed this approach using a particular kind of American **semiotics** to explain the popularity of the Disney visit. Briefly, as soon as visitors arrive, they begin to make favourable comparisons with other tourist destinations; Disney sites are usually perceived as much safer, cleaner, and more welcoming.

There are other studies that point to the fundamental mechanisms of human conversation as crucial in this process of joining events so as to make sense of them. Thus, in his analysis of the 'documentary method', Garfinkel (in Manis and Meltzer, 1972) points to the skilled and creative ways in which we try to ascribe meaning to conversations by seeing them in terms of relations to some underlying 'document' which we think lies beneath the conversation of the other. Most of the practical examples here refer to interactions between students and counsellors, or between various officials and their clients, but it is easy to see how conversations in a leisure context (between hosts and visitors, for example, or between players in a game) might be analysed in the same way.

A particularly powerful form of analysis, usually known as 'structuralism', or 'semiotics' takes a different tack. Here, the idea is to see how meanings develop in cultural products such as film, television programmes, novels, or other kinds of texts. These meanings are articulated in various ways, and this process provides pleasure for the spectator or reader. It is clear that the **narrative** structures of film are very important in providing pleasurable understandings. We can see this best, perhaps, in the structure of a murder mystery, where the film provides certain insights, some blind alleys, some problems, and then delivers a pleasurable resolution. Sometimes this is a politically loaded pleasure for the critics, since the narrative can also be used to demonstrate the superiority of a political viewpoint as a resolution of difficulties – Bond's adventures eventually lead us to see that male intervention is needed to manage various wayward women, that the English virtues of stylish improvisation are still required in the modern world, or that people from other nations and 'races' cannot be trusted (I am paraphrasing a famous analysis of Bond movies and their pleasures by Bennett and Woollacott, 1987). Tourist brochures, or the layout of them, can be understood as 'texts' with narratives in a similar way (see Selwyn, 1996).

I have mentioned above that meanings might also be articulated in structures 'across space', and this is another insight provided by structuralist analysis. To be brief and general, individual signs which bear meaning are related to other signs, collected together in whole sets (sometimes called 'paradigms', which is not, incidentally, used in quite the same way as in those discussions referring to different scientific approaches). When a sign appears, it evokes these other members of the set. Thus, when I see the word 'Freud' in a sentence, it evokes all sorts of meanings connected with other German theorists, other psychologists, other work on the Unconscious, and so on. Writers sometimes consciously try to evoke these 'paradigmatic' meanings when they use literary forms such as metaphor or analogy, that deliberately make us think of parallel meanings. Bearing in mind that the term 'text' is meant to be taken very generally, we can begin to understand the ways in which meanings 'attach' to just about any human activity, including leisure pursuits such as watching a football match.

Dedicated fans will not need to be reminded of the metaphorical elements in a major football match – it is far more than just two teams kicking a ball around. Guttmann's (1986) study of spectators in the USA points to another 'literary' form of meaning, when the game becomes an allegory; briefly, spectators see in the course of a game another story about their own character, the qualities of different nations, some sign or indication as to the course of future events, and so on (see also Dunning and Waddington, 2003). For any excessively literally-minded spectators, television commentators will gladly provide cultural material of this kind, and few tourists can escape similar commentary by brochures, tour guides, documentaries, promotional videos, souvenir photographs, and so on. There are also implications for **authentic** experience.

There is also a more specific sense in which the term 'articulation' is used in leisure studies. A particular approach to understanding culture, associated with the Centre for Contemporary Cultural Studies (CCCS), originally based at Birmingham University in the UK, tried to develop this specific sense as part of their project (discussed in the entry on **gramscianism**). Drawing on marxist and other theoretical sources, including semiotics, the project tried to decide how particular elements were woven together into subcultures or, later, political world-views or **ideologies**. Thus in their classic discussion of **youth subcultures**, CCCS writers attempted to demonstrate the influence of both the social class of members, and their age. The effects of class and age were not necessarily combined automatically, or consciously, or in a way which was apparent to members themselves. Nor had someone else combined these elements deliberately – suspects here might include some representatives of the ruling class, such as the media, for example. Somehow, in this case, class and age were 'articulated' without deliberate intervention or awareness, and both impacted on experience in a connected way.

The approach makes sense in terms of a broader interest in trying to analyse the effects of the economy and of cultural elements. The relationship between the economy and culture had long been a problem for marxist theorists. Marx himself had placed a great deal of emphasis on the way in which the economy worked 'behind the backs' of social actors to affect very deeply both what they actually did, and the shape of the institutions which had emerged in society. We can see this fairly clearly if we consider economic behaviour and the emergence of economic institutions such as free markets, but the issue becomes more complex if we want to consider political behaviour and political institutions such as parliamentary democracy, or, as in our major interest, cultural and leisure behaviour. To be brief, the main alternatives seemed equally unsuitable. Some marxists took the view that the economy still did tightly affect behaviour even in these apparently spontaneous and creative areas. Other critics thought that the economy had no important role to play, or that other factors were equally important. Any modern marxist analysis would have to take this sort of debate into account, and we can see the issues emerging in several other entries in this book, including those on ideology or **postmodernism**.

The concept of 'articulation' might suggest a way forward here. As we have seen, economic factors, such as social class position, and social factors, such as age, can be seen as articulated, or interconnected, without necessarily insisting that one set of factors tightly determines the other. In youth subcultures, the argument is that social class is the main factor in providing youth with various social problems (unemployment, alienation), but that age is an equally important factor which shapes a specific response from young working-class people. It would be quite dogmatic just to look at the social class factors on their own, and very non-marxist to look at age in isolation as well, as many rival theories did. In this interpretation, then, specific articulations could be studied scientifically, from a marxist perspective, but without dogmatically insisting that everything must be simply reduced to social class. This is indeed an appealing research programme, with almost limitless potential, but it will bring problems of theoretical coherence, as we shall see.

Gramscian analysts went on to investigate political programmes, for example. These can also be seen as articulations, weaving together various cultural and political themes in order to gain the support of the voting population. Here, we can trace the role of actual agents, political theorists, media commentators, political advisers, and so on. Famous analyses were developed of Thatcherism, Hall (1988) for example, showing how the UK Conservative Party was able to enjoy a spell of 13 years in power by appealing to quite different segments of the population. Thus, Thatcherism contained appeals to nationalism, alongside the appeals to support Britain's entry into Europe in order to achieve modernization; a promise to modernize British society was articulated with a promise to return to traditional values, including those that looked fairly racist on occasion. There was no necessary logical coherence to these policies, nor should they be understood as the straightforward manipulation of the voting public by a small ruling elite. The concept of articulation promised to explain the connection between these elements as partly accidental, partly opportunist, picking up on issues of the day as they emerged, but also somehow connected to the underlying need to modernize the economy. A similar analysis of British politics was also used to understand the immediate electoral appeal of a third party that had emerged in Britain in the 1980s – the Social Democrats. Here, the party programme was seen as a form of 'pure articulation', so to speak, based entirely upon embracing plausible policies, with no connection to any real social base or social movement. The gramscians were quite right to predict the rapid demise of the Social Democrats, and they have been quite successful in criticizing New Labour on the same general grounds (Hall, 2003).

Before we leave these political examples, it might be worth making some initial critical comments. It is possible to see that a successful political articulation must still combine economic bases and cultural elements. Thatcherism did show signs of clever political articulations at the level of policy, of writing party statements and manifestos, and more generally in introducing a whole political vocabulary to describe the social and economic problems of Britain in such a way as to lead naturally to a Conservative vote. Yet there was also a connection with real economic forces in the form of a necessary drive to modernization. But the temporary success of the Social Democrats, and, arguably the longer-term success of New Labour since, seem to suggest that political articulations can have a decisive effect on their own. This makes acute the longer-term theoretical problem with marxism which arises as societies develop levels of cultural, social and political activity which drift away from any roots in economic activity. Marxist analysis of economic forces seems to be less and less relevant in explaining the specifics and the detail of the activity in question.

This problem arises even more acutely if we turn to leisure examples. To revert to youth subcultures for a moment, these seem to have developed more and more specifically cultural elements, as we argue in the relevant entry, so that their original foundation in the problems provided by social classes becomes less and less relevant. Current youth cultures seem to owe much more to the effects of the media, or to cultural materials provided by earlier subcultures, it could be argued. The same point can be made about modern leisure activities such as consuming leisure goods. We do know that leisure goods are produced in a capitalist economy, and so there still seems to be some mileage in a marxist analysis, pointing to the exploitation of the workforce in the production of modern trainers, or burgers, or leisurewear generally. And yet tracing these objects back to their origins in production does not help us explain the considerable amount of meaning and significance that those goods attract once they are bought and consumed. There is, however, an attempt to deploy the concept of articulation to explain how additional meanings and values are actually integrated into production in the case of the Sony Walkman (see **adding leisure values**).

At this point, we seem to have several meanings of the term articulation. A social system articulates effects derived from both class and age (and later gender). Political theorists articulate concerns in the form of an electoral programme. Companies producing leisure goods also articulate their efforts so as to join together good engineering at the production phase, and leisure values added at the advertising and consumption phase. In these later examples there is a definite agent performing the articulation, although there is still a sense in which the economy is limiting or constraining what can be done. Is this coherent and satisfactory, or evasive?

Post-marxists like Laclau and Mouffe (1987) have gone the whole way and suggested that elements can only be articulated by a definite discourse, but this means almost anything can be articulated with anything else, especially given the specialist skills outlined in sections such the one on adding leisure values. Culture in general, and politics in particular, are left rootless, and the way is opened for the dominance of advertising, promotion, opinion polls and spin (which is indeed the position for Baudrillard, discussed in the entry on **postmodernism**). This is a depressing conclusion for all those who feel that some 'real' political issues are at stake, working 'beneath the surface', and which can be analysed with marxist concepts. It seems impossible to have both positions, and critics like Geras (1988) suggest the whole analysis is tactically ambiguous to avoid having to choose.

See also: *posts.*

Articulation

On the theoretical and political level, try Hall (1988) on the end of Thatcherism, and Hall (2003) on the responses to New Labour. For the classic work on youth subcultures as 'doubly articulated', read the Introduction to Hall and Jefferson (1976). On the debates between articulation and various 'posts' including postmodernism, see Grossberg (1986).

REFERENCES

Bennett, T. and Woollacott, J. (1987) *Bond and Beyond: The Political Career of a Popular Hero*, London: Macmillan Education.

Dunning, E. and Waddington, I. (2003) 'Sport as a Drug and Drugs in Sport', *International Review for the Sociology of Sport*, 38 (3): 351–68.

Geras, N. (1988) 'Ex-Marxism Without Substance', *New Left Review*, 169: 34–62.

Gottdiener, M. (1995) *Postmodern Semiotics: Material Culture and the Formations of Postmodern Life*, Cambridge, MA: Blackwell.

Grossberg, L. (1986) 'On Postmodernism and Articulation: An Interview with Stuart Hall', *Journal of Communications Inquiry*, 10 (2): 45–61.

Guttmann, A. (1986) *Sports Spectators*, New York: Columbia Press.

Hall, S. (1988) *The Hard Road to Renewal: Thatcherism and the Crisis of the Left*, London: Verso.

Hall, S. (2003) 'New Labour Has Picked Up Where Thatcherism Left Off', *The Guardian*, 6 August 2003, and [online] http://www.guardian.co.uk/comment/story/0,3604,1012982,00.html

Hall, S. and Jefferson, T. (eds) (1976) *Resistance through Rituals*, London: Hutchinson.

Laclau, E. and Mouffe, C. (1987) 'Post-Marxism Without Apologies', *New Left Review*, 166: 79–106.

Manis, J. and Meltzer, B. (1972) *Symbolic Interaction: A Reader in Social Psychology*, 2nd edn, Boston: Allyn and Bacon, Inc.

Selwyn, T. (ed.) (1996) *The Tourist Image: Myths and Myth-Making in Tourism*, New York: John Wiley and Sons.

24

Authenticity

A state of preferred existence usually contrasted with the falseness and artificiality of modern life. The production of objects, actions and experiences are uncontaminated with commercial motives. Authentic locations are contrasted with commercialized tourist and leisure sites.

Section Outline: *Authenticity as a central term in debates about the effects of tourism. The construction of authenticity in the media and in colonial anthropology: Australian aborigines. 'Otherness' and its paradoxical relation to the self.*

In tourism studies, a considerable debate began after MacCannell (1989) stated that a major impulse for travel was a search for authenticity, the desire to encounter cultures and people that were not contaminated by industrial societies and their synthetic, commercialized mass cultures. MacCannell's views cannot be taken as support for the common distinction between cheap, vulgar, packaged tourism and proper, sophisticated, independent travel, however: that distinction is clearly based on bourgeois values and, increasingly, reflects the categories of the tourist business itself.

Something had happened to place modern people on the edges of their own societies. Rojek (2000) calls this process 'alienation', while MacCannell prefers the term 'modernization'. The old ways of living have changed and disappeared – communities, families, neighbourhoods and occupational cultures are not what they were. All social life is subject to constant change, and it is increasingly differentiated as more and more alternative ways of living and gaining **identity** are on offer. The mass media have a clear role to play here in offering alternative role models and ways of life, in exposing us to different ways of living. I would suggest that the role of the mass media is by far the most important one, although classical work on leisure and tourism tends to neglect it. More substantial social processes are important too as cultures travel to us (a theme in Rojek and Urry, 1997), borne both by visitors and settlers. Faced with such changes, a number of responses are possible – the ones that interest us here involve an increasing role for tourism, and, I would argue, for other leisure activities too, as a source of some dimly perceived alternative, some real encounter with an authentic self and genuine others.

However, the paradox is that tourism itself threatened authenticity, as those on the receiving end developed synthetic and commercialized versions of their own culture specially for tourists: I encountered a recent example of this in the simulated Arab village at Aswan in Egypt, where people donned traditional dress and performed traditional activities solely for the benefit of the paying customers. At the Temple of Hatshepsut and at the granite quarry in Aswan, locals simulate work of the kind once undertaken for real, as they chip at stones. MacCannell (1989) was one of the first commentators to notice that tourism now offers simulated work of this kind as a tourist experience (or real work, with tours of actual organizations, even slaughterhouses, available to the Paris visitor), and he found it sinister: the tourist experience now offers a whole picture of society, with work and leisure and the relationship between them all nicely organized.

This original insight has been much developed since, and the concept of authenticity itself has been subdivided. To summarize the excellent article by Cohen (2002), there is now a concern for the authenticity of 'objects', including ways of life, which has become separated from a more personal or existential notion of authenticity, a perception held by individuals that one is having an authentic experience. In between these two is what Cohen calls the 'social constructivist' conception of authenticity, which opens up the possibility that authenticity is socially constructed, an effect of both previous experience on the part of the tourist, and the efforts of the tourist industry to construct plausible stories about the scenes which are unfolding, sometimes in the form of a very tightly organized 'tourist gaze', as Urry (1990) puts it. Finally, Cohen goes on to point out some implications for the notion of 'sustainable tourism' as it interacts with the discourses of authenticity. Even those attempts to resist commercialization usually encounter it quickly enough; as Munt (1994) points out, for example, 'wilderness tours' offer the visitor an encounter with 'unspoiled wilderness', but only after considerable effort to co-ordinate the itinerary so that none of the other wilderness seekers are perceived as this would spoil the enjoyment of the individual.

This whole discussion is an example of a much larger concept, found in social theory more widely, about what happens when people encounter novel social experiences, and meet others who seem to be quite different and who lead different social lives. There is a real difficulty in understanding others. Indeed, social sciences, including anthropology and sociology, have long tried to develop a reliable method for understanding other people, such as field work, **ethnography**, or special interview techniques.

It is not surprising that most accounts of 'first contact' with other peoples show a considerable lack of understanding, often leading quickly to armed aggression. Even the best of colonial administrators struggled to begin to understand Australian aboriginal societies, for example, to apply European notions of law to interactions with them, to relate to them without just wiping them out and destroying their cultures. To do this, they had to manage the authenticity of those peoples, which involved trying to model it in such a way as would make it compatible with European cultures. Reece (in Chapman and Read, 1996: 28–9) says that:

> Aborigines are both an invention and a product of European colonisation . . . when the British first came to Australia . . . there were no Aboriginals . . . Instead there were possibly as many as 600 identifiable groups or peoples . . . differentiated in their own eyes by very specific kin, geographical, linguistic and other associations.

Attwood (1996) points out that anthropological theory itself helped to construct an image of Aboriginals as 'early humankind' or as 'timeless', notions with clear links to the evolutionary theory of the day, and to early ethnography (itself associated with British imperialism). This image helped Europeans to separate off Aboriginal cultures, ignore them and deny their specificity, playing a major part in the 'great Australian silence' about the colonial period (ibid.: xv).

When encountering other cultures, and lacking a systematic method to understand them, most people are forced to relate it to their own experiences, often quite crudely, at least initially. As MacCannell (1989) notes, if visitors or researchers do not speak the local language and the locals do not speak English, an encounter with authenticity is unlikely to happen.

These debates seem quite similar to ones that have taken place in media studies. I have already suggested that we gain most of our understandings of ourselves and of others from the mass media, but there are some interesting problems revealed by examining how the media actually work. The concern to distinguish between authentic and inauthentic televised reporting still surfaces in fierce political debates about the neutrality of documentaries, for example. A great deal of work has been done to examine the ways in which films actually construct a sense of authenticity and realism, noting devices that range from accurately reconstructing historical costumes and buildings to the less obvious filmic devices such as unobtrusive editing and camerawork, which can lend a 'naturalistic' look to what is a carefully assembled piece of filming. Much work has also been done on showing how the 'realism' of a film or programme depends on the **narrative** structure of the piece, how the story is told in such a way as to deliver a pleasing 'knowledge effect'. This arises when viewers are able to confirm their own accounts of reality in the 'discovery' delivered by the film, and must resemble the 'existential authenticity' noted by Cohen (2002). To take an obvious example, we know, from watching *The Lord of the Rings*, that the virtues of honour, loyalty, and honesty will triumph over all the dreadful machinations of industrialized evil, and it is very pleasant when, despite all their trials and tribulations, the hobbits win through in the end.

Media studies has also done much to explore the reactions of viewers, as a way of investigating personal views of authenticity. We know, for example, that viewers have to learn to use the conventions of film actively in order to make sense of them. We take this for granted these days, but early viewers had to learn about such devices as cuts and fade-outs, close-ups and mid-shots. Rose (2002) helps us to understand the shock of the new conventions by reminding us that many early viewers were quite unable to distinguish between the film and reality, and would flee in panic from a shot of an advancing locomotive. Modern viewers are far more sophisticated, of course, and have simply learned to ignore the obvious artifices in cinema, such as the all-seeing camera showing us a lifeboat apparently isolated in mid-ocean, or appearing in the middle of a battle, for example. Modern viewers also have the capacity to bring previous experiences to their understanding of film, including their knowledge of earlier films – they view the latest Schwarzenegger film with a whole series of expectations and comparisons in mind, based on their viewings of the earlier ones. Sometimes personal experience is engaged, as in the kind of 'emotional realism' identified by Lovell (1990). In this sense, viewing is always intertextual, implying that a range of texts – other films, novels, posters, documentaries about films, websites, video games, memories – are always invoked by any encounter with a film or television programme.

Let us explore some more implications for leisure studies. Some writers still want to insist that there is a boundary between leisure and tourism, for example, because tourism specifically requires an organized gaze directed at particular object (see Carr, 2002). There is also an assumption that tourism involves actual physical travel. However, much leisure activity involves encounters with objects too, including the symbolic or virtual ones provided by film and television. The issue of the authenticity of the objects involved also arises when we discuss **heritage** and leisure. For this entry, however, it might be appropriate to discuss the idea of personal authenticity in particular.

What is it about leisure activity that makes us think we are expressing our authentic selves? Clues can be found in some of the earliest work on leisure that stressed qualities such as freedom from compulsion, choice, self-expression and, later, 'peak experiences'. Much of this gained force from a comparison with work, of course, especially the 'free time' of the weekend compared to that the dull compulsion of manual labour conducted in factories or involving assembly lines. However, this work–leisure relationship as an explanatory concept seems to share as many paradoxes as the self–other relationship.

The suspicion arises again that the authenticity of leisure is itself a socially constructed one: this sort of argument is developed in Adorno's work on free time, for example (Adorno, 1991), which argues that officially approved leisure, in his case the development of hobbies, is really a work-like activity after all. Hite (1981) reported widespread perceptions among young American males that sex was becoming work-like as well, with an emphasis on performance and work-rate. Sport is another clear example of work-like leisure activity, and we consider the effects of **disciplinary apparatuses** more generally. As Marx himself once argued, human work is the authentic form of self-expression, which has become perverted, limited and alienated under capitalism. Similar suspicions inform marxist work on the 'rational recreation' interlude in the ninteenth century in Britain, where more popular forms of leisure, often involving a good deal of social disorder, were banned or regulated so as not to threaten the industrial discipline required of the workforce (see **social class**).

Nevertheless, the notion of leisure as authentic persists, especially, perhaps, in discussions of unofficial or even **illegal leisure** such as drug-taking or crime. We consider leisure as **escape** in another entry, but, to be brief, it is still possible to think of ourselves as truly individual when we slip away from the constraints that bind us to social groups and undertake what Becker (1973) once called a 'moral holiday'. These offer a form of licensed disorder, much as did the carnivals and wakes of medieval society, where we can abandon our normal polite restraint, and get outrageously drunk in public, or leave aside our reservations about ecology and enjoy using a jet-ski. We can experiment sexually, or try illegal drugs, visit a cockfight or bullfight, spend money on ourselves in moments of guilt-free consumerism, and so on. If our tastes turn to more to more cerebral pleasures, we can attempt to lose ourselves in an alien culture, in one of those adventurous encounters with ' otherness' discussed above.

How far can we go with this analysis? Rojek (2000) provides one of the more disturbing accounts in suggesting that one response to a perception of inauthenticity is to turn against the self, to repress parts of it. An unfortunate interest in 'abnormal leisure', sometimes even in outright criminal activity, can result. It is fairly easy to see how the search for oblivion and retreat can be one such response, and how an attraction for illegal drugs can be seen as one way to satisfy the search. Rojek also wants to suggest that violence towards others is another response, one which might explain the persistent connections between leisure activity and violence, whether this is sporting violence on the pitch, symbolic or real violence among spectators off the pitch, or even the search for 'peak experiences' apparently delivered by serial and mass killing. We have come a long way from the search for authenticity in tourism with these examples, perhaps too far for Rojek's critics.

However, whether we can leave aside all constraints and social influences is much more uncertain. That which has been left behind is hard to renounce. Indeed, we have one of those dialectic relations again, as with 'otherness' in general: the whole point and fun of pretending to be a Californian biker for ten days is that one is really an elderly English academic all along. To develop a **postmodernist** twist, intertextuality is always with us, always governing our perceptions – it is impossible to leave behind or abandon our knowledge and experience. As Baudrillard (1983) points out quite rightly, this undercuts the whole notion of authenticity. Authentic and inauthentic experiences alike are informed by experiences and perceptions provided by a range of texts, quite often film or television programmes. Standing in front of the Egyptian pyramids, it becomes impossible to leave behind the many photographs, films, and television documentaries that have already provided interpretations of and lent significance to the sight one is trying to interpret authentically. Otherness has already been constructed in ways which make it familiar.

FURTHER READING

MacCannell (1992) follows on from the classic 1989 work with more examples and a debate with postmodernists especially. Rojek (2000) has the controversial section on violence and leisure which led to much debate with feminists when it originally appeared in the form of a conference paper. Given the frequent appearance of Australian aboriginal people in discussion of the impact of tourism on indigenous peoples, it is useful to look at some history via Attwood (1996) or Chapman and Read (1996).

REFERENCES

Adorno T. (1991) 'Free Time', in T. Adorno *The Culture Industry: Selected Essays on Mass Culture* (edited and with an Introduction by J. Bernstein), London: Routledge.

Attwood, B. (ed.) (1996) *In the Age of MABO: History, Aborigines and Australia*, St Leonards, NSW: Allen and Unwin.

Baudrillard, J. (1983) *Simulations*, London: Semiotext(e).

Becker, H. (1973) *Outsiders: Studies in the Sociology of Deviance*, New York: The Free Press of Glencoe.

30

Carr, N. (2002) 'The Tourism–Leisure Behavioural Continuum', *Annals of Tourism Research*, 29 (4): 972–86.

Chapman, V. and Read, P. (eds) (1996) *Terrible Hard Biscuits: A Reader in Aboriginal History*, St Leonards, NSW: Allen and Unwin.

Cohen, E. (2002) 'Authenticity, Equity and Sustainability in Tourism', *Journal of Sustainable Tourism*, 10 (4): 267–76.

Hite, S. (1981) *The Hite Report on Male Sexuality*, London: MacDonald.

Lovell, T. (1990) 'Landscapes and Stories in British Realism', *Screen*, 31 (4): 357-76.

MacCannell, D. (1989) *The Tourist: A New Theory of the Leisure Class*, revised edn, New York: Schocken Books.

MacCannell, D. (1992) *Empty Meeting Grounds: The Tourist Papers*, London: Routledge.

Munt, I. (1994) 'The "Other" Postmodern Tourism: Culture, Travel and the New Middle Classes', *Theory, Culture and Society*, 11 (3): 101–24.

Rojek, C. (2000) *Leisure and Culture*, Basingstoke: Macmillan Press Ltd.

Rojek, C. and Urry, J. (eds) (1997) *Touring Cultures: Transformations of Travel and Theory*, London: Routledge.

Rose, J. (2002) *The Intellectual Life of the British Working Classes*, New Haven, CT: Yale University Press.

Urry, J. (1990) *The Tourist Gaze: Leisure and Travel in Contemporary Societies*, London: Sage.

Bodies

Human bodies have a social dimension revealed in their appearance, which can help us understand the social significance of leisure activity.

31

Section Outline: *The sociology of the body as an alternative to understanding consciousness abstractly. Bodies, stigma and disability. Body language, bodily regimes and the cultivation of the body: piercing, tattooing, and the sporting body in the work of Bourdieu.*

We commonly think of an individual as a living being whose limits are defined by a body, but it is much more complex than that. For one thing, we have a mind and consciousness as well, and, not long ago, a soul. For another, we live in complex social relationships and our sense of individuality depends a great deal on how these are understood, and how we are understood as social beings – we have a social dimension to our body as well.

A prevailing philosophical tradition in the West has assumed that bodies and souls or spirits are separate entities, and that the mental entities are superior to the physical ones. The Christian notion that the soul survives, while the body perishes, offers a classic example of such dualism, but there are cultural traditions which see consciousness as the defining aspects of human beings, while their bodies are seen as unfortunate lesser partners that offer all kinds of bodily temptations and limitations. As a result, bodies have to be controlled, subordinated to consciousness, mastered. This mastery sometimes was clearly marked on the body itself – the scars left by the whips of religious penitents, or the desperately thin body of the fasting mystic. In monasteries, the body was never allowed to be comfortable, but was subject to the strict controls of what we might now call a behaviour-shaping regime – an artificial timetable was inflicted on the body's biorhythms, the body was ignored, purged or scarified, constantly submerged in cold water, put to hard manual work, and so on. The idea was to purify the mind. My own grammar school expressed this idea and had as its motto *validus in corpore animoque* (strong in body and in mind). We disciplined our bodies with strict timetables, rules of behaviour, military activity and, of course, plenty of exercise in the fresh air.

Before we go on to sport, however, it is worth noting the emergence of a specific sociology of the body, which attempted to chart the social role of the body more generally. Bodies, or the visible surface of them, can be seen as offering important signs, used in the exchange of meaning, discussed in the entry on **semiotics**. The obvious ones refer to gender and age, but there are clear signs of the social class of the person involved for those who know where to look. Thus, for Turner, 'major political and personal problems are both problematised in the body and expressed through it' (1996: 1). Until fairly recently, for example, it was possible to own people's bodies, not just those of slaves, but those of women as well, so that monogamy could be enforced as a form of social discipline, justified as necessary to guarantee legitimate inheritance. Similarly, the mysteries of embodiment in Christianity became important political issues dividing different fractions of the Church. To turn to modern examples, the **postmodern** body has escaped from the old social controls and can be used socially much more flexibly. For example, it now channels 'new emotional intensities' (ibid.: 3), offering signs indicating how we engage in consumerism and lifestyles. As a result, we now treat our bodies deliberately as 'projects', surfaces on which we can display signs of belonging and difference.

The recent fashion for tattooing or body piercing has been read as a

Bodies

sign of this kind of neo-tribal involvement, as well as a sign of being an adult, being aware of the erogenous potential of the body, and indicating a new awareness of, and respect for, the body (see Curry, 1993; Fisher, 2002). Our bodies are now integral parts of our lifestyles and are subject to more and more cosmetic manipulations – plastic surgery (from breast enlargement to hair transplants); dieting, working out; wearing suitable combinations of revealing and concealing clothing (exposing and erogenizing the midriff is perhaps a way to validate youthful female bodies against the proliferation of surgically enhanced breasts and liposuctioned thighs); taking body-shaping drugs (steroids allegedly became popular among male ravers who wanted to show a six-pack as they danced with their shirts off, while anti-depressants put one more at ease with the body but threaten weight gain). Modern youths have had to become skilled in taking those difficult decisions faced by the stigmatized – to alter one part of the body may be to invite additional stigmatization as a vain person or drug taker, while it is hard to judge whether being depressive or fat is the worse stigma.

Perhaps the most fascinating aspect of this new attention to the body is Turner's argument that bodily metaphors are at the heart of some of the most important cultural distinctions. For example, the asymmetry of the body, its tendency to be divided according to left- and right-handedness may be the source of the binary systems of classification that we note as being crucial in the entry on semiotics. Body and soul distinctions produced the extremely important sacred and profane distinctions that are important in **functionalist** accounts of social solidarity. Rational control over the body is a kind of bedrock for much broader beliefs associated with Protestantism, the work ethic, and the spread of capitalism. Dance is an important art expressing dominant cultural ideas (echoed in modern work on dancing and reviewed in the entry on **ecstasy**). Leisure activities such as taking theme park rides, swimming, bungee jumping or trying extreme sports might have the effect of 'putting things in perspective' by reminding us we all have bodies after all. A less reassuring reminder of the foundational nature of the body is also found in the process of ageing, says Turner (1996).

The sociology and politics of disability focus another clear set of concerns. One of the classics in studies of human interaction is Goffman's (1968) work on stigmatization, which focuses upon a range of perceived imperfections, including physical deformities and disabilities, ranging from scarring and baldness to paraplegia, genetic malformation or the results of amputations. Quite the most interesting part of this substantial exploration is the way in which the stigmatized manage their social encounters with 'normals'. The careful control of information and knowledge about the stigma, and a very close attention to the details of interaction are the hallmarks of this management. If interaction cannot be avoided altogether, one strategy is to attempt to be true to oneself while assisting 'normals' to interact without hostility or embarrassment. There is, apparently, a set of rules: assume normal people are ignorant rather than malicious, and thus do not react to offence or clumsiness; try to reduce the tension, perhaps by trying humour, including self-mockery; co-operate by allowing intrusive questions and agreeing to be helped. Goffman also notes a 'disclosure etiquette' – 'a formula whereby the individual admits his [sic] own failing in a matter-of-fact way, supporting the assumption that those present are above such concerns while preventing them from trapping themselves into showing they are not' (1968: 124). It should be added that these strategies are for those who are skilful enough to recognize that they are the appropriate course in the circumstances: in other circumstances, avoiding interaction might be better (or the only technique available), or using one of the ingenious 'passing' techniques to conceal the stigmatizing feature.

Goffman is also frank about the price that the stigmatized pay in managing interactions in this way. It is a skilled performance designed to conceal the pain and sense of unfairness felt by the stigmatized. If done successfully, the stigmatized person emerges as possessing exceptional character, courage, or whatever, but this is equally inauthentic. At best, the stigmatized achieves 'phantom acceptance ... [and] ... phantom normality' (1968: 148). It goes without saying that Goffman is referring to western democracies here – the disabled in Nazi Germany faced a far worse fate than inauthenticity, and no amount of skilled interaction would convince the Gestapo that a Jewish body (itself defined in extraordinarily unforgiving and arbitrary ways) was acceptably normal.

This pessimism is echoed by Hughes who points out that the concept of 'normal' has always required a corresponding 'stranger' or 'other', and that this is rooted in the very cultural strategy and cognitive formations centred in modernity itself (which always assumed narrow and falsely universal notions of 'normal' bodies). Thus 'modernity has had a great deal of difficulty in incorporating impairment' (Hughes, 2002: 576) because of its ultra-rational tendencies and penchant for simple categories: 'modernity and mess are incompatible' (ibid.: 577). Postmodernism is potentially far more liberating and tolerant of difference, although it is still primarily visual difference that is celebrated, not corporeal difference. Apart from anything else, this should warn us against the idea that there are easy answers in policy initiatives such as merely increasing disabled access to leisure without changing the culture of leisure. The interaction with 'normals' (or the more accurately named 'temporarily able-bodied' persons) that this provides is by no means simply and obviously beneficial, although, obviously, nor is the idea that the stigmatized should always stay isolated from others. Perhaps the receiving 'normals' should be 'wised up' first, or the disabled allowed to control the interaction according to their own probably heightened interactive skills?

Goffman has always argued that examination of strategies used by marginal groups can be extremely informative, and it is clear that the body and its social management play a major part in mainstream interactions as well. We have to move away from local interaction as the focus, though, and consider wider structural matters. Bourdieu (1988) discusses the basis of judgements made about people's ability and suitability in French universities, and notes the important part played by 'bodily hexis'. This not only concerns the shape and size of the body, but also the ability to manage it and to feel at home in it – the physical discomfort felt and manifested by cramming working-class male bodies into mass-produced suits is a classic example of visible unease. The recent interest in 'body language' is rooted in this urge to judge, in my view, helping teachers or policemen to find some 'objective' evidence to find out what people are 'really' thinking despite their attempts to conceal it behind words and appearances. A self-conscious attempt to conceal or control 'body language' is one obvious response, and sportspersons in particular know very well how to indicate aggression, confidence, ease or determination deliberately, in the very way they stand or walk (see Light and Kirk, 2000).

More generally, it is clear that sport in particular is centred on 'struggles over the definition of the legitimate body and the legitimate use of the body' (Bourdieu, 1993: 122), struggles which invite participation from all sorts of other contributors, moralists, the clergy, doctors, educators and clothes designers. Sciences of the body emerge, to rival aesthetics of the body. Claims are made about the inner effects of developing the body, turning on the cultivation of leadership and discipline, or the benefits of disciplinary regimes in schools or other total institutions. Controlling movements of the body produces dispositions, which supplement other mechanisms, and are 'reinserted into the unity of the system of dispositions, the habitus' (ibid.: 127). Bourdieu (1977) offers examples from his own fieldwork to support this point, showing how social relations are taught to children among the Kabilya (in Algeria) by teaching them how and where to stand, and how to move their bodies within and through their houses. Different sorts of bodies are the outward signs of these dispositions – in our culture, strong bodies or healthy bodies represent examples of working-class and middle-class dispositions respectively.

Other sports offer chances to relate to the body differently, to establish that one can endure pain and suffering (boxing, see Wacquant, 1995), or to demonstrate a willingness to gamble the body (motorcycling, athletics, dangerous sports). Some physical activities work on the outside of the body and its surface, such as those used to develop '"physique", that is, the body for others' (Bourdieu, 1988: 130). There is a working-class instrumentalism towards the body, while the middle-class preference is for activities designed to maintain and invest in the body as an end in itself. Keep-fit regimes express an interest in scientific and anatomical knowledge about the body (such as that of the specific muscle groups), and demonstrate a willingness to undergo deferred gratification which fulfils 'the ascetic dispositions of upwardly-mobile individuals' (ibid.: 130). Finally, there is the female body that shows the trends particularly, such as the intersection between the concern for health and the concern for beauty: 'women . . . are more imperatively required to submit to the norms defining what the body ought to be, not only in its perceptible configuration but also in its motion, its gait, etc.' (Bourdieu, 1993: 130).

See also: *disciplinary apparatuses, social class.*

FURTHER READING

Light and Kirk (2000) offer a detailed account of a body-shaping regime in their study of Australian high-school rugby. Wacquant (1995) has a good 'application' of Bourdieu in his piece on boxers, and discusses images of the body and 'bodily capital'. The journal *Body and Society*, has a special edition on disabled bodies (Volume 5, 1999). Fussell (1992) has an insider's account of the pleasures and risks of bodybuilding. The Body Modification Ezine (2003) discusses piercing and other practices from the point of view of enthusiasts.

REFERENCES

Body Modification Ezine (2003) [online] http://www.bmezine.com/
Bourdieu, P. (1977) *Outline of a Theory of Practice*, Cambridge: Cambridge University Press.
Bourdieu, P. (1988) *Homo Academicus*, Cambridge: Polity Press.
Bourdieu, P. (1993) *Sociology in Question*, London: Sage.
Curry, D. (1993) 'Decorating the Body Politic', *New Formations*, 19: 69–82.

36

Fisher, J. (2002) 'Tattooing the Body, Making Culture', in *Body and Society*, 8 (4): 91–107.

Fussell, S. (1992) *Muscle: Confessions of an Unlikely Bodybuilder*, London: Abacus.

Goffman, E. (1968) *Stigma: Notes on the Management of Spoiled Identity*, Harmondsworth: Pelican Books.

Hughes, B. (2002) 'Bauman's Strangers: Impairment and the Invalidation of Disabled People in Modern and Postmodern Cultures', *Disability and Society*, 17 (54): 571–84.

Light, R. and Kirk, D. (2000) 'High School Rugby, the Body and the Reproduction of Hegemonic Masculinity', *Sport, Education and Society*, 5 (2): 163–76.

Turner, B. (1996) *The Body and Society: Explorations in Social Theory*, London: Sage.

Wacquant, L. (1995) 'Pugs at Work: Bodily Capital and Bodily Labour Among Professional Boxers', *Body and Society*, 1 (1): 65–93.

Cultural Capital

A stock of unconscious and taken-for-granted 'predispositions' used to guide everyday decisions and actions in social and cultural matters, including the development of 'tastes' in leisure. Like all forms of capital, cultural capital is unevenly distributed. It has a complex relation with other kinds of capital in the work of Bourdieu – economic and social capital especially.

37

Section Outline: Bourdieu's work on education, taste, and social distinction, with implications for leisure activities. Criticisms of his work. Notions of 'popular cultural capital' in clubbing and watching TV. Cultural capital as a commercial resource to make money out of cultural attractions: Disney and city gentrification.

'Cultural capital' is one of a number of remarkable concepts developed by the French sociologist Pierre Bourdieu. These concepts were deployed to examine some classic problems in the sociology of education, such as why the children of particular elite groups tend to do so well in a modern education system which is supposed to select people strictly on the basis of their measured ability. Without going into the sociology of education too far, we can summarize very briefly Bourdieu's account (for example, in Young, 1970). First, children of elite groups do very well on tests of measured ability, partly because measured ability reflects what elite groups know in the first place and, second, and more importantly, children are judged in schools not just on the basis of measured ability, but according to their general cultural abilities as well. Children are judged on the basis of whether they 'fit in', know how to behave, respond to the tasks they are set with good humour and a certain amount of nonchalance, whether they can converse easily with their teachers, whether they feel 'at home' with and in their **bodies**.

These qualities are most easily acquired by being raised in aristocratic families, who pass on a cultural inheritance as often as they pass on capital in the usual sense (that is economic capital in the form of stocks and shares, cash, houses, land, and so on). Children living in that sort of family will simply grow up knowing what is best, without ever bringing those choices and judgements to consciousness. It will seem simply 'natural' to like particular kinds of novels, films, meals, holiday destinations, and sports. Such children will never feel they have to justify their choices, and may well be simply ignorant of alternatives, but they will have the additional bonus of feeling that those alternatives simply do not matter, and that they should not feel ashamed of not knowing about them. These choices and judgements are rarely made explicit, but take the form of practical 'know how'. This prevents them being rationally discussed or criticized, and also has the great benefit of offering a set of unconscious categories which can be used automatically when encountering entirely new experiences: together, they make up a systematic set of predispositions, a 'habitus'. They are also responsible for the fractions, divisions and development of 'a cultural field', which can be used to explain the development of particular sports (Bourdieu, 1986). Sporting activities help to demonstrate Bourdieu's point that acquiring these procedures often occurs at a bodily level – knowing how to stand, how to space oneself in company, how to occupy a space without feeling self-conscious, what sort of body shapes are best, how to think of one's body, and so on (see **bodies**).

There is an early connection with leisure made in this work, since Bourdieu points out that a great deal of free time is required to develop sufficient cultural capital in the first place – no one can develop the right kind of confident yet distant judgements without feeling that they are above worrying about money. Economic security is a prerequisite for cultural security. There is also a sense that leisure for those with cultural capital takes on quite a different meaning. It is not just a release from work, but a chance to further apply and extend the underlying set of judgements and categorizations in a habitus, to try these out on the world. No doubt there are the **pleasures** of being able to locate new experiences in the categories installed from birth. As we have said in several entries as well, leisure activities also offer a chance to display one's cultural capital actively, to engage in what Bourdieu calls 'social distanciation', consolidating one's **social class** position, drawing social boundaries between oneself and others. This is what is going on in those elevated conversations that one can sometimes overhear (or participate in) in the foyers of cinemas, theatres or opera houses as people place and manage each other's knowledge and interests.

Cultural capital relates to a number of other forms of capital, and Bourdieu specifically mentions economic capital, social capital, educational capital, and even physical capital (in his discussion of the body). These combinations explain the emergence of particular fractions in social classes, and also their particular tastes in leisure activities. Members of the traditional elite simply possess most kinds of capital, and have become entirely adept at transforming one kind into another: for them, there is an easy transition between cultural capital and educational capital, since their cultural background provides them with a smooth entry into and a successful route through higher education, as we suggested. While at university, they are likely to stock up their social capital, by adding to their important 'connections', and for this group it will be easy to cash in on their investments, go on to occupy well-paid jobs and positions of power, and thus end with a great deal of economic capital as well.

For other class fractions, there are contradictions and compromises. A particularly interesting group, one that is growing in (post)modernity, is the new petite bourgeoisie, for example. This group lacks much in the way of economic capital, and, because of social mobility, stocks of social capital are low, at least at first. Cultural capital and educational capital tend to be high, although intellectual careers have often been 'interrupted' without leading to elite universities (Bourdieu, 1986: 357), which provides this group with the usual cultural insecurity associated with all bourgeois groups. Thus, the occupations they tend to occupy are those often described as a 'vocation', which provides status compensations. Increasingly, though, this group is found in 'all institutions providing symbolic goods and services' (ibid.: 359). In other words, these are the people who occupy the professions that are involved in symbolic power, such as advertising, public relations, and media and it is this sort of capital that tends to be used as a claim for prestige and differentiation in those fields. The new petite bourgeoisie often also embrace 'an erudite, even an "academic" disposition which is inspired by a clear intention of rehabilitation' (ibid.: 360), especially for those who have fallen from social classes above. This downwardly mobile group takes care to differentiate itself from other bourgeois groups in cultural terms, preferring leisure activities which are 'stylish', or 'refined', rather than 'sentimental'.

Members of the petite bourgeoisie have characteristic leisure tastes, which Bourdieu charts for France (we can recognize some of these tastes as those of the urban young professional in other countries). They are the ones who have fully embraced the 'therapeutic ethic', and the 'morality of pleasure as a duty' (ibdi.: 367). It is this group who are the cultural trendsetters, pursuing 'a practical utopianism': they want to avoid apparent classifications and 'hierarchies of knowledge, theoretical abstractions or technical competences . . . [arising from a] . . . sort of dream of social flying, a desperate effort to defy the gravity of the social field' (ibid.: 370). Analysing the cultural and leisure preferences of this group also shows Bourdieu's attempt to connect social location and gender into the discussion of cultural capital. This group is frequently feminized, in terms of their choice of 'stylish' leisure goods, and in their interest in 'the self presentations which are often an essential condition' for success (ibid.: 362). The import of location arises because the new petite bourgeoisie realizes its assets 'only in Paris' (ibid.: 363), where there are far more cultural goods, and more chances for contact with fellows. Thus, it is in the leisure pursuits of the new petite bourgeois that the strongest cultural and leisure differences exist between Parisians and provincials (and perhaps between metropolitans and provincials in other countries too?).

Finally, Bourdieu suggests that it is in the cultural dispositions of the new petite bourgeois that we find the ideal (post)modern consumer. People in this group are perpetually insecure, never sure that their 'social bluff' will work, much more isolated than members of other groups, not guided by cultural constraint or anything as old-fashioned as a work ethic, nor the notion of duty or continuity across the generations. As a result, they are constantly predisposed 'to consume and to consume the latest thing' (1986: 371). If anyone can develop a flexible **identity** in our society, it will be a member of this group.

It is tempting to go on and on quoting from Bourdieu's massive work, which crackles with insight on every page. I have found myself thinking continuously of his arguments to explain a number of reactions that I encounter every day, including the responses of colleagues to my body, my own response on overhearing discussions of weekends spent in New Age retreats, or the characteristic mixture of 'hostility' and 'panic' from students from non-traditional backgrounds when they first encounter the 'high aesthetic' developed in an avant-garde film.

Bourdieu's work has also been heavily criticized. One sort of criticism turns on its 'sociologism', that is the tendency to explain even the most minute detail of cultural preference or leisure pursuit as due to sociological factors, in this case turning on the possession and distribution of cultural capital. It is impossible to convey immediately how plausibly Bourdieu's work does this, and this is a source of suspicion for critics such as de Certeau (1984). It is too well done, and the suspicion is that the whole thing is actually closely contrived: what Bourdieu does is to provide so much detail that we cannot see the trick, that is managing 'discovery' so it always shows the same mechanisms underneath. It is not a real discovery at all for de Certeau but a circularity, using empirical detail to justify basic sociological categories (ultimately, those of social class), while seeming to work with the detail first, from which the categories emerge. I have explored this critique more extensively, and Bourdieu's response to it, in Harris (2003).

Lash's (1990) critique is more abstract, but we can borrow some of the more specific points here. One is where Bourdieu stands in the discussions of **postmodernism**. He has acknowledged differences between the habituses and cultural fields of pre-modern and modern societies, for example, but has not embraced the full idea of cultural implosion in postmodernism (in other words, the collapse of internal boundaries that we discuss in that entry). He comes close to using a connection with the economy to defend the current boundaries of cultural fields, but there is something distinctive about postmodern culture here. A new mass audience for culture emerges, partly driven by an explosion in student numbers and by the growth in the cultural industries: these changes produce looser schemes of classification, independent to some extent of social class origins.

This point is made specifically by those who have emphasized the role of mass media in providing cultural materials much more widely. Bourdieu (1986) has certainly discussed the role of the education system in increasing people's cultural capital, although he tends to be fairly pessimistic about its effects – people who have been deliberately educated about them, or who have taught themselves, can still never quite feel at home in the system of classifications, can never effortlessly produce 'correct' cultural commentary, and are always in fear of error ('allodoxia'). Nevertheless, there have been changes, perhaps more markedly with 'popular cultural capital', which modifies the effects of dominant cultural capital. Fiske (1987) and Thornton (1995) both agree that Bourdieu has left popular cultural capital relatively unexamined, and both argue that it plays a substantial role. In Fiske's case, circuits of networked knowledge, culture and criticism provide a valuable resource for the 'active viewer' of television programmes, who talk about their viewing and draw upon shared experiences to find their own meanings. There is also the semi-secret shared understanding of the language of emotions that feminist analysts have discovered among women viewers of the melodrama (see Kuhn, in Gledhill, 1987). Bourdieu has minimized the importance of such 'emotional capital' too.

Thornton's (1995) work, which we discuss in the entry on **ecstasy**, points to the apparently effortless reproduction of distinctions among clubbers, who seem to be able to distinguish between one club or one set of musical tastes and another with a similar sort of unconscious ease that gourmets display on finding their way around a menu. However, she sees such popular cultural capital as being deeply influenced by mass and local media (such as fanzines and flyers). It might be possible to generalize from this work too and refer to the enormous amount of material informing consumer choices in just about every sphere of cultural activity: Bourdieu (1986) acknowledges the effects of consumer guides of various kinds, but sees them as having an effect on top of the basic structure of discriminations so to speak – for most people, choice is still limited by what apparently seems natural and necessary.

Finally, there is another sense of the term 'cultural capital' which points to the ways in which cultural assets are commonly converted into real economic capital ones, but by companies not individuals. We discuss the mechanism in general in the entry on **adding leisure values**, but there are specific cases in Zukin's (1990) account. Zukin's first example is the Disney Company. Here, the cultural values of the Disney Company are used to disguise its economic activities. These activities are typical of a global company – take-overs and mergers, re-locations to low-pay areas, land speculation, and so on – but they are covered by the sentimental, nostalgic, popular and family-loving images of Mickey Mouse. One recent image sums this up for me – the Company cut a deal with Microsoft and both CEOs were photographed 'just having fun' with Minnie Mouse.

Another Zukin example involves 'gentrification', the ways in which certain areas of the city become valuable because of some cultural characteristics. Islington, in London, is a famous example: the area remains attractively picturesque with Georgian and Victorian architecture, a village green and a traditional high street, even though it is not far from the City area. As a result, it began to attract well-off commuters. This led to a process whereby shops and services to cater for them began to move in – delicatessens, antique shops, restaurants, specialist food shops, street markets, and so on. These facilities attracted more middle-class families and finally celebrities. In turn, house prices and land values rose, and the spiral unwound once more. This strategy is now widely encouraged in city tourism generally, using almost any facility to launch the strategy – a university, or even an academically certified 'postmodern' area will serve, says Soja (1989). Indeed, a search for 'cultural capital' brings up many websites promoting various cities under that title. Some have decided to use architecture, heritage or shopping centres as 'attractors' to seed the process. Businesses like to locate to areas where their managerial staff can enjoy cultural benefits and, of course, the usual paradoxes are involved: original inhabitants are excluded by high housing prices, and the 'authentic' attractions that sparked off the whole thing are turned into tourist sights.

See also: *Disneyfication, ideology, gazes.*

FURTHER READING

Bourdieu and Wacquant (1992) offer an extended discussion of the concepts of cultural capital and habitus, and an indication of the connections with Bourdieu's wider project. Loesberg (1993) has an excellent if slightly technical discussion of the concept. Bourdieu applies the idea of cultural capital in the essays in Bourdieu (1993), especially the ones on becoming a sportsman, haute couture, and the ways of defining the types of capital in 'The Sociologist in Question'. A controversial definition and some useful insights are provided in work on American sport and social class (Wilson, 2002).

REFERENCES

Bourdieu, P. (1986) *Distinction: A Social Critique of the Judgement of Taste*, London: Routledge.
Bourdieu, P. (1993) *Sociology in Question*, London: Sage.
Bourdieu, P. and Wacquant, L. (1992) *An Invitation to Reflexive Sociology*, Cambridge: Polity Press.
De Certeau, M. (1984) *The Practice of Everyday Life*, Berkeley, CA: University of California Press.
Fiske, J. (1987) *Television Culture*, London and New York: Routledge.
Gledhill, C. (ed.) (1987) *Home is Where the Heart Is: Studies in Melodrama and the Woman's Film*, London: BFI Publishing.

43

Harris, D. (2003) *Teaching Yourself Social Theory*, London: Sage.

Lash, S. (1990) *The Sociology of Postmodernism*, London: Routledge.

Loesberg, J. (1993) 'Bourdieu and the Sociology of Aesthetics', *ELH*, 60 (4): 1033–56, [online] http://muse.jhu.edu/demo/elh/60.4loesberg.html

Soja, E. (1989) *Postmodern Geographies: The Reassertion of Space in Critical Social Theory*, London: Verso.

Thornton, S. (1995) *Club Cultures: Music, Media and Subcultural Capital*, Cambridge: Polity Press.

Wilson, T. (2002) 'The Paradox of Social Class and Sports Involvement: The Roles of Cultural and Economic Capital', *International Review for the Sociology of Sport*, 37 (1): 5–16.

Young M. (ed.) (1970) *Knowledge and Control: New Directions in the Sociology of Knowledge*, London: Collier Macmillan.

Zukin, S. (1990) 'Socio-Spatial Prototypes of a New Organization of Consumption: The Role of Real Cultural Capital', *Sociology*, 24 (1): 37–56.

Disciplinary Apparatuses

Since the work of Foucault, attention has focused on the ways in which social discipline is instilled into individuals in order to make them conform. Specific 'apparatuses' (social organizations) have been developed to do this, including sports teams and gyms.

Section Outline: *Functionalist views. Foucault's work extended into Hargreaves's studies on sport and fitness discourses as disciplinary apparatuses. Current social policy: activity to counter obesity among the young. Problems, including the ability of consumers to resist discipline and gain alternative pleasures*

Partly because of the particular theoretical tradition that informed earlier studies of leisure, it is common to think of leisure as having purely positive functions. Leisure is traditionally seen as a moment of personal freedom and choice, away from the dull compulsion of work, for example, although there are some problems with that view of the **work–leisure relationship**. Similarly, **functionalist** analysis tends to point to the recreational aspects of leisure, the way it helps us to renew ourselves and our relationships with others, to reassert genuine social relations of friendship and mutual respect as a compensation for the more ruthless and competitive world of work. Marxist analysis tends to reveal a slightly more sinister and politicized 'function' for leisure in enabling a ruling class to go on dominating social life (see **social class**). However, leisure has also been seen as a source of resistance to the values of capitalist society, even as a zone of social life which permits experiments with social identities and a certain amount of political thinking of alternatives (Rojek, 2000). To some marxist critics, leisure offers about the only alternative to the alienated social relations of life in capitalism, and this kind of theme is picked up in the use of terms such as leisure (originally tourism) as a 'utopia of difference' (see MacCannell, 1989, and the entry on **authenticity**).

However, some new critical resources derived from the work of Foucault return to the more sinister aspects of leisure as a form of social control. This particular approach is best exemplified, perhaps in the work of Hargreaves (1986). Just to sketch in the background, Foucault (1980) offers a particular analysis of the way that power is deployed in societies. It is not just something that is exercised by a ruling class or its representatives in the law or in Parliament, nor is it deployed entirely negatively, as a force to compel people to act against their will (to echo a particular definition by the German sociologist, Max Weber). Instead, forms of power play are found throughout social life. Indeed, for Foucault, the very existence of social life means that there must be resources of power to make things happen, and thus knowledge and power are linked. The examples that he analyses tend to refer to particular kinds of power, often but not always state-sponsored forms of applied knowledge – official discourses. Thus, the emergence of a particular discourse about crime and punishment leads to widespread changes in policy towards convicted criminals (directed towards reforming them rather than spectacularly punishing them), and the emergence of a whole new set of institutions such as modern reformatory or penitentiary prisons. These institutions in turn enable the development of a particular science of understanding crime and criminals, the better to reform them (Foucault, 1977).

Hargreaves (1986) attempts to connect this particular tradition back to a **gramscian** analysis, of the kind we have seen developed by Clarke and Critcher (see **social class**). Indeed, Hargreaves describes the 'rational recreation' period of leisure policy pretty much as conventional marxists

45

do, that is, as an attempt to regulate dangerous and unruly forms of leisure, and to encourage safer and more commercialized and individualized forms in order to preserve social and political order. Sports such as football offer a 'corporatist' model of the social order, with its localism, its 'myths' of social mobility for the working-class lad (and black people and perhaps girls), and its convenient nationalism. However, he borrows more explicitly from Foucault in stressing the centrality of the need to discipline the body, and he has reservations about whether the class struggle alone is responsible for the developments he cites. This emphasis reappears when discussing more modern examples.

One theme in Foucault's account of modern society is the rise of self-discipline. A shift towards getting people to discipline themselves is just about detectable, perhaps, in the example above about the reform of the prison system: the idea is to use prisons not just to punish people, but to force them to reflect upon their bad choices and miscalculations. In other words, they are to become self-disciplined, to rein in their immediate impulses, to think of long-term consequences, and to realize that it is in their interests in the end to be law-abiding. This is a far more effective way of regulating people, of course, since you do not need to supervise them closely after a while – it is the awareness that they are likely to be supervised (or subject to a **gaze**) that is crucial in producing the shift towards self-regulation.

It is in this sense that Hargreaves sees much modern leisure as consisting of disciplinary apparatuses, offering ways of producing disciplined subjects who will be docile, obedient, restrained, and willing to follow rules and regulations. Perhaps the most obvious examples involve participation in sports, which require participants to follow a disciplined and healthy lifestyle, and to subject themselves to punishing work-like regimes in order to get fit and to develop their skills. However, Hargreaves also talks plausibly about health and fitness crazes, or the cult of the slim toned body that seems so widespread, especially among girls. He borrows another idea from Foucault here and points out that ways of talking about these activities and acting on them can be combined together to form a whole discourse, a more institutionalized way of speaking and acting. Indeed, it is the power of particular discourses to be able to articulate together various themes that ensures their widespread social availability and connections to power. For Foucault, talk about sex, for example, is very widespread in our society because it offers so many chances to launch forth on important social themes – the body, individual self-expression, relations between the genders, family life, care of the vulnerable, sexually transmitted diseases, over-population, the role of the

46

media, anxiety about immigrants, and so on. For Hargreaves, similarly, talk about fitness enables a number of important social themes to be brought together, including some of those above, and, in addition, for a number of commercial purposes to be served as well – the importance of the right brand name for athletic clothing, of proprietary diets, slimming aids and supplements, keep-fit apparatuses including sports centres and gyms, sun tanning and beauty equipment. The aim is to produce not only a socially disciplined subject, but a consuming subject, ready to participate in the extensive consumption of leisure goods.

Hargreaves does allow for leisure activities being pleasurable, but rather like the analysts of Disney sites, and many other attractions, this pleasure comes at a price. As you walk away from the gym with that healthy glow resulting from pleasant exercise, you also take away significant messages about desirable body types and lifestyles. You also find yourself wanting to conform to ideal body types, or feeling guilty and unhappy with your body as it is. You are in exactly the right frame of mind to consume more leisure goods and services.

This sort of analysis represents the kind of academic discussion that leisure students can find quite challenging. Partly because leisure choices are so important to some people in their maintenance of an **identity**, any analysis that suggests that fitness regimes are not a matter of personal choice at all, but the result of manipulation, seems not only wildly exaggerated but personally unwelcome. Again, the challenge is to remain calm about analyses with which you do not agree, and try to assess them objectively. Is there anything of merit in Hargreaves's analysis?

That there are deeper social functions for sport and leisure seems fairly well accepted, for example, although they are usually seen as the wholly beneficial and nice ones I began with – organized leisure integrates young people into social life, gives a sense of social responsibility, offers them a socially acceptable channel to discharge their energies, and bestows definite benefits in terms of health, for example. Thinking in Foucludian terms for a moment, though, it is clear that these often cited functions must involve some deployment of power, if only to act upon people who may be unwilling initially to participate. The claimed outcomes do not look too different either – 'developing a disciplined subject' will serve as a rather more abstract description for phrases such as 'channelling aggression'. I think that for Foucault himself, there is certainly no immediate condemnation of such outcomes, although his position on this is notoriously debatable (see Fraser, 1989, for example). For Hargreaves, however, the development of disciplinary apparatuses such as those found in sport and leisure seems to be unreservedly bad, stifling the creativity of young people, channelling their activities into consumerism, and preparing their bodies for more effective exploitation at work.

Whatever the political objections might be to such analysis, it seems that there are slightly more technical problems. There is an assumption here that disciplinary apparatuses actually do work in the ways intended, for example, and that no-one is able to resist their effects or turn them to their own purposes. This is actually a slightly surprising assumption given the **gramscian** analysis that Hargreaves associates himself with, which does usually allow for some limited resistance to these attempts at social control. Foucault himself has been accused of neglecting resistance, by critics who include de Certeau (1984) and Baudrillard and Lotringer (1987) although he is ambiguous here, and has supported and actually joined organizations aiming to resist the effects of disciplinary apparatuses of various kinds.

Another obvious problem is that Hargreaves has picked the example of sport and sport-like activities, while leisure itself covers a much broader span of activities. Some of those activities do not seem to involve quite the same sort of self-discipline as does sport or fitness. Indeed, if current popular scares are correct, there is an epidemic of obesity sweeping the young in Britain and the UK. 'Couch potato'-type leisure – watching TV or playing electronic games – seems to indicate that the young are perfectly capable of resisting calls for bodily self-discipline! It is still interesting to consider whether Hargreaves's arguments might apply more widely though. Defenders of electronic games have indeed pointed to the 'work-like' nature of the tasks required, and noted the mental discipline needed to achieve high levels of competence (see Greenfield, 1984). Meanwhile, calls for more vigorous exercise regimes for the obese make Hargreaves's point rather well; there is a perceived need for more discipline among the young, which is usually developed in discourses about health, social responsibility, under-achievement and deviancy, as well as aesthetics, and sport and fitness can be the recommended disciplinary technology.

As usual, we need to know much more about what is actually happening to the people who subject themselves to the necessary disciplines of sport and leisure. We might compare Hargreaves here to the work of Bourdieu (1986) which has been outlined in the entries on **social class** and **bodies**. Bourdieu seems to locate the drive to self-discipline, especially of the body, in petit bourgeois groups specifically, and would trace the pleasure in self-punishing gym workouts to much broader sets of 'tastes'. It is not just a desire to discipline working-class bodies. Hargreaves's study seems to follow a purely theoretical path instead of investigating the specifics – marxist and (some) Foucauldian theory implies a general interest in discipline and control of the lower orders, which some articulate spokespersons have managed to develop as modern discourses about health and work aimed at the working-classes. Fitness has become popular, therefore it must all be connected (even **articulated**) together.

We are starting to learn a little more about the **pleasures** of physical regimes too, and we discuss some options in that entry. Much is made of the notion of 'flow', for example. Such a state seems to involve getting so absorbed in the activity that it is possible to close your eyes to the more propagandist social messages plastered on the walls of the gym, and to the more superficial social concerns for beauty and conformity. However, we still lack much in the way of study of long-term social effects of such participation, especially the effects on social attitudes or ways of life.

Finally, as an example of the marvellous flexibility that leisure offers, there have been press reports of a New York gym run by a dominatrix offering an 'S & M inspired workout' (Mowbray, 2003). This is certainly a take on 'disciplinary apparatus' that Hargreaves seems to have overlooked. Apparently, the sessions usually start with personal abuse and then develop into more specialized services: a compulsive snack-eater can be offered aversion therapy by having the snacks hurled into their face, while 'A foot fetishist . . . gets extra push-ups at the Mistress's feet' (ibid.). As one would expect, there is even a DVD for those unable to attend: its intended audience is described as 'fat losers who haven't worked out in a long time' (ibid.).

See also: *adding leisure values, fantasy, postmodernism.*

FURTHER READING

Foucault's work might be explored further, especially Foucault (1980). Le Breton (2000) offers an insider's account of the pleasures of disciplining the body in extreme sports. Discussion of the relationship between obesity and exercise can be found on the websites for the UK Department for Culture, Media and Sport (2003), and for the USA on the Virtual Office of the Surgeon General (2003). Maguire (2002) analyses discourses about fitness and consumerism in fitness magazines.

49

REFERENCES

Baudrillard, J. and Lotringer, S. (1987) *Forget Foucault and Forget Baudrillard*, New York: Semiotext(e).

Bourdieu, P. (1986) *Distinction: A Social Critique of the Judgement of Taste*, London: Routledge.

De Certeau, M. (1984) *The Practice of Everyday Life*, Berkeley, CA: University of California Press.

Department for Culture, Media and Sport (2003) [online] http://www.culture.gov.uk/sport/default.htm

Foucault, M. (1977) *Discipline and Punish: The Birth of the Prison*, London: Peregrine Books Ltd.

Foucault, M. (1980) *Power/Knowledge: Selected Interviews and Other Writings*, Brighton: Harvester Press.

Fraser, N. (1989) *Unruly Practices: Power Discourse and Agenda in Contemporary Social theory*, Cambridge: Polity Press.

Greenfield, P. (1984) *Mind and Media: The Effects of Television, Video Games and Computers*, London: Collins.

Hargreaves, J. (1986) *Sport, Power and Culture*, Cambridge: Polity Press.

Le Breton, D. (2000) 'Playing Symbolically With Death in Extreme Sports', *Body and Society*, 6 (1): 1–11.

MacCannell, D. (1989) *The Tourist: A New Theory of the Leisure Class*, revised edn, New York: Schocken Books.

Maguire, J. (2002) 'Body Lessons: Fitness Publishing and the Cultural Production of the Fitness Consumer', *International Review for the Sociology of Sport*, 37 (3–4): 449–64.

Mowbray, N. (2003) 'You've Been Very Naughty . . . so it's Step Aerobics for you', *The Observer*, 28 September.

Rojek, C. (2000) *Leisure and Culture*, Basingstoke: Macmillan.

Virtual Office of the Surgeon General (2003) [online] http://www.surgeongeneral.gov/topics/obesity/

50

Disneyfication

Characteristic forms of organization involved in running a global leisure business have been developed by the Disney Company, and these have been much imitated and applied by other leisure businesses. This can be seen as converting cultural capital to economic capital. This entry focuses on attempts to understand how history, culture and consumerism are developed by the Company.

> **Section Outline:** *Academic criticisms of the Disney Company and its operations, based on marxist, feminist and postmodernist positions: commercialism and big business; history and tradition; America and international relations. Specific criticisms of the ideological elements in theme parks (with some brief examples of the movies). Comparisons with 'normal' visitor reactions. Academic criticism as elite pleasure.*

The academic work analysing the appeal of Disney sites is almost entirely critical. This can be a shock for the leisure studies student, especially if they have memories of happy childhood visits to Disney sites or Disney films: the critical literature seems either unfair, or exaggerated, or just pointless. Of course, this is only further evidence of the devastating cultural effects of Disneyfication, for critics such as Willis (in The Project on Disney, 1995). Students therefore encounter quite a profound challenge from the academic work, in that their own personal views are also treated as a resource instead of being taken seriously and at face value. The topic is therefore an ideal one to explore the difference between academic and popular perceptions of leisure. In order to fully experience this challenge, you might well begin by just reflecting upon your own views and experiences of Disney sites.

Academic visitors to Disney sites have found much to criticize. The sites offer much more than innocent pleasures to the visitor. Underneath the surface, discernible only to those with special research methods, but with serious unconscious effects on the visitors, lie a whole series of highly dubious ideologies and values embedded in the very structure of the parks, and expressed in the attractions themselves.

First, the Disney Company runs a highly commercial organization, hidden behind a family image. This begins with the clever ticket pricing system, whereby an expensive pass leads to 'free' rides. This is one of the many tricks of consumerism which we all have to learn to deal with, but apparently it impresses children who think that the Disney Company is really kind to offer such 'free' rides (Willis, in The Project on Disney, 1995). Once in the park, as any parent will tell you, there is sustained pressure to part with your money, not only to keep everyone supplied with food and drink, but also to buy souvenirs. As Eco (1987) points out, such consumption can even be disguised as participation in the fun: the shops on Main Street are designed to look like authentic 1920s' shops, but are also real shops, and they want your money.

There is a more general level of support for commerce and big business

51

as well. Big corporations such as Exxon or AT&T sponsor exhibitions that inform the visitor of the importance of energy extraction or communication respectively. They also manage to suggest a new innocence for themselves as mere agents of some basic human drives to develop society: the AT&T ride at EPCOT tells us an evolutionary story as it progresses, with images of cavemen at the start, images of early signalling systems in the middle, and the latest products of the company right at the peak of human evolution, which we reach at the end. The ride is an embodied **narrative** delivering its knowledge effect. Finally, according to Bryman (1995), the rides and exhibitions are telling us, in effect, that the same big corporations can be trusted with America's future as they lead the way into some wonderful utopia.

Second, the Disney Company peddles its own versions of history. Disney history is so one-sided that some critics have labelled it 'Distory' (Smoodin, 1994). If you visit the American Pavilion at EPCOT in Walt Disney World, Florida, for example, you will witness the Disney version of American history, presented to you in a multimedia experience of cameos and soundbites, together with some familiar but highly emotive images, such as Martin Luther King's 'dream' speech, shots of the Kennedys, film of the first nuclear explosions, shots of famous Hollywood celebrities including Marilyn Monroe, and so on. Walt Disney himself appears in this illustrious company as one of the people who have made America great. Statues and animatronic figures express the theme, which is how the natural American qualities of enterprise and self-reliance have shaped modern America (actually rather a contrast to the support for big corporations, as Bryman (1995) has noted). The downside is depicted, in the form of little dramas re-enacted from the Depression, or an ecologically-friendly speech by a displaced Native American ('Chief Joseph'), but the impression is clearly given that these sad events are in the past, that the American spirit prevailed over them anyway, and that the future offers nothing but prosperity and glory.

Third, there is a simple depiction of international relations on offer too, most obviously in the form of the national pavilions in EPCOT. These display stereotyped characteristics of various other countries, in exhibition sites arranged around a lagoon with the American Pavilion right in the centre offering protection to the rest. England is depicted as a series of cottages with thatched roofs clustered around a village green with an allegedly typically English pub. France has Parisian street scenes and another one of those multimedia multi-screen presentations showing sturdy French peasants enjoying agricultural produce, with lots of shots of the French countryside. China is strictly pre-revolutionary. Germany is a ludicrous assemblage of buildings in different regional styles, men in *Lederhosen* and all the other clichés you would expect. Mexico is dark and exotic, and visitors can take a ride offering a potted history of the country, which nearly manages to avoid mentioning the Conquest altogether, and offers a conveniently rapid leap from Aztecs to modern Mexico without the nastiness of smallpox epidemics, colonization and social upheaval.

Fourth, on a more localized scale, the Disney Company represents traditional America, a nostalgic time of real community and real families, one which is far away from modern multi-ethnic communities and modern family life. Critics have noticed the same themes in famous Disney films. To take one example of many analyses, Byrne and McQuillan (1999) discuss the depiction of women in films such as *The Little Mermaid*, and find them horribly conventional and sexist. Good and evil women are indicated by their ages and body types, and there is a transition narrative which suggests that girls become real women only when they participate in consumer society.

There are several other specific themes identified by the critics, including excessive entrepreneurialism and poor employment practices of the Company itself (see Kuenz, in The Project on Disney, 1995). There are also some rather more abstract criticisms of the obviously totally constructed nature of the Disney sites, which relate back to the debates on **authenticity** and a tendency to saturate the public with '**hyperreal**' meanings and messages (Eco, 1987; MacCannell, 1989). There have been specific consumer campaigns against the Company's policies towards clothing manufacture (Clean Clothes Campaign, 2003) and 'family values' (Christians Boycotting Disney, 2003). However, the overall impression of academic critics is summarized best by Fjellman: 'I think this 27,400 acres of central Florida swamp and scrub forest . . . is the most ideologically important piece of land in the United States. What goes on here is the quintessence of the American way' (1992: 10).

It might be useful at this point to return to the perception of the typical visitor, if there is such a thing. Some very modest local research of my own in Plymouth, UK, found that there were a few gripes about the prices of drinks, and a few asides about the exaggerations of American hospitality, especially the phoney wish that visitors 'have a nice day'. However, no-one seemed to share the academic critics' perceptions of ideological saturation, and no-one felt particularly manipulated into taking a particular view of America's role in world history. Some did display a tendency to reproduce the Disney slogans about their experiences, as fulfilling a 'dream', for example, and there was some evidence that Disney had persuaded them that no childhood would be complete without a visit. The reaction to a quick summary of most of the academics' views was as described above – they were seen as exaggerated, mean-spirited, or as missing the whole point of the Disney experience, which was to have fun.

There is a certain mean-spiritedness about some of the academic commentaries, in my view, and some academics seemed determined not to enjoy themselves, shown best in their rather self-righteous accounts of their activities as 'work' – Klugman (The Project on Disney, 1995: 14) felt both anxious and 'professional' because 'everybody else was on holiday and just goofing off, whereas I felt this obligation to make my family's sacrifices worthwhile'. This claim to be doing work also leads to another that therefore the results are more reliable than the impressions gathered by people who are merely on holiday – we might want to agree with this one. Yet what is really missing from the academic accounts is any consideration that the visitors themselves might be actively involved in constructing the pleasures of the Disney site. We know that the viewers of films are actively involved, as suggested in entries like the one on **effects analysis**, or **pleasures**, and in the many accounts of viewer interpretation or 'reading'. We also know that the intertextuality of the Disney sites is almost bound to provide a source of alternative readings beyond the control of the Company. Despite the legendary attempts to regulate the use of the Disney images, there are many commentaries, including websites, about the Company itself as well as on many connected aspects of American life, not all of them sympathetic. As I point out in my own contribution on my website (Harris, 2003), I have heard a failing Scottish newspaper referred to as a Disney organization, because 'this dis'nae work and that dis'nae work', while it has long been common in the UK to decry the quality of work, or even of certain degree courses, by referring to them as 'Mickey Mouse'. I am not suggesting that all Disney visitors are capable of ironic detachment, nor that most of them would want to be, but I think there are initial grounds to doubt that they are quite the 'cultural dopes' that academic critics often assume they are, gullibly drinking in Disney ideologies along with their over-priced Coca-Cola.

In virtually all the writing about other aspects of popular culture, this is now the orthodoxy. In film criticism, for example, it has long been possible to offer a 'redemptive reading' of such apparently flawed forms as melodramas and soap operas, and to discover skilled and ironic viewers who are quite capable of reinterpreting these forms. Ang's (1985) study showed that viewers of *Dallas* were capable of seeing that soap opera as a kind of parody of womanhood, and its women stars as female impersonators. In the field of popular culture generally, there have been

Disneyfication

constant efforts to assert the active consumer as a kind of necessary counterpart to the clever and manipulative culture industry. Why is the Disney site such an obvious exception?

One possible answer also reveals something about academic analysis, in my view. It is pleasurable in itself. Academic work does deliver a genuine sense of achievement to the researcher who eschews the normal pleasures of the visit and goes around actively and systematically gathering impressions, doing interviews, or trying to do **semiotic** analysis. There is certainly plenty to get your teeth into with the Disney visit, and producing a publication based on research must deliver a wonderful sense of achievement. There are other pleasures too, ones which perhaps academics are less happy to disclose. It is pleasurable to see a stock of **cultural capital** usefully put to work, and, as Bourdieu (1986) points out, it enables us to establish a pleasurable social distance too. When academics visit the Disney site, we are not going as mere tourists. Indeed, we are doing something diametrically opposed to what the tourists are doing, that is working and analysing critically. We are doing the equivalent of 'authentic' travel, trying to organize a systematic understanding, rather than mere tourism. This gives us a feeling of social and cultural superiority. The final irony arises in the possibility that the Disney Company itself might eventually become complicit in providing this kind of 'authentic' experience, perhaps even advertising itself as the most ideologically saturated site in the world or whatever, precisely to attract a new segment of tourists.

See also: ideology, narratives, McDonaldization, postmodernism.

FURTHER READING

I have merely skimmed excellent commentaries like Bryman (1995) and these are worth pursuing. Fjellman (1992) has a comprehensive if dated set of descriptions of the attractions and some useful accounts of background terms such as 'commodification', 'hegemony' and 'ideology', and he develops a robust Marxist commentary on and critique of postmodernism. A useful shorter piece is Rojek (1993a), and the underlying theoretical themes are followed more generally in Rojek (1993b) and Rojek (1995). Disney movies are reviewed in Byrne and McQuillan (1999). A remarkable piece by Hansen (1993) offers an excellent Freudian and marxist reading of Disney cartoons. The Disney Company's own website (Disney Online, 2003) is another source for news of projects and expansions. There is an account of my own visit as an 'ironic tourist' on my website (Harris, 2003).

Ang, I. (1985) *Watching Dallas: Soap Opera and the Melodramatic Imagination*, London: Methuen.

Bourdieu, P. (1986) *Distinction: A Social Critique of the Judgement of Taste*, London: Routledge.

Bryman, A. (1995) *Disney and His Worlds*, London: Routledge.

Byrne, E. and McQuillan, M. (1999) *Deconstructing Disney*, London: Pluto Press.

Christians Boycotting Disney (2003) [online] http://www.christianitytoday.com/ct/7tb/7tb84a.html

Clean Clothes Campaign (2003) [online] http://www.cleanclothes.org/companies/disney.htm

Disney Online (2003) [online] http://disney.go.com/park/homepage/today/flash/index.html

Eco, U. (1987) *Travels in Hyperreality*, London: Picador.

Fjellman, S. (1992) *Vinyl Leaves: Walt Disney World and America*, Oxford: Westview Press.

Hansen, M. (1993) 'Of Mice and Ducks: Benjamin and Adorno on Disney', *The South Atlantic Quarterly*, 92 (1): 27–61

Harris, D. (2003) 'Dave Harris (and Colleagues): Essays, Papers and Courses' [online] http://www.arasite.org/

MacCannell, D. (1989) *The Tourist: A New Theory of the Leisure Class*, revised edn, New York: Schocken Books.

Rojek, C. (1993a) 'Disney Culture', *Leisure Studies*, (12): 121–35.

Rojek, C. (1993b) *Ways of Escape*, Basingstoke: Macmillan.

Rojek, C. (1995) *Decentring Leisure: Rethinking Leisure Theory*, London: Sage.

Smoodin, E. (ed.) (1994) *Disney Discourse: Producing the Magic Kingdom*, New York: Routledge.

The Project on Disney (1995) *Inside the Mouse: Work and Play at Disney World*, London: Rivers Oram Press.

56

Ecstasy

The word 'ecstasy' is derived from the Greek *ek-stasis*, which is usually translated as 'standing outside' (of the self and of normal life). This pleasurable state can be induced in exciting social situations, especially leisure activities. Ecstasy is also the street name for a popular recreational drug which can induce this effect.

> **Section Outline:** *Sociological work on religious ecstasy. Rave and clubbing and their characteristic pleasures according to Thornton, Malbon and Redhead: social and chemical ecstasy. Different approaches to understanding rave: new forms of old pleasures or postmodern 'disappearance'?*

There are heightened personal experiences where normal understanding ceases to apply, and where some special relationship develops with others and with the world at large. Such relationships are described as being particularly meaningful, insightful, and fulfilling, while one also gains a deeper knowledge of oneself and one's true nature. This unusual state provides great pleasure as the undesirable parts of the self are left behind – the petty worries, fears, anxieties and limits. A feeling of being outside constraint emerges – in the entry on **pleasure**, we describe this as 'jouissance'. Ecstasy can offer an opportunity for learning as well as gaining great pleasure, and therefore plays a major role in social life.

Religiosity has been described in exactly these terms. Based on the analyses in Durkheim (discussed in Ritzer, 1996), religiosity involves becoming aware of a special part of life, the sacred realm, where the most important and deeply shared values apply, and where mundane everyday worries and limits are left behind. Durkheim emphasized the important role of collective ritual in helping to generate ecstasy. Briefly, members of a congregation engaged in a common ritual offer all kinds of subtle signals to each other that an unusual state of mind is about to occur – behaviour such as uninhibited dancing, shouts of encouragement to those acting strangely, and so on. This permits participants to display signs of collective excitement themselves, and these are acknowledged and rewarded in turn by other members of the crowd, so that a collective excitation and amplification take place, until an extraordinary feeling is generated among all participants. As experience of these collective excitement grows, the stages of the ritual themselves can act as signals to the members that a state of ecstasy is imminent. Durkheim was particularly interested in analysing early forms of religious experience, but some contemporary religious experiences can also offer this kind of extra-ordinary consciousness. Pentecostal churches that feature 'speaking in tongues', or charismatic churches that offer 'the Toronto experience' (see Strom, 2003) can also involve people uninhibitedly babbling, swaying, jerking, or rolling around consumed by laughter.

In the entry on **functionalist** analysis, we suggest that this Durkheimian

57

work can be used to explain other modern mass rituals as well, including the collective excitement generated among spectators at football matches. Here, though, we are going to attempt to explore the collective excitement generated among clubbers. This collective excitement and its pursuit are one of the reasons why clubbing offers such appeal to young people: Thornton, for example, suggests that 'Admission to dance clubs are substantially higher than those to sporting event, cinemas, and all the "live arts" combined' (1995: 14–15), and she estimated the value of the rave scene in 1993 to be approaching two billion pounds. Analysing ecstasy as a central experience becomes crucial in understanding the pleasures of clubbing. I should say immediately that we need to discuss the collective social rituals of club life as well as the consumption of the drug given the street name of Ecstasy: I shall use the capital letter to indicate the drug, and lower case to indicate the state of collective excitement.

Malbon's (1999) account begins by insisting that clubbing is an important activity for young people yet one which is routinely underestimated by non-participants, including researchers. Clubbing went on in a semi-secret world separated from normal life, and analysing its pleasures involved new theoretical ventures into areas that have classically been ignored or downgraded as trivial, especially popular music and dance. Malbon argues that clubbing has a context, including preparation for the event, and managing the 'afterglow' on return to normality. These activities also demonstrate the pleasures of clubbing, especially the ability to conceive of oneself as separate from 'straights', such as taxi drivers or parents, and to share in a semi-secret world, removed from both work and domesticity.

Malbon organizes his perceptions around a number of analytic themes based on what happens at clubs. Vitality plays a major part, as a distinctive form of adult play involving self-expression and excitement. A great deal of skill is deployed to manage public dancing, which is vitality's bodily expression, especially in the way that 'interactional spacings' have to be negotiated. Vitality also seems to express oppositional energy to the routinization of normal life, a life-giving assertion and determination to enjoy the moment. Experience of clubbing produces an intense collection of sensations, produced there and then 'out of a mix of bodily practices, emotions and imaginations' (Malbon, 1999: 183). Participants experience 'a flux between egocentric and logocentric identities' (ibid.: 183), as they become aware of themselves both as individuals and as members of the crowd. The latter involves ecstatic loss of self, pleasures which fit the description of 'flow' (see **pleasures**), and something that could be explained as 'tension balance' (discussed in the entry on **figurationalism**). One version of the tension is expressed best in dancing, needing to dance in a skilful way that is not obtrusively different, that demonstrates the requisite level of 'coolness', and combines dancing on one's own and with the crowd while achieving that lack of self-consciousness and fellow feeling that Malbon describes as an 'oceanic' sensation (he reserves the term 'ecstatic' to refer to chemically induced oceanic feelings).

Malbon notes the neglect of music as a factor in clubbing, and examines its role in helping to create imaginary space, to co-ordinate activity, to amplify responses and to manage participation: music has the remarkable capacity to help people develop 'cultural narratives' (1999: 81) which are shared and yet also local and unique. Dance has similarly been neglected, although it should be restored as a 'prominent form of creative listening' (ibid.: 82) based on shared understandings and tastes. Despite this ability to generate embodied listening, dance also requires particular techniques and competences: dancers manage to convey a number of meanings referring to sexuality and personal vitality, for example, and dance acquires a particular status in clubs that are so noisy that normal verbal communication cannot be pursued.

Overall, it is the overwhelming of the senses, especially hearing, in clubs that produces altered states in participants, leading to tranquillity, an awareness of self and environment, feelings of warmth and of peace. It is not surprising that the term 'ecstasy' is also used to describe the state arising from a similar overwhelming of the senses in sexual orgasm. Although the consumption of Ecstasy also produces such alterations of the mind as chemical effects, Malbon points out that it is difficult to explain every aspect of the atmosphere of clubbing in terms of chemical effects, not least because the dosage and composition of drugs taken tends to vary considerably. Nor does an ecstatic experience happen to every clubber, even if they have taken drugs, since so much also depends on the crowd and the music. In particular, the practice of playing 'anthems', recognized by all, is likely to trigger involvement and thus that transition from individual to crowd. Generally, Ecstasy amplifies rather than causes ecstasy. We do learn something about the context of Ecstasy use from Malbon's study, such as how the tensions involved in buying tablets contrasts with the warm sharing atmosphere of the club, and how the drug apparently has the effect of heightening perception rather than inducing the 'mindlessness' feared by so many critics (ibid.: 120).

Generally though, Malbon struggles with the serious difficulties of attempting to use rational discourse to capture ecstatic experiences. He tries to analyse what constitutes 'coolness', for example, which apparently affects the ability to identify with the crowd and respond to the music, or the emotional climate more generally. Ecstasy is variously described as letting oneself go, entering a state of 'flow', finding one's true self, or feeling as if one belongs immediately to the crowd. Malbon analyses the complexities of an evening spent dancing in terms of conventional social science terms such as 'impression management', or the ability to manage 'backstage and front stage' regions. He also tends to 'talk up' the responses to his inquiries, describing the 'wonderfully evocative, almost poetic' (ibid.: 139) qualities of one response, and the 'captivating exchange' he noted as two girls discussed their experiences (ibid.: 159). He is also at pains to list the skills, competencies and knowledge required to participate, and the practice needed to dance in the required manner, despite the appearance of effortless performance; in this way, clubbing almost becomes work-like.

Malbon's account certainly makes clubbing far more familiar than one might expect. In his attempt to analyse the unanalysable, clubbing seems to offer the same kinds of responses that most people would experience in listening to any kind of music in any kind of public arena (except that no-one dances when doing 'serious listening' in concert halls, of course). I feel sure the same sort of analysis could stress the skills and liminality involved in 'moshing'.

The same goes for Thornton's (1995) ground-breaking efforts; her description of clubbing evokes values familiar to any student of leisure studies – 'flow', **escape**, and so on. What is new for her is that clubs offer a much-needed public space for the young in Britain to escape the confines of the domestic – unlike American youth, British youth cannot escape into the interiors of their cars. Luckily, clubs are spaces where hardly any adults intrude, and barriers can be erected to discourage adult participation, not the least of which involves the loud playing of music which would repel. Clubs have taken over from pubs for the British young, Thornton suggests, since the leisure spaces they offer are far more attuned to the specific audience.

There is a different account, of 'rave' in this case, that suggests that something new really has happened. Melechi (in Redhead, 1993) suggests that rave displays characteristics that one would expect of **postmodernism**. In fact, the analysis takes on particular relevance for this book since it begins with an insistence that rave began as a tourist experience. Young British holiday-makers visiting Ibiza were not attracted to the packaged experience on offer featuring British food, British people and mainstream music, organized by a controlling 'tourist **gaze**'. In search of something more challenging, British youth encountered some more upmarket Ibizan dance clubs offering 'an eclectic mish-mash' of styles (Redhead, 1993: 31). This original attempt to flee, to become invisible to the tourist gaze, deeply affected the rave scene, and Melechi draws parallels with Baudrillard on the effects of **hyperreality**. Baudrillard, on holiday in America, noticed that in the intensive hyperreality of the USA, Europe had disappeared, an effect he describes as part of the 'ecstasy of communication' (Melechi, in Redhead, 1993: 32). As an aside, Deleuze's (1992) influential and huge study of the cognitive impact of photography and the cinema also refers to the ecstatic qualities of being able to look at oneself from the outside on the screen, or to distort time with slow-motion effects, or to allude to something unrepresentable altogether.

Attempting to reproduce the holiday rave scene back home in London, Ibiza ravers sought the 'pleasures of loss and abandonment . . . signalled by the "trance dance"' (Redhead, 1993: 33) (relating to an early rave anthem). In summary, rave culture represents a postmodern disappearance for Melechi. There is an escape from the gaze, an indifference towards sexuality and the body, and a lack of interest in previous youth groups, so that ravers can include fans of 'football, indie, traveller amongst others' (ibid.: 36). Even the music represents postmodern pastiche or weaving, a new impersonality that denies a subject, whether represented by an individual singer or by some notion of the 'soul' of a community. Although this sounds dreadful and alienating, it has produced a new kind of sociability, a selflessness and sense of belonging, a space to escape 'A place where nobody is, but everybody belongs' (ibid.: 37).

See also: *cultural capital, fantasy, youth subcultures.*

FURTHER READING

Thornton (1995) and Malbon (1999) offer detailed accounts of the reactions of clubbers to their experiences, and it should be possible to test my suspicion that they are slightly exaggerated and 'talked up'. Redhead (1998) offers a collection of fairly recent articles about British clubs. Hammersley et al. (2002) report the results of an empirical study of Ecstasy users in Glasgow, pursued over ten years. Steins (2003) offers an insider's account of the rave scene (actually from 1997).

There have been several discussions of social and political reactions to rave in particular. Critcher (2000) is one of the most comprehensive, but see also Glover (2003). Hill (2002) is useful and is also discussed at more length in the entry on **gramscianism**.

REFERENCES

Critcher, C. (2000) '"Still raving": Social Reaction to Ecstasy', *Leisure Studies*, 19: 145–62.

Deleuze, G. (1992) *Cinema 1: The Movement-Image*, London: The Athlone Press.

Glover, T. (2003) 'Regulating the Rave Scene: Exploring the Policy Alternatives of Government', *Leisure Sciences*, 25: 307–25.

Hammersley, R., Khan, F. and Ditton, J. (2002) *Ecstasy and the Rise of the Chemical Generation*, London: Routledge.

Hill, A. (2002) 'Acid House and Thatcherism: Noise, the Mob and the English Countryside', *British Journal of Sociology*, 53 (1): 89–105.

Malbon, B. (1999) *Clubbing: Dancing, Ecstasy and Vitality*, London: Routledge.

Redhead, S. (ed.) (1993) *Rave Off: Politics and Deviance in Contemporary Youth Culture*, Aldershot: Avebury Press.

Redhead, S. (ed.) (1998) *The Clubcultures Reader*, London: Routledge.

Ritzer, G. (1996) *Sociological Theory*, 4th edn, Singapore: McGraw-Hill.

Steins, E. (2003) [1997] 'On Peace, Love, Dancing and Drugs' [online] http://www.phantasmagoria.f2s.com/writings/raveindex.html

Strom, A. (2003) 'The "Toronto" Controversy: Disturbing New Facts from History', [online] http://homepages.ihug.co.nz/~revival/toronto.html.

Thornton, S. (1995) *Club Cultures: Music, Media and Subcultural Capital*, Cambridge: Polity Press.

— Education as Leisure —

Education is often thought of in instrumental terms, as supplying knowledge, skills and experience as a preparation for work. However, studying can also be a leisure activity in several senses, supplying pleasures of the kind found in more conventional leisure activities for example.

Section Outline: *The connection between work and education in the provision of mass education: rationalization and McDonaldization of the university. The traditions of education for its own sake as an element of popular culture in the past. Non-vocational interests and 'cognitive tourism' in current mature students: the pleasures of learning, education as 'serious leisure'. Virtual leisure and electronic teaching. Connections with niche tourism.*

If you are taking a university or college course while reading this book, you will probably think of education as far more like work than leisure. There has certainly been in recent years a noticeable institutionalization, professionalization and bureaucratization of education. Education has become defined almost exclusively as something that specialist educational institutions provide, and the ways in which they provide them has been affected by a view that education is for something else – for qualifications, for work – and as a result increasingly like work itself. A key factor has been the emergence of the view that we should use work-like bureaucratic mechanisms both to provide education and to monitor people's progress through it. The paraphernalia of setting specific objectives, tasks, and measurable criteria, and then tying funding to measured performance on these criteria, as in the burgeoning UK 'quality' apparatus, or the highly controversial Research Assessment Exercise, have all been imported from the logic of business practice. Another key factor has been the extension of educational opportunity, mass schooling, and, increasingly, a mass higher education system. Such extension, welcome though it is in many ways, has been shaped by assumptions about the need to rationalize and bureaucratize education in order to make it available. For some critics, this is akin to the process of **McDonaldization** (see Parker and Jary, 1995).

Providing mass education using rational principles is a project with a long history that began in the 1800s in the UK with the establishment of primary education in a peculiarly industrial 'monitorial' form, and came to fruition in the establishment of the UK Open University. As I have argued before (Harris, 1987), there was an assumption that new students from non-elite backgrounds could only cope if they were offered new forms of knowledge, involving simplification and rationalization. They could also only be motivated through the usual mechanisms found at work – behaviour-shaping, assessment and supervision, stressing the immediate rewards of education in the form of qualifications and certificates, with a promise of promotion, a job, or social mobility at the end of it. These assumptions remained largely in place when the conventional system of higher education in the UK was expanded recently.

The old system of higher education clearly preserved the values and 'aesthetics' (see **social class**) of elite groups in its practice. These values were unconsciously held and taken for granted, yet they deeply affected the whole basis of judgement which informed curriculum design, teaching, and the assessment of students. Bourdieu (1988) shows exactly how this structure of judgement worked, in French traditional universities at least. Yet the new system never fully replaced the old elite system, and it currently offers access but at the price we have discussed – students are admitted to universities in order to work hard at gaining instrumental or vocational knowledge (at least as far as the government is concerned).

It is clear that there was once a tradition of education taking place outside of the formal system of schools and universities altogether. Johnson (in Clarke et al., 1979) has talked of the high demand for 'really useful knowledge' among working-class groups in Britain, which included a level of practical skill and know-how, but not what the State came to think of as vocational education. Rose (2002) offers a remarkable history showing British working-class interest in a number of non-vocational 'cultural' areas as well, nourished and stimulated by the private purchase of books, sometimes through book clubs, and the provision of libraries in places such as Working Men's Institutes. Some of the comments he has collected serve to refute the normal professional educational view of working-class people as traditionally uninterested and unmotivated: 'a . . . Derbyshire collier recalled a sister, a worker in a hosiery factory, who was steeped in the poetry of Byron, Shelley, Keats and D. H. Lawrence . . . [while his mother read] . . . Tolstoy, Dostoevsky, Turgenev, Dumas, Hugo, Thackeray, Meredith, Scott, Dickens' (ibid.: 181); 'The seventeenth-century waterman-poet John Taylor had read More's *Utopia*, Plato's *Republic*, Montaigne and Cervantes' (ibid.: 223); 'I remember one youth . . . who used to console himself after losing a game of billiards by quoting Bishop Berkeley' (ibid.: 229).

Rose cites a number of examples of readership surveys, book sales and attendances at evening classes to support this more qualitative material. However, an apparent lack of interest and motivation has been charted ever since among working-class parents in a number of sociological surveys (such as Douglas, 1967). This might have extended to the kind of education offered by schooling, ignoring this long tradition of interest in another kind of education outside of school altogether. One of the founding fathers of British Cultural Studies, Richard Hoggart (1981), also famously described the rich cultural leisure pursuits of the working classes in Northern England more recently, which included brass bands, choirs and classical music.

Other hints of alternatives also suggest that education has a value 'for its own sake', or, to focus the issue for our purposes here, that it is a leisure activity. For example, I have interviewed Open University students who clearly have wanted to pursue courses in higher education for other than vocational reasons, like the ones who studied three modules in order to acquire an MA but then proceeded to study additional modules for fun,

Education as Leisure

or those who undertook the course but did not attend the examination to acquire an actual certificate. These were known informally as 'cognitive tourists': like normal tourists, they were out to explore unusual terrains, see the sights, encounter otherness and novelty, and have intellectual **escapes** and adventures. The effects of their intellectual explorations were sometimes quite profound in terms of their personal **identities** or their views of the world. Some read social science and decided to re-order their lives as a result (in one particular case to end a marriage that seemed to be 'inauthentic'). Some have achieved something like a conversion experience, speaking of their delight in being now able to think things through clearly and realize how limited their earlier conceptions had been. I have just read an essay by one of my own current students reporting something similar. Higher education can deliver a range of pleasures associated with leisure, including 'flow', as one becomes absorbed in an intellectual activity, *plaisir* as one follows an educational narrative to its conclusion, or even *jouissance* (see the entry on **pleasures** for a discussion of these terms).

Mature female students, a growing segment in British higher education, also offer an interesting case. Many mature students are unlikely to receive much of an instrumental benefit from gaining a degree in higher education, it might be argued, especially since promotional and occupational opportunities decrease markedly with age. A classic sociological survey of social mobility (Goldthorpe et al., 1980) suggested that the age of 32 was a threshold here. Female career patterns could continue past that threshold, but women faced additional constraints, since many had sacrificed careers of their own in order to support husbands or raise children, and thus had followed their families around the country or the world. Re-entry into the labour market would be limited by the availability of local opportunities, a particularly serious problem in some areas. Yet this did not seem to deter females from applying to the UK Open University, and it gradually emerged that they might have had other reasons, not involving vocational preferment at all. Some work suggests, for example, that the rewards were much more to do with personal status and identity, see Harris (1987).

Of course, the education system, as it is presently institutionalized, has many features that limit pleasure as well. We have mentioned the considerable and possibly increasing amount of work-like activity in the form of continuous (continual in some cases) assessment, and it is worth remembering that assessment processes can also hurt people badly, demoralize and demotivate them, and produce high rates of drop-out. Some students have developed ways to reconceptualize the work tasks they have been given, to cope with them by 'selective neglect' and sometimes by plagiarism or cheating. We could analyse this behaviour too in the terms used to understand **illegal leisure** with its balance of risks and benefits; as a **youth subcultural** reaction (following another famous study by Becker et al., [1968] 1995); as a classic tactic of the powerless negotiating their way around **disciplinary apparatuses** using 'proletarian cultural capital' as de Certeau (1984) suggests; or even as a form of resistance to hegemony, every bit as penetrating and limited as the reactions of Willis's (1977) 'lads' to secondary school. Again, this requires a shift in perception, perhaps even a betrayal of professional solidarity on my part – we are supposed simply to condemn student activities like these and police them severely, not to try and understand them in leisure terms!

It has become almost impossible to discuss the leisure aspects of education in the current political climate in the UK, since a thoroughly instrumental and calculative attitude prevails. In the days when the government supplied students with maintenance grants, I suppose they were entitled to demand value for money, a return on their investment, and other benefits which could be calculated in instrumental terms. There may be a shift occurring as the higher education system moves towards a more consumer-based relationship with students, who will pay for their own education. Consumerism is often condemned but it has its good sides too, for example, in permitting students to begin to demand the rights of any other consumer to receive the goods that they particularly want, and to use them how they want, once bought and paid for – no-one tests your knowledge of a film as you walk out of the cinema. Demand for both vocationally relevant and traditionally elite forms of knowledge may be much more volatile in the future as a result.

One possible scenario is that there will be a move towards the long-awaited 'permanent' or 'lifelong' education, but again thinking here seem to be limited to a vocational model, assuming people returning to universities want to be topped up with knowledge as their vocational skills become redundant. Jones and Symon (2001) suggest that a new angle might be developed by considering lifelong learning as a form of 'serious leisure'; this term refers to leisure pursuits that involve commitment, skill and dedication and yet are not entirely like work (see Stebbins, 1982, 1997). Serious leisure is discussed further in the entry on **escape**, but it would be useful as a way to get politicians to realize that there may be a market in lifelong learning for those with interests in education as leisure. As an example of what might be in store, in Britain the University of the Third Age is pioneering a de-institutionalized way of learning for its own sake, based on local groups (see University of the

Third Age, 2003), and there are developments of this idea in Australia too (see U3A Hobart, 2003).

The appeal of having some interesting educational material to grasp lies behind the growth of niche tourism in areas such as archaeology, languages, learning to fly, and so on. Israel seems to be developing activities in this field (see, for example, Keshet Educational Tours, 2003), and so does Australia (National Capital Educational Tourism Project, 2003), but there are many other examples. Whether there will be an increased market in universities themselves for education as leisure seems to have been less well explored. If there is one, we can expect to find considerable changes in the ways in which it is provided, not least of which concerns the social relationship between students and university. At the moment, considerable work-like discipline is expected of the student who has to acquire knowledge that has been defined by an organization. Whether this requirement will prove to be popular in the future could be in doubt, especially given what looks like an emerging alternative in the provision of education via electronic means. We discuss the possibilities for the development of non-hierarchical relationships among respondents in the entry on **virtual leisure**. It is obvious that there are whole university courses which are online, as in the Massachusetts Institute of Technology (2003) experiment with OpenCourseWare, but the Web is awash with educational materials, lecture notes, seminar papers, essays and theses as well as commentaries on film, painting and architecture, reviews of novels, online novels for that matter, collections of avant-garde video, historical documents and diaries, fragments of Dead Sea scrolls, lessons in Sign Language, and the like, offering an unparalleled series of rich materials for the cognitive tourist. However, we do need to see how much and what type of cultural capital is required to exploit and enjoy these resources.

FURTHER READING

Rose (2002) is packed with examples of early education as leisure and is excellent at exposing some of the myths about UK working-class culture. Try out some of the latest online educational resources collected at the Distance Education Surf Shack (Ed Surf, 2003), a website that began as a project on a higher education course, developed as an example of 'serious leisure', and then became an occupation. There have been several applications of the term 'serious leisure', traceable from Stebbins (1997).

Becker, H., Geer, B. and Hughes, E. ([1968]1995) *Making the Grade: The Academic Side of College Life*, with a new Introduction by Howard S. Becker, London: Transaction Publishers.

Bourdieu, P. (1988) *Homo Academicus*, Cambridge: Polity Press.

Clarke, J., Critcher, C. and Johnson, R. (eds) (1979) *Working Class Culture: Studies in History and Theory*, London: Hutchinson.

De Certeau, M. (1984) *The Practice of Everyday Life*, Berkeley, CA: University of California Press.

Douglas, J. (1967) *The Home and the School: A Study of Ability and Attainment in the Primary School*, St Albans: Panther Books Ltd.

Ed Surf (2003) [online] http://www.edsurf.net/

Goldthorpe, J., Llewellyn, C. and Payne, C. (1980) *Social Mobility and Class Structure in Modern Britain*, Oxford: Clarendon Press.

Harris, D. (1987) *Openness and Closure in Distance Education*, Barcombe: The Falmer Press.

Hoggart, R. (1981) *The Uses of Literacy*, Harmondsworth: Penguin Books.

Jones, I. and Symon, G. (2001) 'Lifelong Learning as Serious Leisure: Policy Practice and Potential', *Leisure Studies*, 20: 269–83.

Keshet Educational Tours (2003) [online] http://www.keshetisrael.co.il/

Massachusetts Institute of Technology (2003) [online] http://web.mit.edu/

National Capital Educational Tourism Project (2003) [online] http://www.nationalcapital.gov.au/edtourism/home.htm.

Parker, M. and Jary, D. (1995) 'The McUniversity: Organization, Management and Academic Subjectivity', *Organization*, 2:1–20.

Rose, J. (2002) *The Intellectual Life of the British Working Classes*, New Haven and London: Yale University Press.

Stebbins, R. (1982) 'Serious Leisure: A Conceptual Statement', *Pacific Sociological Review*, 25: 251–72.

Stebbins, R. (1997) 'Casual Leisure: A Conceptual Statement', *Leisure Studies*, 16: 17–25.

U3A Hobart (2003) [online] http://www.tased.edu.au/tasonline/uni3age/

University of the Third Age (2003) [online] http://www.u3a.org.uk/

Willis, P. (1977) *Learning to Labour: How Working-class Kids Get Working-class Jobs*, Farnborough: Saxon House.

68

Effects Analysis

The social effects of exposure to violent TV or electronic games have been much researched and are of great interest to policy-makers in the field of leisure. Several research traditions have been developed. The term 'effects analysis' is used here to describe the overall effort to research effects, but it can also refer to a particular approach.

Section Outline: *Concern about the effects of electronic leisure, especially among the working classes: moral panics. Violent behaviour as an effect. Research in different traditions and its general difficulties. Reviews of the findings of examples of research across the range – Anderson and Dill, Buckingham, and Gauntlett and Hill.*

Social commentators have raised all sorts of concerns about the effects on the audience of exposure to anti-social behaviour depicted in films, television and video games, including politicians, teachers and various 'moral entrepreneurs' (Becker's, (1973) term for those whose role it is to develop various moral campaigns or concerns). As a result, there has been a large amount of research devoted to these themes, especially on the effects of exposure to sex and violence. As I have noted before in other entries, research tends to be directed particularly at the sort of leisure activities enjoyed by the working classes; there is no research that I know on possible undesirable effects arising from elderly accountants watching violent and sexually arousing plays or operas. It is believed that only certain sections of the population are likely to be adversely affected, such as children, or those adults who have not developed suitable intellectual skills to discriminate between fact and **fantasy**. It is easy to see the social agenda here, and it might be tempting to dismiss the whole interest in violent video or electronic games as a classic moral panic (see McRobbie and Thornton, 1995) by those who are personally repelled. Indeed, I have found, when reviewing the research, that people tend to polarize in their opinions: some people are convinced that the electronic games are deeply harmful, for example, while others can see absolutely no harm in them at all. In what follows, I concentrate on the research on the effects of violence: the possible effects of depictions of sex are discussed in the entry on **pornography**.

Research has been undertaken for some time. It is possible to think of different approaches to research, depending on how the media are supposed to affect people. One school of thought thinks that watching violence on the screen produces an immediate attempt to imitate or copy what has been just seen. This school believes it possible to note a number of effects, arising from behaviour or from various kinds of more subjective phenomena such as attitude or opinions. One particular piece of work, which we shall review below, suggests that the mass media might provide people with 'scripts', vocabularies and narratives which they can use in explaining or guiding subsequent narratives. In general, research here proceeds to test whether or not these effects are created or amplified by exposure to violent material. This is the tradition that is normally thought of when discussing effects analysis (see Gauntlett, 1998).

There are, however, alternative approaches. Some analysts, for example, are worried about a number of indirect or unconscious effects on the viewer, some of which may be long term and therefore escape short-term testing. Other researchers take quite a different view about the process involved in watching television or playing electronic games, and try to look at the ways in which images and **narratives** are actively interpreted: one way in which this might be done would be for players to disapprove of violence, or to enjoy it on the screen but as a fantasy, resisting any attempt to apply it in practice. While the first approach tends to lead to psychological testing and statistical analysis of the results, the second tends to lead to something more like an **ethnography** of the television viewer, focusing on subjective meanings already developed in the player or viewer, and tracing how they are maintained and related to what is being viewed.

It is obvious that there will be considerable difficulties for any study attempting to pin down the effects of on-screen violence on subsequent behaviour. An initial difficulty will be to get some agreed definition of what counts as violence, for example. It is easy to rely on subjective opinion here, although that does seem to vary considerably, from those who would see *Tom and Jerry* as a violent cartoon, to those who would worry most about graphic death and mutilation on news bulletins. One classic study of television violence (Belson, 1978) relied upon a panel of experts to define violence and the particular categories of violence that they thought might be worrying, but even this technique has obvious problems in that the actual viewers might not share these definitions. The same problem arises with trying to pin down what counts as violent attitudes, opinions or actions.

Even when the data have been secured, problems arise with any attempt to show the relationship between violence on the screen and violent action. As Belson (1978) notes, one obvious connection might be, for example, that those who are violent already tend to want to watch more violence on TV, and not the other way about. The Belson study is one of the few that did try to address this problem, using a set of statistical analyses to test the relationship first one way and then the other: the result in his case was to show a slightly stronger connection overall in the direction that worries the critics (in other words, that exposure to violence on television leads to violent action, rather than the other way about). However, even this careful study openly discussed a number of problems and flaws which remained, not the least of which is that the expected intervening variable – attitudes – seemed not to be strongly affected by violence on the screen, leaving the results without an obvious explanation at all.

It is impossible to summarize all the work, of course, and I have tended to cite some of the 'best' ones, methodologically speaking. In one recent case, the study has also been extremely influential in policy debates. Anderson has much experience in researching the connections between violent video games and violent feelings, as in the early work with an associate, Ford (Anderson and Ford, 1987). He has recently returned with an authoritative study undertaken with another associate (Anderson and Dill, 2000), and the piece has been selected as exemplary by the American Psychological Association. It is worth summarizing this classic piece of work in slightly more detail.

Two studies are involved. The first began by asking the student sample to provide information about their video-game playing habits, name their five favourite video games, and then rate them for violent content. Information was then sought about aggressive behaviour and attitudes to a number of other matters of concern, including 'world-view' (basically, whether they saw their society as a crime-ridden and unsafe place). Gender and academic achievement were recorded. Participants were also psychologically tested to see whether or not they already had an aggressive personality, using apparently standard measures. The study then attempted to correlate the findings to test the strength of the association between playing video games and aggressive behaviour or attitudes.

The findings are typically rather inconclusive and patchy. For example, overall: 'Aggressive delinquent behaviour was positively related to both trait aggressiveness [aggressive personality] and exposure to video game violence' (Anderson and Dill, 2000: 788), and measures of the strength of these correlations are given as 0.36, and 0.46, respectively. Similar but lower correlations were established between both trait aggressiveness and exposure to video game violence and non-aggressive delinquent behaviour. Unfortunately for seekers of simple answers, there were also connections between exposure to video-game violence and aggressive personality. Gender was strongly related to several of the variables, especially 'perceived safety . . . video-game violence . . . and time spent playing video games' (ibid.: 789). Individual differences also had an effect though, and here, aggressive personality in particular showed a link with aggressive behaviour. Anderson and Dill note a particular large effect produced by combining exposure to video-game violence and aggressive personality factors – 'the VGV [video-game violence] effect on aggression occurred primarily among participants with high AP [aggressive personality] scores' (ibid.: 790), especially for men.

To take an example of the definitional problems mentioned above, Anderson and Dill wanted to classify the most popular game (*Super Mario Brothers*) as violent, even thought they recognized that many others would not see it that way. In the end, they included all the ambiguous examples in the category 'violent games'. We do not know what the analysis would have looked like if they had not done so. Further, the sample was drawn from college students, who may not be typical of games players. Anderson and Dill think they may be less prone to violence than the population as a whole, but we do not know. Finally, there are reservations about correlational studies:

> the correlational nature . . . [of this first study] . . . means that causal statements are risky at best. It could be that the obtained video-game violence links to aggressive and non-aggressive delinquency are wholly due to the fact that highly aggressive individuals are especially attracted to violent video games. Longitudinal work . . . would be very informative. (ibid.: 794)

The second study took place in the laboratory and adopted a more experimental design. This time, participants (still psychology students) were asked to play a variety of electronic games assessed (after a pilot study) as equally exciting but differing in terms of violent content. This would help pin down the effects of violent content as such, which is not often done in studies of the effects of video games – as a result, researchers in the past may have been measuring the arousal caused by the excitement or frustration involved in playing any sort of game. After playing, participants were given various tests to measure likely outcomes such as aggression. Again, these were classic psychology tests, apparently well accepted. One of them involved students taking part in a competition to press a buzzer before a (simulated) opponent: if they won, they could punish their opponent with a blast of noise, and receive a blast if they lost. The intensity level of the noise chosen and the duration of the blast give a measure of aggressiveness, apparently. The task was to pin down the effects of the game they had just been playing, rather than whether they had lost, or whether they had themselves just been blasted and were retaliating.

The results are rather frustrating again – playing a violent game had no effect on the intensity of the blast delivered, but it did affect the duration of the punishment! This is a rather complex form of aggression then. Gender also affected the duration of the punishment, with women giving longer blasts. Anderson and Dill want to dismiss this as an artificial finding, though, based on women's lack of ease with playing video games. The findings overall are ambiguous as well. In explaining 'state hostility' overall irritability was a main factor, and so was gender. All other effects, including the effect of playing violent games, 'were nonsignificant' (Anderson and Dill, 2000: 201). Accessibility to aggressive thoughts, as measured by another test involving gauging reactions to particular words 'did not produce a significant . . . [relationship with] . . . game type'. However, when reactions to three types of words were combined into a single measure (a pretty controversial step, especially when the resultant composite was called the 'Aggression Accessibility Index'), game type did seem to have a main effect in that those who had played a violent video game scored higher than those who had not. 'In other words, the violent video game primed aggressive thoughts' (a highly dubious conclusion, in my view, mixing correlations and causes despite the earlier caution). Gender also had an effect, with higher scores for men in this case. However, this time there seemed to be no connection between aggression accessibility and the trait irritability measure (aggressive personality), which is apparently quite unusual and not found in the other literature. Anderson and Dill suggest that this may be due to another artificial effect, because playing the games themselves is 'sufficient to temporarily override the usual differences between people high and low in irritability' (ibid.: 202). It is not clear how they came to this conclusion.

What can we conclude overall, for policy purposes? Anderson and Dill rely here on other studies as much as their own, and we do not have access to them, so we cannot satisfy ourselves about their methodology. However, 'parents, educators and society in general should be concerned about the prevalence of violent video games in modern society' (ibid.: 205). Yet the effects of violent video games were moderated by individual differences in aggression. Overall, it looks as if aggressive personality and video-game violence offer a 'long-term bidirectional causality effect in which frequent playing of violent video games increases aggressiveness, which in turn increases the desire and actual playing of even more violent video games' (ibid.: 205). Overall, 'the danger in exposure to violent video games seems to be in the ideas they teach and not primarily in the emotions they incite in the player. The more realistic the violence, the more the players identify with the aggressor' (ibid.: 206). I did not see any evidence in the actual study to support this view about realism, however. Video games may offer more dangers than television or movies since in video games 'the player assumes the identity of the hero . . . and usually sees the video game world through that character's eyes' (ibid.: 207). (There seem to be some major assumptions here, and again the authors are straying beyond the findings of their own study.) Anderson and Dill think that active participation may also increase aggressive behaviour, since the video game player chooses to be the aggressor, helping 'the construction of a more complete aggressive script than would occur . . . [from]. . . watching violent movies or TV shows' (ibid.: 208). (There is a much to argue about here too, because this view seems to be based on a naïve view of 'participation' as meaning actually controlling the action instead of imaginative participation, for example.) Finally, video games have 'an addictive nature' (ibid.: 208), and more research is quoted here, including the view that 'one in five adolescents can be classified as pathologically dependent on computer games' (Anderson and Dill, citing Griffiths and Hunt, p. 208) (we would need to look very carefully at definitions and correlations here before we accept this, though).

The article also develops a theoretical model, which is of some general interest and could well be applied to other leisure pursuits. The GAAM (general affective aggression model) is based on much earlier research on aggression. Basically, what it does is to describe a 'multi-stage process' whereby individuals and situational factors can lead to aggression. This involves 'input variables' such as aggressive personalities, or situational variables such as 'video game play' or 'provocation'. These can affect 'present internal states', not just affects or emotions, and arousal, but also 'cognitions' or 'aggression related knowledge structures' (Anderson and Dill, 2000: 776). These can involve, for example, 'a behavioural script' guiding people in how to respond to aggression, or other ways to psychologically access 'aggressive cognitions'.

The three internal states are thought to be interconnected. One important implication is that the arousal effect is not specific to violent video games 'but could occur with any game that happens to be very exciting' (ibid.: 777). We have seen that this point is used to criticize early research, but it is also an implied invitation to try out the model on sport, cinema, opera and ballet. Before these internal states can be released in behaviour, people also have to go through an appraisal process, which can be either 'automatic' or 'controlled'. The latter requires more cognitive resources and time. Apparently, appraisal processes can also activate 'behavioural scripts' – 'Well-learned scripts come to mind relatively easily and quickly and can be emitted fairly automatically' (ibid.: 778). People with aggressive personalities have lots of aggression scripts, and are also more ready to react with aggressive means. Anderson and Dill 'believe that video-game violence also primes aggressive thought, including aggressive scripts' (ibid.: 778). There are writers who disagree with this 'script' metaphor altogether, however, since it minimizes the powers we all have to choose and interpret, or 'appraise' in Anderson's and Dill's terms (see the entry on **identities**).

The authors go on to adapt the general model to try to pin down the long-term effects of video-game violence as they do their research. The hypothesis is that violent video games help people

> rehearse aggressive scripts that teach and reinforce vigilance for enemies . . . increase hostile perception, develop aggressive action against others, expectations that others will behave aggressively, positive attitudes towards use of violence, and beliefs that violent solutions are effective and appropriate. (ibid.: 778)

The main effect operates through the individual variables, making people more aggressive, and the authors invoke a kind of labelling theory here to explain how personal aggression can be amplified as other people react adversely. It is also worth noting that the diagram of their specific hypothesis seems much more deterministic, with all the arrows pointing in one direction, leading from repeated violent game playing, through aggressive beliefs and behaviour scripts, to an increase in aggressive personality, and then a reinforcement of that personality. The appraisal processes seem to have been missed out altogether, and I could find no trace of it being measured in the actual studies.

In clear contrast to this famous American study, a British researcher, David Buckingham, has been closely associated with the ethnographic approach that we discussed briefly earlier, and has produced a number of studies showing how 'active' the audience can be (for example, Buckingham, 1987, 1991, 1996). On an interesting methodological note, Buckingham (1991) showed the effects of the discussion itself among the group of children viewing and discussing what they had seen (sexism on television) – whether individual children would have reported the same effects if they had not been prompted or provoked by their fellows is more in doubt. Annoying as this must be for studies which aim to pin down specific effects in specific individuals, this shows the important effects of social groups (such as peers and family) and the ability to come to some collective reading. It also shows that discussion itself can produce statements about 'attitudes' as well as the actual programmes in question: this may have affected Buckingham's own later research too, of course.

To focus on the study most immediately relevant to the problem of violence, Buckingham (1996) carried out a number of intensive

75

interviews with children and their parents which began by asking them what they found to be violent or disturbing on television. One finding is that almost anything can be disturbing to children, not just the obvious scenes of carnage or fierce fighting – the news can be frightening, *Dr Who* can be frightening (in my own case, early *Tarzan* films were very frightening). Overall, however, the study seemed to show that children had a number of ways of managing the fear that was aroused by television, and did not seem to be in any danger of simply being affected by it uncritically. As with Anderson and Dill, Buckingham's study claims additional relevance by referring to a shocking child murder, this time in Britain in the 1990s. The death of James Bulger at the hands of two other children caused a great deal of upset and earnest discussion in Britain, and, at one stage the violent horror video *Child's Play III* was blamed for desensitizing the killers, or even for deliberately teaching them some techniques that they used in the murder. However, Buckingham is at pains to point out that there was never any hard evidence that the killers ever watched that video, and the suggestion that it might have had a causal impact was actually made by the judge in summing up rather than by any researchers. However, the belief that violent video was involved still seems widespread.

The overall findings of his approach are summarized for us in Buckingham (1996). They include that children are often able to make complicated assessments of what is fictional or factual using their knowledge of how the media works, and that they are more likely to identify with the victim than the perpetrator of violence. Further, children develop a range of coping strategies themselves, such as group viewing, ridicule, hiding, and so on. Overall, there is no evidence that watching violence makes children act more violently or that continued exposure desensitizes them to violent actions. Violent behaviour should be seen best as the result of various influences, above all, the family. Again, the research offers a model which could be used in studying a variety of leisure pursuits – how people cope with the tension in the dressing room before a game or come to terms with the violent aspects of grouse shooting, perhaps.

Finally, a long-term study of television watching is worth citing here, based on a panel of 450 adults keeping a record of what they watched and how they reacted to it over a period of five years (Gauntlett and Hill, 1999). The results are almost entirely unspectacular and 'ordinary', which indicates how most people may actually react to television. Some people did have strong objections to televised violence, for example, but they were in a minority (Gauntlett and Hill do not quantify their findings very precisely). Many respondents felt it was a complex issue and a matter of subjective taste, some changed their minds over the course of the research, and 'It is not uncommon in diarists' written responses to find contradictory arguments' (ibid.: 268). Many people could see the general problem and thought it might affect others more strongly than themselves, especially children, but their own reactions showed a general satisfaction with existing ways of regulating TV violence. People watched a lot of television but felt mildly guilty about doing so; they could condemn violent action (especially in fictional forms), but continued to watch it; they saw a number of benefits and pleasures in watching; their attention varied a good deal as they watched; they did use the technology for their own distinctive purposes; there was more evidence of gender equality in terms of who controlled watching. This sort of thing hardly makes for dramatic findings and headlines, but it may well be valid in describing the most common reactions.

There is much research which supports either side of the argument about violence, and yet not all of it is as carefully laid out as the examples we have seen. However, the ambiguity and ambivalence of most of the careful research simply disqualify it in the view of many social commentators who already have strong views and wish to see them supported and confirmed. It is always possible to invoke 'common sense', or the experience and views of selected parents or teachers. For such people, violence is increasing, and the prevalence of violent images on the screen is increasing, therefore it is simple to argue that one must have caused the other. Sometimes, the issue is combined with a rather nostalgic view of a golden age when there was no street violence or criminal assault on people. Historical evidence tends not to support this view, of course. Slightly more abstractly, it is also possible to suggest the existence of a series of subtle and unconscious effects that are not easily measured; for some reason, it can seem easier to believe in these even though there is no actual evidence of their influence.

FURTHER READING

I have some notes offering more depth on the articles by Belson (1978), Anderson and Ford (1987), and Anderson and Dill (2000) on my website (Harris, 2003). Studies such as Buckingham (1998), and Gauntlett and Hill (1999) are worth pursuing for the detailed case studies and extracts that I have had to omit here.

Anderson, C. and Dill, K. (2000) 'Video Games and Aggressive Thoughts, Feelings and Behavior in the Laboratory and in Life', *Journal of Personality and Social Psychology*, 78 (4): 772–90.

Anderson, C. and Ford, C. (1987) 'Affect of the Game Player: Short Term Effects of Highly and Mildly Aggressive Video Games', *Personality and Social Psychology Bulletin*, 12 (4): 390–402.

Becker, H. (1973) *Outsiders: Studies in the Sociology of Deviance*, New York: The Free Press of Glencoe.

Belson, W. (1978) *Television Violence and the Adolescent Boy*, London: Saxon House.

Buckingham, D. (1987) *Public Secrets: EastEnders and its Audience*, London: BFI Publishing.

Buckingham, D. (1991) 'What Are Words Worth? Interpreting Talk about Children's Television', *Cultural Studies*, 5 (2): 228–44.

Buckingham, D. (1996) *Moving Images: Understanding Children's Emotional Responses to Television*, Manchester: Manchester University Press.

Gauntlett, D. (1998) 'Ten Things Wrong with the "Effects Model"', in R. Dickinson, R. Harindrath and O. Linné (eds) *Approaches to Audiences*, London: Arnold. [online] at http://www.leeds.ac.uk/ics/david.htm

Gauntlett, D. and Hill, A. (1999) *TV Living: Television, Culture and Everyday Life*, London: Routledge.

Harris, D. (2003) 'Dave Harris (and Colleagues): Essays, Papers and Courses' [online] http://www.arasite.org/

McRobbie, A. and Thornton, S. (1995) 'Rethinking "Moral Panic" for multi-mediated social worlds', *British Journal of Sociology*, 46 (4): 559–74.

Escape

78

Escaping the routines of social life is a theme with increasing appeal in leisure and tourism. Escapism is also a theme in the enjoyment of popular film and television. However, escape is not easy to achieve and is usually far more closely tied to those social routines than appears to be the case.

> **Section Outline:** *Leisure as adventure and as escape in the work of Rojek, Beezer, and Kjølsrød. Debates about authentic tourism revisited. The increasing levels of social control and the difficulties of leaving social identities at home. Postmodernist 'flatness' and banality. Clubbing, drugs, extreme sports and hobbies as adventures.*

A number of pieces, including Rojek (1993), suggest that the growth of interest in escape is linked to social changes and developments, and that, as usual, it reveals some complex issues, despite its apparent simplicity. Indeed, this is Rojek's general technique – to take a theme and use it to open out discussion on leisure and to question the usual approaches (which are often based on the **work–leisure** distinction).

In many ways, there is a similar approach in discussions of 'escapism' in media studies. Many people think that those who watch soap operas, for example, do so to escape into a fictional world. However, most analyses of the pleasures of soap operas (such as Geraghty, 1991) suggest that it is the very familiarity of that world that permits people to identify easily with the characters and their fate. The same might be said of other genres, of course – the worlds they offer, for all their exoticism, are largely the same worlds as we inhabit, complete with familiar social divisions or recognizably modern individuals. Even the most pleasurable **fantasies** flirt with the familiar.

What do people want to escape from? Is escape more important now than it was? There is a view, found in much sociological theory, that social changes have produced acute social problems for people. Weber, for example, predicted increased rationalization and bureaucratization of work and of life itself. Ritzer (1993, 1999) has recently revived these themes with his notions of **McDonaldization** and disenchantment. Marxists might describe the changes in terms of increased alienation, as individuals lose control over their lives to powerful corporations and government agencies – particular variants of this approach stress the increased de-skilling or intensification of work (Fjellman, 1992, has an excellent survey of this work applied to leisure, and we also discuss some applications in the entry on **youth subcultures**).

Foucault (1977) described the changes in the type and extent of surveillance in public life – in the last century especially, whole new mechanisms of surveillance were established to regulate our conduct in minute detail and at all times. We discuss this in the entry on **disciplinary apparatuses**. In this century, we have seen the rise of electronic

79

surveillance in workplaces, universities, shops, roads and public spaces. These technologies aim (not always successfully) at producing the self-regulating citizen who controls his or her actions even when there is no actual surveillance. These powerful trends are dehumanizing and intrusive for the critics, and although some people may be able to resist, it is not surprising to find an urge to escape from them from time to time.

Rojek (1993) argues that the traditional areas which offered a chance to escape were thought of as childhood; the adventure (especially as in Simmel's work – gambling and promiscuity are his examples and we discuss other variants below); dreams or hallucinations; madness, and moments of collective excitement. Such excitement was sometimes interpreted as a validation of religious feeling, although in reality it was the exchange of permissions to behave abnormally and the amplification of abnormal behaviour that explained the feeling (see **ecstasy**). All these areas have been rationalized or regulated as well by now, Rojek suggests. Childhood has been colonized by pedagogues and child psychiatrists and is now an ever briefer prelude to systematic education thanks to 'hothousing' parents and nursery schools. Foucault blames Freud for regulating the unconscious and its activities such dreams and fantasies or hallucinations. Freud is out to regulate and control these areas, says Foucault, and to bring them back under the sway of reason and he uses therapeutic techniques that themselves derive from authoritarian and regulating techniques such as the Catholic confessional. Madness has been medicalized. Adventurous activity and collective activity have been regulated and licensed. We know how the collective aspects of leisure have been subject to increasing regulation, licensing and commercialization, as in the discussion of rational recreation (see **social class**).

We could think of another example, not elaborated by Rojek (although hinted at in his chapter on women and the control of their **bodies**) – sex, long seen as a source of ecstasy, a loss of self, a truly human and liberated zone of activity. Sex has also been regulated and controlled though, by a combination of 'discourses' – religious prohibitions, sexual hygiene movements, the childhood movement, campaigns against over-population, an increasing concern with performance, or the new sexual ethics of American teenage life (see Silver Ring Thing, 2004). Even the view that sees a kind of sexual ecstasy in **semiotic** adventures (in Barthes, 1977) seems limited – you probably have to be a professor of semiotics to get much of a charge at being joyfully lost in poetry or in the semiotic promiscuity of a video game (as in Fiske's 1989 example). Some writers and critics still hold out hope for personal liberation in 'rebellious

Escape

subjectivity' (Marcuse), or in occasions of deliberate excess (Bataille) although Habermas is less optimistic (Bernstein, 1985).

Other obvious escape activities such as travel and tourism also show the deeper links with normal life, and the difficulties of escape. The first travellers, the aristocracy on the 'grand tours' of Europe in the eighteenth century onwards, had no intention of leaving their normal values behind, it could be argued. Indeed, travel confirmed and supported their overall value systems, argues Rojek (1993) in two directions: contrasts with some countries supported the social Darwinism and racism of the day, while visits to the seats of classical civilizations lent support to the myth that British culture was a direct descendant of those classic traditions (a powerful idea embedded in educational policy too). These ideas might be 'broadened' by travel but confirmed, not challenged. As an aside, Rojek mentions the growth of archaeology as confirming the **authenticity** of those visits. Clifford (1988) suggests that **ethnography** as a discipline did the same job in a later period – it was closely tied to the military, administrative and ideological requirements of imperialistic powers and helped confirm the more liberal, benevolent 'common-sense' views of the relations between cultures.

A later phase of travel and tourism emphasizes **authenticity** too. The 'quest' for it reflects all sorts of anxieties about industrialization and the threat to culture and to privilege based on culture. Travel offered the chance to find authentic cultures, and indeed, to be authentic oneself – a visit would confirm one as a sensitive person with 'proper' values and proper cultural skills, able to understand and empathize coolly with others, without all the artificiality of bourgeois civility (or, indeed, social scientific methods). Travelling and being intellectually moved by the encounter was a way of confirming a standard upper-class identity, to put it rather bluntly (and a gendered one, argues Beezer, 1995). Similar points arise for encounters between 'individuals' and 'Nature' in travels in wildernesses. Both are bourgeois concepts, (Rojek, 1993), and travel confirms the strength of both. **Cultural capital** seems to be required to manage such cultural encounters and to regulate the challenge they offer.

It is increasingly difficult now to deliver such encounters – simple authenticity has disappeared with globalization, so that Papua New Guineans drive Honda mopeds, and one encounters large Mercedes lorries loaded with Coca-Cola on remote African dirt roads. Tourism has spoiled the encounter (Rojek argues that the division between travel and tourism is also largely a matter of class distinction), and 'authenticity' is as corruptible a marketing device as 'green'. As a result, the quest for authenticity has power these days mostly as a matter of nostalgia, which, in **postmodernist** thought, stresses the sentimental and political attachments to a bygone era and to the concepts that described it. In practice, the romantic **gaze** is a very selective one, usually offering telephoto shots of the landscape, or close-ups of the fauna and flora but very few mid-shots with people in them (especially ill, starving or exploited people).

As Rojek argues, in order to control or regulate ourselves to fit the modern order we have to become very self-conscious and analytical, constantly monitoring our 'passions'. As a result, it becomes difficult to enjoy anything any more – we frantically search for pleasure and release but can never find them, since we can never leave ourselves at home (as he puts it). This is demonstrated well in the work on the constantly dissatisfied consumer (see **shopping**), in the self-conscious raver (see Malbon, 1999), or in the self-conscious display of youth cultures as members 'hide in the light' (Hebdige, 1988).

Finally, Rojek (1993) builds on Urry's work to discuss post-tourism (see **posts**). The whole enterprise of tourism as travel, as a quest, as a release, as an escape has now been abandoned (by the tourists, and thus it should also be abandoned by the theorists). Tourism and travel are nothing special, compared with normal life – the experiences delivered have become routine additions to the normal state of affairs in modernity. There are no core values left to break out of or invert or confirm.

Life in postmodernism features a radical tolerance (or indifference), a de-differentiation, fragmentation and relativism right at the heart of our everyday life (or, at least, life in metropolitan centres). There is a liberating side to this in that, paradoxically, we can all relax and feel at home when we travel, abandon 'serious' quests, and take what we find as useful experience, no matter how staged it might be. The ironic enjoyment of tourism, precisely as a staged event, is a major source of pleasure. The dominating experience of travel for Rojek is experiencing the flat and banal wherever we go and however hard we try to escape. The exciting idea of 'abroad' as a place of licence is clearly involved here as an element of fantasy but, of course, one soon returns, 're-created'.

There may well be, nevertheless, activities not involving actual travel that approach the sensation of escape. We could add the concept of a 'moral holiday' to this discussion, based on the work of Becker (1973) who coined the term to describe the occasional foray into deviance undertaken by everybody, including respectable youths. It is a temporary suspension of morality and responsibility, often, but not always, undertaken away from the home turf. Victims are often foreign people too, as British youths carouse in Mediterranean resorts, but local inhabitants of British cities also know the syndrome. The idea of a 'moral holiday' might also explain the recreational use of illegal drugs as a form of escape, dealt with in a recent survey by Parker et al. (1998) (see **illegal leisure**). There is also a connection to the development of modern forms of clubbing, itself a form of temporary escape or even 'disappearance' (see Melechi in Redhead, 1993).

There are also extreme sports. Le Breton (2000) explains participation in these as a kind of escape back into the body, a retreat to basics, an encounter with pain, endurance, and sometimes danger. Extreme activities like this are probably not the more balanced kind that generate 'flow' (see **pleasures**), although mountain-climbing is one of the examples discussed in Csikszentmihalyi (1975). For Le Breton, there is another drama being played out, where willpower overcomes suffering, and, as a result, the individual achieves 'a renewed significance and value to his life' (2000: 1).

On a different tack, Kjølsrød (2003) takes up the idea of an adventure in Simmel that we mentioned earlier, but applies it to apparently quite safe and moderate pursuits, such as collecting or pursuing a hobby. There is no need to be a fit young person to undergo an adventure in this sense. These activities might well appear as 'serious leisure' (Stebbins, 1982), but they do appear to have exciting undertones for participants: Kjølsrød talks of the thrill of the hunt, or a passion that approaches obsession. Dramatic opportunities to experience emotion are often involved, and success can be seen in terms of heroic or other admirable personal qualities. Participants do not exactly escape, but they are successful in maintaining a boundary around these activities, and they can be playful or creative within the boundary of the adventure. These activities also seem to be far more in balance with modernity, unlike the disappointing cycle of escape and return in Rojek (1993), or the boredom and disengagement of the *flâneur* (see **hyperreality**).

83

FURTHER READING

The theme of escape can be followed through subsequent pieces by Rojek (1995, 2000). The paradoxes of 'escape holidays' can be seen in the journeys on offer in the promotional materials of the major companies (such as Explore Worldwide, 2003). Critical commentary on the gendered nature of adventure and adventure narratives is provided by Jokinen and Veijola (in Rojek and Urry, 1997) and Beezer (1995).

Barthes, R. (1977) *Image-Music-Text*, London: Collins.

Becker, H. (1973) *Outsiders: Studies in the Sociology of Deviance*, New York: The Free Press of Glencoe.

Beezer, A. (1995) 'Women and "Adventure Travel" Tourism', *New Formations*, 21: 119–30.

Bernstein, R. (ed.) (1985) *Habermas and Modernity*, Oxford: Polity Press.

Clifford, J. (1988) *The Predicament of Culture: Twentieth Century Ethnography, Literature and Art*, London: Harvard University Press.

Csikszentmihalyi, M. (1975) *Beyond Boredom and Anxiety*, San Francisco: Jossey-Bass.

Explore Worldwide (2003) [online] http://www.exploreworldwide.com/

Fiske, J. (1989) *Reading the Popular*, London: Unwin Hyman.

Fjellman, S. (1992) *Vinyl Leaves: Walt Disney World and America*, Oxford: Westview Press.

Foucault, M. (1977) *Discipline and Punish: The Birth of the Prison*, London: Peregrine Books Ltd.

Geraghty, C. (1991) *Women and Soap Operas*, Cambridge: Polity Press.

Hebdige, D. (1988) *Hiding in the Light*, London: Comedia/Routledge.

Kjølsrød, L. (2003) 'Adventure Revisited: On Structure and Metaphor in Specialized Play', *Sociology*, 37 (3): 459–76.

Le Breton, D. (2000) 'Playing Symbolically With Death in Extreme Sports', *Body and Society*, 6 (1): 1–11.

Malbon, B. (1999) *Clubbing: Dancing, Ecstasy and Vitality*, London: Routledge.

Parker, H., Aldridge, J. and Measham, F. (1998) *Illegal Leisure: The Normalization of Adolescent Recreational Drug Use*, London: Routledge.

Redhead, S. (ed.) (1993) *Rave Off: Politics and Deviance in Contemporary Youth Culture*, Aldershot: Avebury Press.

Ritzer, G. (1993) *The McDonaldization of Society: An Investigation into the Changing Character of Contemporary Social Life*, London: Sage.

Ritzer, G. (1999) *Enchanting a Disenchanted World: Revolutionizing the Means of Consumption*, Thousand Oaks, CA: Pine Forge Press.

Rojek, C. (1993) *Ways of Escape*, Basingstoke: Macmillan.

Rojek, C. (1995) *Decentring Leisure: Rethinking Leisure Theory*, London: Sage.

Rojek, C. (2000) *Leisure and Culture*, Basingstoke: Macmillan.

Rojek, C. and Urry, J. (eds) (1997) *Touring Cultures: Transformations of Travel and Theory*, London: Routledge.

Silver Ring Thing (2004) [online] http://www.silverringthing.com/about.html

Stebbins, R. (1982) 'Serious Leisure: A Conceptual Statement', *Pacific Sociological Review*, 25: 251–72.

key concepts

84

Ethnography

Ethnography refers to a range of methods used in the social sciences that involve trying to come to an understanding of the way a group lives, and then to write about it analytically (which is almost the literal definition). The methods used seem very similar to the ways in which people ordinarily understand the actions of other people, although they are more rigorously developed. The techniques have been used particularly successfully for understanding detailed sequences of unusual, deviant or semi-secret activity which are unlikely to be disclosed using questionnaires. It has the great advantage of being relatively cheap and straightforward, if time-consuming, and is widely used as a result.

Section Outline: Theoretical background and claims. Examples of ethnographic understanding of unusual leisure activities: casual homosexual encounters, illegal leisure, 'having a laff'. Problems with the approach and some solutions to threats to validity: exhausting the data, feminist 'disclosure' approaches. Theoretically informed ethnography: Bourdieu and Willis. Ethnographic writing, 'surprise' and realism.

American interactionism, which includes symbolic interactionism, is often seen to be the guiding theory for ethnographic work (see Joas, in Giddens and Turner, 1987). It is because human individuals already do work toward shared understandings through interacting with each other, internalizing each other's roles and perceptions, and negotiating some shared understandings of symbols that ethnographic research becomes possible. Ethnographers rely on the same subjective capabilities, although they also have particular interests and face the requirement to offer rigour and precision. More 'positivistic' research, employing questionnaires, say, offered a much more limited view of human subjective capacity. At one stage, during the 'battle of the schools' in sociology in the 1970s, these general theoretical disputes became matters of great importance, although it is fair to say that research these days tends to be based much more upon using a range of different techniques according to costs, funding requirements and publication deadlines rather than upon any purist commitment to underlying beliefs about human beings. The theoretical debates concerning symbolic interactionist work in leisure specifically are well reviewed in Kelly (1994).

In order to understand the ways of life of other people, it seems obvious that the best thing to do is go and live among them, observe, participate, and then try to organize any observations into a coherent account. We find ethnographic methods used in situations where understanding the lives of other people seemed to pose a particular problem. The University of Chicago, for example, found itself in a city in the 1920s that contained a large variety of people of different ethnic origins, immigrants to the USA, and it became quite important to find out how they were living together, integrating, and adapting to the American way of life. In Europe, during the colonial period, similar issues arose, this time with the need to understand the ways of life and culture of people who were being colonized. Such understanding would lead to social policy, it was hoped, to assist social integration, and colonization, or, alternatively, to protect threatened ways of life and help them survive in the new conditions. We have already seen, in the discussion of Australian aboriginal people in the entry on **authenticity**, that this often involved the deployment of suitable discourses justifying colonialism as well.

Understanding these ways of life obviously presents particular problems in those contexts. Researchers need to learn the languages of the communities they intend to study, and to become aware of some of their basic values and customs, so as to avoid early embarrassment and perhaps rejection. In some cases, this could be more of a problem than in others – coming to terms with local practices such as torturing animals during religious ceremonies, circumcising women, or abandoning infants if food became short might well require considerable effort from Western liberals.

Having gained entry and initial acceptance to a particular community, the technique involves allowing oneself to become socialized by that community, so that more and more social life becomes understandable. There are some obvious difficulties to manage here – one might become too involved, and 'go native', adopting a largely unreflexive and uncritical understanding of everyday social life. On the other hand, insufficient integration may mean that people never quite feel relaxed or able to perform naturally in front of the researcher, and instead act in a way that takes full account of the fact that they are being observed and researched – one of several possible 'observer effects', where the presence of a researcher prevents natural behaviour from occurring. Bourdieu (1977) points out that the ethnographer actually needs to find people who are themselves willing to help translate their practice into terms the researcher can grasp and then theorize about – which raises questions about the validity of what is being written about.

So far, we have used examples of researchers attempting to understand people of different ethnic origins living quite different social lives from what might be taken as the norm in European or American academic society. However, the same sort of approach might be used at home to understand cultural minorities or members of subcultures, or even members of particular audiences, or those undertaking particular leisure activities. The same kind of social policy initiative sometimes drives these efforts to understand, as we argue in the entry on **illegal leisure**. To understand drug-takers, in this case, might help us develop more effective policies to control and regulate illegal drug-taking, or to minimize its harmful effects. Ethnography appears an obvious technique to guide research. In some of the best examples, which I outline below, considerable knowledge of other worlds has been generated by the technique. I should also warn the reader that these studies may present cultural or ethical challenges: the groups studied are often deviant ones. There is also the danger of titillation – too much ethnography has focused on 'exotic' groups and far too little on mainstream, powerful or straight ones. Young has referred to this tendency to display the exotic for the entertainment of polite society as 'zookeeping' (Young, in Taylor et al., 1975).

A challenging classic study was undertaken by Humphreys (1970) of the ways in which homosexual encounters were organized between men in public toilets in the USA, for example. Humphreys denies that he is homosexual himself, and therefore clearly had to overcome a number of matters of personal distaste or disinterest in his study. Posing as a lookout and voyeur, he was able to record the interactions that took place between men who visited particular public lavatories, known in the USA as 'tearooms' (the equivalent term in the UK at the time was 'cottages'). Those men who were interested in having homosexual encounters had to learn which particular public toilets were likely to host the encounters, and also how to manage the encounters once they had entered. Few words were exchanged, and there was little to indicate what was going on to the naïve 'normal' person who had entered by accident. Encounters were concluded very rapidly on the whole. Humphreys then pursued the ethically dubious technique of noting down the registration numbers of the vehicles driven by the participants and using his contacts with the local police to trace and then interview some of the men involved. When he did so, he discovered that the majority of them were otherwise 'normal' heterosexual married men with families. Whatever your personal views and tastes, I think that Humphreys provided knowledge about an otherwise completely unresearched leisure activity with some important implications for the debates about (sexual) **identities** and how flexible they are.

The same might be said of many recent studies, such as one of African street traders in New York (Stoller, 2002), or one reporting the reactions of American girls to outdoor education experiences (Hurtes, 2002). The classic works also had a great impact at the time, as represented by Becker's (1973) studies of cannabis users and jazz musicians – both repay study in the present. For example, Thornton (1995) in her study of clubbers refers to the work on jazz musicians who also thought they led a life unknown to and more authentic than the world of 'straights'.

Willis published influential studies of working-class 'lads' and how they resist schooling (1977), of **youth subcultures**, especially bikers and hippies (Willis, 1978), and of the common cultural activities of unemployed or marginally employed youth (Willis, 1990). Perhaps the first one offers the best example of a useful but controversial approach. Willis conducted a series of interviews with young male school students in a town in northern England, and recorded their views about schooling, jobs, and attitudes to girls and to parents. The study makes for very lively reading: 'the lads' are intelligent and witty, and spend much of their time 'having a laff' (engaging in subversive casual leisure activities). They realize early on that the route to social mobility through educational qualifications is not for them (quite an accurate perception, given the statistics), and see their future in manual labour. Their ability to outwit the teachers is a source of some cultural pride. When discussing their notion of masculinity, however, Willis detects a more defensive note. Being masculine is a source of pride as well, but this leads to contempt for women and for middle-class workers (teachers are described as 'poofs'), and offers a dubious cultural consolation for the perils of working-class life. As a result, this stance disqualifies the lads from a proper understanding of gender and gender politics, and from gaining an academic understanding of their condition. 'Having a laff' may be an effective coping strategy at school but it is an ineffective politics, which delivers the young men to the fate that capitalism had waiting for them all along – manual labour. This study has been much quoted since, and its underlying mechanism also appears in studies of young women and their leisure as an equally limited form of resistance (for example, see McRobbie, in Women's Study Group, 1978; Hobson, in Hall et al., 1980).

In the second part of Willis's study, however, much more abstract and theoretically informed analysis appears. This permits Willis to be theoretically critical of the way of life he is studying, in the sense that he sees it as highly limited in its ability to 'penetrate' the workings of the social system. He also wants to explain the development of this intriguing but limited working-class culture, by using marxist theory, and developing his own notion of 'ideology'. Of course, this introduces new problems into the analysis, and Willis never satisfactorily explains how you actually move from ethnographic data to theory of this kind. The book is written in a way which can seem to suggest that theoretical commentary grows out of the ethnographic data, but it is quite likely that the theory predisposed him to find certain themes in the ethnographic data in the first place. It is interesting to note that in a return visit to the study, Willis found slightly different theoretical and political themes in the data (in Barton and Walker, 1983). How exactly can abstract concepts like ideology be grounded in detailed descriptions of people's lives and activities, if at all?

This problem emerges in a different guise in some of the later work too. Willis (in Hall et al., 1980) feels it necessary to defend the need to do ethnographic research against a particularly powerful theoretical argument, found in an influential variety of marxism (Althusserianism) that tended to condemn it as 'empiricist'. Very briefly, empiricism is a belief that somehow the facts can speak for themselves, that research aimed at uncovering detailed factual findings about the world can somehow deliver a privileged knowledge. This is absurd, for followers of Althusser, since theory is needed to generate knowledge, and theory takes place at a different level from description. Willis's argument in 1980 was to be repeated in his 'Manifesto' for a new journal to celebrate ethnography (Willis and Trondman, 2000). Theory on its own can tend to be self-referential, and to close off options for learning about the world. Ethnography's role is to deliver 'surprise' to counter this tendency.

There most certainly was a tendency towards 'lazy theorizing' in the traditions associated with British Cultural Studies, as we argue in the entry on **gramscianism**. At the same time, there are some obvious objections. Any kind of empirical social research can deliver 'surprise', even the most positivist statistical demonstration of trends that were not immediately apparent. Second, the amount of surprise generated depends on how naïve the theory, or the theorist, was in the first place. I have expressed quite low enthusiasm for the 'surprising' insights delivered by the research by Grimshaw in his study of the Boy Scouts, for example (see Harris, 1992).

As ethnographic techniques have become more and more professionalized, thanks to the growth of social sciences, these difficulties have come to the fore. Social science makes ethnographers much more aware of the effects of their own values and culture on the things that we see and the ways in which we interpret them (see the entry on **authenticity**). Social science also provides us with a specialist body of theoretical knowledge that should relate to ethnographic observation: an innocent recording of a local way of life has little interest for social scientists these days, unless it tells us about something generalizable. The goal should be to provide 'a theoretically informed methodology for ethnography' (Willis and Trondman, 2000: 11). Willis's early studies, reviewed above, attempted this, and Hammersley (1985) suggests another particular example of this sort of development. Bourdieu et al. (1999) offer powerful examples of such theoretically informed ethnography in their studies of life among the deprived, and the closing essay in that book is a classic on the need to develop open yet informed understanding. Unfortunately, there are few direct studies of leisure as such in the collection, except perhaps for the ones on drug use and the general habits of 'hanging around'.

For some ethnographers, there are particular methods or techniques that might be used to guard against the most obvious sources of bias. These are well discussed in the introductory literature (such as Hammersley and Atkinson, 1995), and include attempting to 'ground' observations carefully in actual data (as in 'grounded theory', see Glaser and Strauss, 1967). Some researchers recommend checking the validity of observations gained with others, such as respondents themselves (respondent validity), or with results gained from other studies ('triangulation' as it is called, especially if there are three sources, people, or methods that can be used to check results). Some of the best studies (such as Becker et al., 1995) have taken care to attempt to gain as wide a range of observations as possible, and especially to record 'negative cases', where respondents do not appear to agree with general conclusions, where they offer exceptions, or where they present data that are ambiguous or difficult to understand. The same research team also took care to note whether comments or behaviour appeared to be spontaneous, or as the result of an observer effect.

A particularly interesting strand of ethnographic work, often associated with feminist researchers, offers a form of 'disclosure', a running commentary on the threats to validity encountered during the research, with no attempt to hide these away in footnotes. Thus Fuller (in Burgess, 1984) relates her own difficulties in trying to manage encounters with the black girls she was studying, and Walkerdine (in Burgin et al., 1987) recalls her own feelings of pain, embarrassment, and deep-seated regret stemming from her own childhood, and openly announces that these may well have influenced the observations she was making (we discuss her work in the entry on **fantasy**). Ethnographers such as Hammersley (1990) have encouraged people to be more rigorous and open in the way they present their data. A common technique is simply to pick examples from a range of observations or interviews which support a particular point, for example, but this leaves the whole issue of validity very much in the hands of the researcher, since readers have no idea of whether these examples are typical, how actually they occurred (spontaneously or as the result of prompts), and so on. A more challenging approach would be to present whole transcripts or records of observations, and then to try to explain everything that happened, to 'exhaust the data', much as does rigorous structuralist analysis (see **semiotics**) rather than just pick examples that seem to confirm understandings.

There is still much debate about whether these procedures and strictures are sufficient to reassure readers about the validity of what ethnographers have uncovered. Those researchers preferring more 'scientific' approaches argue that we are still very much in the hands of the researcher, who can simply assure us that he or she has 'grounded' their findings, or 'triangulated' them or whatever – Butters (in Hall and Jefferson, 1976) has an excellent critique. There are no hard and fast rules about how to accomplish these procedures, and there is no guarantee that intersubjective agreement about interpretations represents real validity. After all, only the researchers really know how the data have been generated from what went on, and we are very much dependent on them, even when they assure us that they have disclosed all the factors that might affect their work.

A particularly acute criticism of ethnographic writing has arisen from the work of post-structuralists and deconstructionists (Clifford, 1988; Clough, 1992). This work directs attention to the suppressed problems, difficulties, and incoherencies of the text and to the writing techniques that are used to gloss these over. Clough, in particular, has focused on the writing techniques that are used to develop a sense of authenticity and co-presence, and the narratives and other devices designed to involve viewers and to deliver a 'knowledge effect'. It would be perfectly possible to apply this analysis to study how ethnographic writings generate 'surprise' as well. Of course, this is not to deny the importance of ethnography, merely to ask for more self-awareness about the effects of writing. It is self-awareness and expertise that inform the close and constructive interrogation of ethnographic findings that Hammersley demonstrates so clearly (for example, in Woods and Hammersley, 1993). This is the role of critical ethnographers, perhaps, to check the research base and demand justification, instead of letting the narrative convince us.

See also: *Disneyfication, ecstasy, effects analysis, shopping.*

FURTHER READING

You might want to explore some ethnographic studies, perhaps the ones cited here, or some in the journal *Ethnography*, such as Bernstein (2001), an ethnographic study of the male clients of prostitutes, or Wacquant (2003), a 'progress report' on ethnography as a method. Ethnographic studies informed by a figurationalist approach are found on the online Centre for Research into Sport and Society (2003). There are many classic studies available online, not all of them about leisure, including those selected under the relevant heading by the UK Social Sciences Information Gateway (a portal), referenced as SOSIG (2003).

REFERENCES

Barton, L. and Walker, S. (1983) *Race, Class and Education*, London: Croom Helm.

Becker, H. (1973) *Outsiders: Studies in the Sociology of Deviance*, New York: The Free Press of Glencoe.

Becker, H., Geer, B. and Hughes, E. ([1968]1995) *Making the Grade: The Academic Side of College Life*, with a new introduction by Howard S. Becker, London: Transaction Publishers.

Bernstein, E. (2001) 'The Meaning of the Purchase: Desire, Demand and the Commerce of Sex', *Ethnography*, 4, (1): 389–420.

Bourdieu, P. (1977) *Outline of a Theory of Practice*, Cambridge: Cambridge University Press.

Bourdieu, P. and Accardo. A., Balazs, G., Beaud, S., Bonvin, F., Bourdieu, E., Bourgois, P., Broccolichi, S., Champagne, P., Christin, R., Faguer, J-P., Garcia, S., Lenoir, R., Françoise, Œ., Pialoux, M., Pinto, L., Podalydès, D., Sayard, A., Soulié, C., Wacquant, L. (1999) *The Weight of the World: Social Suffering in Contemporary Society*, Cambridge: Polity Press.

Burgess, R. (ed.) (1984) *The Research Process in Educational Settings*, London: Falmer Press.

Burgin, V., Donald, J. and Kaplan, C. (eds) (1987) *Formations of Fantasy*, London: Routledge.

Centre for Research into Sport and Society (2003) [online] http://www.le.ac.uk/crss/

Clifford, J. (1988) *The Predicament of Culture: Twentieth Century Ethnography, Literature and Art*, London: Harvard University Press.

Ethnography

Clough, P. (1992) *The End(s) of Ethnography from Realism to Social Criticism*, London: Sage.

Giddens, A. and Turner, J. (eds) (1987) *Social Theory Today*, Cambridge: Polity Press.

Glaser, B. and Strauss, A. (1967) *The Discovery of Grounded Theory*, Chicago: Aldine.

Hall, S., Hobson, D., Lowe, A. and Willis, P. (eds) (1980) *Culture, Media and Language*, London: Hutchinson.

Hall, S. and Jefferson, T. (eds) (1976) *Resistance Through Rituals*, London: Hutchinson.

Hammersley, M. (1985) 'From Ethnography to Theory: A Programme and Paradigm in the Sociology of Education', in *Sociology*, 19 (2): 244–59.

Hammersley, M. (1990) 'What's Wrong with Ethnography? The Myth of Theoretical Description', *Sociology*, 24 (4): 597–616.

Hammersely, M. and Atkinson, P. (1995) *Ethnography: Principles in Practice*, London: Routledge.

Harris, D. (1992) *From Class Struggle to the Politics of Pleasure: The Effects of Gramscianism on Cultural Studies*, London: Routledge.

Humphreys, L. (1970) *Tearoom Trade: A Study of Homosexual Encounters in Public Places*, London: Gerald Duckworth.

Hurtes, K. (2002) 'Social Dependency: The Impact of Adolescent Female Culture', *Leisure Sciences*, 24: 109–121.

Kelly, J. (1994) 'The Symbolic Interactionist Metaphor and Leisure: Critical Challenges', *Leisure Studies*, 13 (2): 81–96.

SOSIG (2003) [online] http://www.sosig.ac.uk/

Stoller, P. (2002) 'Crossroads: Tracing African Paths on New York City Streets', *Ethnography*, 3 (1): 35–62.

Taylor, I., Walton, P. and Young, J. (1975) *Critical Criminology*, London: Routledge and Kegan Paul.

Thornton, S. (1995) *Club Cultures: Music, Media and Subcultural Capital*, Cambridge: Polity Press.

Wacquant, L. (2003) 'Ethnografeast: A Progress Report on the Practice and Promise of Ethnography', *Ethnography*, 4 (1): 5–14.

Willis, P. (1977) *Learning to Labour: How Working-Class Kids Get Working-Class Jobs*. London: Saxon House.

Willis, P. (1978) *Profane Cultures*, London: Routledge and Kegan Paul.

Willis, P. (1990) *Common Culture*, Milton Keynes: Open University Press.

Willis, P. and Trondman, M. (2000) 'Manifesto for *Ethnography*', *Ethnography*, 1 (1): 5–16.

Women's Study Group (1978) *Women Take Issue*, London: Hutchinson.

Woods, P. and Hammersley, M. (eds) (1993) *Gender and Ethnicity in Schools: Ethnographic Accounts*, London: Routledge in association with the Open University.

93

Fantasy

A fantasy arises when a person is able to identify in their imagination with a person or role in an ongoing event or story and thus play a pleasurable part in it. Fantasies seem to be involved with many leisure activities and may even be integral to them, so they are important but difficult to study for obvious reasons.

Section Outline: *The mechanisms of fantasy formation in social psychology and social phenomenology. Fantasies and their role in 'natural' sexual behaviour. Nationalist identification and masculine fantasies in football hooliganism and in watching violent films: controversies and methodological procedures. The importance of fantasy in tourism and leisure.*

The ability to fantasize is possibly a unique characteristic of human beings. Central to this ability are the qualities of human language which we explore in other entries (**articulation, narratives, semiotics**). Our language enables us to name things, categorize them, and organize them in various sequences in order to make sense of them. Equally important are the characteristics of human consciousness, especially the ability to 'attach' personal or subjective meanings to our perceptions of the world. We can simply ignore for now the theoretical debate about whether language or consciousness is the prime source of meaning, and concentrate on the latter in this section.

There are a number of approaches found in interactionist sociology which explore this aspect of consciousness. The term 'empathy' describes the apparent ability we have to place ourselves imaginatively in the positions of other people. Sociologists tend to use slightly different terms such as an ability to 'take the role of the other', which is associated with the work of G.H. Mead and the school called 'symbolic interactionism' (see Joas, in Giddens and Turner, 1987). Another approach, usually called 'social phenomenology' (see Schutz, 1972) analyses the ways in which we can adopt reciprocal perspectives to understand the social world – we simply assume that the social world looks roughly the same to us as it does to other people, and that our understanding of their action fits in some way with how they understand it (the fit need not be identical, of course). Again, human language and interaction enable us to make finer and finer adjustments to these assumptions and abilities and eventually to generalize: we assume that the actions of one specific businessman are typical of all business personnel, for example.

Social phenomenologists also offer an account of the workings of our subjective minds, by developing notions such as 'subjective time'. Perceptions in the present are understood partly by forming relations between some of their elements and events that have happened in the past. Indeed, some people think that this is how all understanding works. To use the slightly obscure language of social phenomenology, present and past are 'united in subjective time'. There is no space here to explore further at this abstract level, but it is important to realize that our consciousness does not deliver a fully transparent, fully understood world to our perception. It is a three-dimensional social world which is formed, populated by what seem to be others just like us: both world and others seem 'objective', that is independent of our understanding of them and thus occasionally mysterious. Our experience certainly contains this effect – we do not feel we are totally in control and able to direct action. Of course, this may be because there really are others and objects in the world, which do things beyond our initial understanding, but, strictly speaking, we cannot decide if the effect is really one of consciousness.

A more specific analogy is developed by Rojek in Rojek and Urry (1997). Noting that 'travel experience involves mobility through an internal landscape which is sculptured by personal experience and cultural influences as well as a journey through space' (1997: 53), Rojek develops a descriptive vocabulary referring to computer files, indexing, and the process of 'dragging elements of files to create new values for . . . [a]. . . sight' (ibid.: 54). Examples include the ways in which customers themselves, and specially produced tourist guides, on the 'Schindler's List tour' combine actual sights with scenes from Spielberg's film. This kind of dragging from files to create collages (PC users might prefer to think of it in terms of cutting and pasting) is widespread, as in 'interactive tourism via mind-voyaging, piecing together different aspects of reports on a sensational event', often provided by TV and radio (ibid.: 63). This activity has a number of important effects which are spelt out in more detail (we discuss some in the entries on **authenticity** and **hyperreality**).

This offers us ways to begin to understand how fantasies work. To revert to our original concepts, it becomes possible for us to attach personal subjective meanings to the objects we perceive, and then begin to develop an understanding about them based on subjective experience. We can tell a story about them in subjective time. We can all experience how this happens – I walk through the streets of Plymouth and see a seagull; that gull causes me to recall other gulls I have seen, perhaps in my childhood during visits to the seaside; I can then 'attach' subjective memories, feelings and understandings from that childhood experience, and then develop a kind of story in which I participate in my imagination. I am still in the present, yet I am recalling the past vividly enough for it still to have current meaning for me. That the human mind has the power to create fictional worlds like this is witnessed by the everyday experience of daydreaming, or getting deeply involved in books, electronic games or films: so involved that we can be brought to tears. The world of dreams offers another powerful example of a realistic and apparently objective world created by mental energy, combining, in the classic analyses of Freud, mixtures of contemporary and infantile material, and driven by strong mental processes. We need not refer to unconscious drives or instincts necessarily, however, if we just need to recognize the importance of fantasy. We can suggest that fantasies are induced by the same motives and interests that drive all leisure activities – the pursuit of some kind of **pleasure**. That pleasure also arises from treating the world as separate and 'other' and yet also familiar – in this way novelty, surprise, and the right level of challenge are also experienced.

That fantasy is important to leisure activities can be demonstrated fairly easily. Let us take the popular and intriguing pastime of engaging in sexual activity of various kinds. There is a common belief that this is a straightforward 'natural' activity, motivated by biological drives, and that pleasure arises from the release of primarily physiological tensions established by these drives. However, many studies of sexual pleasure take quite a different view, and argue that it is one of the least biologically driven of all activities in human beings, and that culture, subjective meaning, and fantasy are absolutely central. Plummer, for example, (in Brake, 1982) argues that human beings are quite capable of directing their sexual interests at a very wide range of objects indeed, so much so that it becomes impossible to talk about sexual activity except in cultural terms. To take his examples, a boy watching a football match might not appear to be taking part in a sexual activity, but he can be fantasising about having sex with the players. A photograph of a naked woman lying on a couch and being fingered by a man could be a record of sexual activity or of a medical examination: the participants would be engaging in sexualizing their contact in the first case, and striving to desexualize it in the second. Sometimes encountering a naked human being is arousing (before you have sex with them) and sometimes not (when queuing for the groceries at a nudist camp).

Apart from demonstrating possibilities like this, though, it is obviously difficult to gather and research actual fantasies, since these are fleeting and often not very respectable. One solution is to ask for voluntary statements, but doing this risks gaining atypical examples. The notorious case of the female fantasies collected by Friday (1993) is obviously open to criticism here, since her volunteer respondents may well have been unusually imaginative or exhibitionist. Certainly, what made this (best-selling) collection particularly controversial was the relatively exotic fantasies of the women, especially those which indicated they took pleasure in imagined non-consensual sex. Clearly some outrage was caused by the implication that such fantasies were 'normal' for women, even though few people suggested that they would lead to imitation in real life.

Kipnis (in Church Gibson and Gibson, 1993) offers another approach in exploring the role of fantasy in the activities of male transsexuals, by examining how they are illustrated in the stories and photographs they submit to specialist magazines aimed at them. However, these will be mediated fantasies, of course, and may well be atypical again. It is interesting to note that some of these fantasies involve attempts to locate the activity in normal life, by choosing domestic setting for the photographs, for example. There is no way of knowing if these fantasises are ever actually realized except in photography, of course, but that they might leak into normal life is a common worry when discussing sexual fantasies especially (we discuss these issues below and in the entries on **effects analysis** and **pornography**).

The issue of the typicality of the fantasies being studied arises again in the quite widespread use of the notorious work of Thewelheit (1987) in exploring male fantasies. This work appeared, most controversially perhaps, in King (1987) writing about male football hooligans. Thewelheit's study is actually a rather abstract one, based on post-Freudian analysis of the desires evident in personal documents, diaries, novels and archive material relating to members of the German Freikorps, a right-wing militia formed largely of ex-servicemen from the First World War who engaged in periods of armed struggle against communist and socialist insurgents in the 1920s. The materials seem suffused with a fear of unrestrained women, especially communist women, and the need to abuse them, even to kill them for pleasure, in order to maintain a necessary masculine purity and a social and cultural hardness and control. Thewelheit admits that he offers a sometimes selective and 'idealized' reading (1987: 151), but generally seems rather casual in treating texts like these as 'evidence' and in attributing motives to Freikorps members in the abstract, finding incestuous longings in fascist writings, and so on. What is even more worrying is when Freikorps members are seen as representing some kind of 'essential' male psychology.

In his critique of King's work, Smith notes that King thinks that 'an insight into the motives and beliefs of this group of proto-fascist, female-slaying, genocidal killers, who eventually formed the vanguard of Hitler's Nazi storm-troopers will help us understand the outlook and actions of young, male football fans in contemporary Britain' (2000: 448). Apparently, both groups are seen to share underlying 'historical conceptual schemes' or 'masculine psychology' (ibid.). Among the specific problems with this are that fascism never really took hold in England, that football fans would never embrace the iron discipline of the Freikorps, and that Thewelheit and even Hitler realized that Freikorps members were very strange people. Turner and Carter (in Burgin et al., 1989) suggest that this is far too literal a reading of Thewelheit anyway, who was more concerned to explain how desire works to generate discourses and chose to illustrate the mechanisms with the Freikorps and their specific resources for producing fascist fantasies.

Walkerdine (also in Burgin et al., 1989) is crammed with insight both about more common male working-class fantasies, and also the petit bourgeois pleasures of intellectualizing about popular culture. Fantasies are by no means a psychological process only, but are mixed with and validated by the practices of everyday life, she argues. It follows that to study them it is not enough to analyse texts and make assumptions about how viewers read them, but rather to sample the everyday life of working-class males to try and understand the cultural 'formations' that they occupy when they view television. Walkerdine observed a working-class family who were watching a video copy of *Rocky II*. A great deal of pleasure was gained from watching one of the fight scenes, and Walkerdine was initially at a loss to understand why anybody would want to watch such violence. She considered the 'bourgeois liberal' option, which is to deplore the violence and sex stereotyping of the working-classes, but she was sensitive enough both to consider her own reactions to the scene, and also to realize that the bourgeois liberal option is not without problems itself. Echoing the terminology we use in the entry on **social class**, Walkerdine says it embraces a particular aesthetic which prefers intellectualizing to involvement, and symbolic violence to real violence.

Walkerdine came to realize that the video also offered empowering

'fantasies of omnipotence, heroism and salvation' (Burgin et al., 1989: 172). Working-class males interpret their lives as a struggle or fight for survival, as providing for their family, and as celebrating a kind of self-reliant masculinity as a survival strategy when faced with real oppression and powerlessness, a determination 'not to sink, to get rights, not to be pushed out' (ibid.: 182). This interpretation emerged from flow between viewers' admiration for the video and actual conversation that took place in the domestic life that went on as well, the relations and interchanges between the men and women, the parents and the children. The need to fight emerged in stories about other struggles to get a decent education for children, for example. This is quite unlike the bourgeois preference for coping by using 'covert regulation and reasoning' (ibid.).

Such regulation lies behind the attempt to intellectualize about the meaning of films. Walkerdine insists that the bourgeois 'will to truth' is an equally specific and perverse way to watch films, even though its pleasure is masked. Wanting to know, intellectually, is also wanting to control, revealing a 'terror of the pleasures of the flesh and the body, the animal passions . . . in sexuality and also in violent uprisings. No surprise then that the regulation of children's consumption of the modern media focuses so obsessively on sex and violence' (ibid.: 196).

Walkerdine is not apologising for working-class masculine fantasies, but trying to understand them as rooted in day-to-day contact with an oppressive system. She is not willing to pretend that her presence had no impact on the interactions she observed or that she had no desire to understand and manage her relationships with those working-class people, quite unlike many other **ethnographic** analyses. She concludes that working-class men like to make ambiguous figures of the women in their lives, sexualizing them through projecting a particular notion of femininity, based on their own suppressed femininity. It is not that these identities are entirely imposed on women, more that women agree to a 'mutually lived-out fantasy' (ibid.: 187). Walkerdine admits her own attraction for being seen as 'small, protected, adored and never growing up' (ibid.: 187). This fantasy too must be connected with everyday life as well as with media depictions. Overall, Walkerdine sees problems in trying to regulate these fantasies, especially on aesthetic grounds – it leaves working-class people with only one option – 'embourgeoisment', that is, becoming middle class (ibid.: 197).

Another set of findings concern the pleasures that spectators 'attach' to the sporting contests that they are watching. Again, these are readily available to any reflective spectator. There is the tendency to 'allegorize' as Guttmann (1986) puts it, which involves a tendency to 'read' the game as a story about something else – the qualities that have made a person, town, or nation 'great', for example. Taking pleasure from some fantastic connection between the players and some wider grouping of this kind is easily experienced (see also Dunning and Waddington, 2003). We also know that television works hard to 'add' meanings to the sporting occasions it covers, spelling out the patriotic implications of British players competing at Wimbledon, or telling us what the World Cup Final means about 'humanity' in general.

Discussions of media and the pleasures that films deliver would be another main site to study the engagement of fantasies, especially the fantastic identification with the characters, or possibly with the narrator or the camera, as is implied in the notion of a **gaze**. That concept also implies, however, that fantasies are not entirely free-floating, but are mediated, focused, or even scripted. We mention this possibility when we discussed the fantastic meanings attached to some consumer goods in the process of **adding leisure values** to them: many advertisements might well be seen as acted-out fantasies with which the consumer can identify. However, Plummer (in Brake, 1982) feels that fantasies are far too subjective ever to be fully controlled or scripted, and we could find some support for this in the theoretical background that suggests that human consciousness is always engaged in the detailed construction of meanings, including fantasies.

The ability to fantasize seems ever available. We walk through a culturally imagined landscape when we walk through cities, suggests de Certeau (1984), acting out a kind of ambulatory fantasy. We can fantasize and daydream, however briefly, even while we are at work, which leads Rojek (1995) to further question the **work–leisure** distinction. Seaton (in Dann, 2002) discusses the growing appeal of tourist packages that offer the chance to 'walk in the footsteps of' some famous individual or group (such as the polar explorers). This tendency relies upon 'metempsychosis' and 'metensomatosis' – the process seems to involve 'taking the role of the other' that we discussed at the beginning of this section. Seaton believes that this capacity may be at the heart of all tourist experiences, and traces its growth to features of modernity such as the boredom, repetition, ennui, and *déjà-vu* experiences at the heart of social life itself, not just work. It is tempting to extend his argument to include virtually all leisure experiences as well.

FURTHER READING

You might want to follow up some of the reading summarized here, especially Plummer (Brake, 1982), Walkerdine (Burgin et al., 1989) or Seaton (Dann, 2002). Thewelheit (1987) is a challenging read but one which is often cited. A largely unresearched area so far is the fantasy game (board or electronic) – see Fantasy Flight Games (2003) for a possible starting point.

REFERENCES

Brake, M. (ed.) (1982) *Human Sexual Relations: A Reader*, London: Penguin.

Burgin, V., Donald, J. and Kaplan, C. (eds) (1989) *Formations of Fantasy*, London: Routledge.

Church Gibson, P. and Gibson, R. (eds) (1993) *Dirty Looks: Women, Pornography, Power*, London: BFI Publishing.

Dann, G. (ed.) (2002) *The Tourist as a Metaphor of the Social World*, New York: CABI Publishing.

De Certeau, M. (1984) *The Practice of Everyday Life*, Berkeley, CA: University of California Press.

Dunning, E. and Waddington, I. (2003) 'Sport as a Drug and Drugs in Sport', in *International Review for the Sociology of Sport*, 38 (3): 351–68.

Fantasy Flight Games (2003) [online] http://www.fantasyflightgames.com/

Friday, N. (1993) *Women on Top*, London: Simon and Schuster.

Giddens, A. and Turner, J. (eds) (1987) *Social Theory Today*, Cambridge: Polity Press.

Guttmann, A. (1986) *Sports Spectators*, New York: Columbia Press.

King, A. (1987) 'The Lads: Masculinity and the New Consumption of Football', *Sociology*, 31 (2): 329–46.

Rojek, C. (1995) *Decentring Leisure: Rethinking Leisure Theory*, London: Sage Publications Ltd.

Rojek, C. and Urry, J. (eds) (1997) *Touring Cultures: Transformations of Travel and Theory*, London: Routledge.

Schutz, A. (1972) *The Phenomenology of the Social World*, London: Heinemann Educational Books.

Smith, T. (2000) 'Bataille's Boys: Postmodernity, Fascists and Football fans', *British Journal of Sociology*, 51 (3): 443–60.

Thewelheit, K. (1987) *Male Fantasies* Vol. I: *Women, Floods, Bodies, History*, Minnesota: University of Minnesota Press.

101

Figurationalism

key concepts

This term describes a general theoretical approach associated with Elias, Dunnning and Mennell (for our purposes) and their associates (many based at Leicester University in the UK). The approach has generated a number of fruitful concepts including 'figuration' and 'the civilization process', and discussions of group formation. A particular interest has always taken in understanding sport and leisure, the specific historical processes involved in their development and their emotional qualities.

Section Outline: Figurations and their characteristics: implications for theory. Politics and a football match as examples of figurations. Tension balances and the process of civilization. Football hooliganism. The modern diet. Problems and debates: complexity, selectivity and the difficulties of detachment.

102

A figuration, which is what figurationalism studies is, is a kind of virtual social group which takes on concrete forms. Actual groups or figures are formed by individuals with certain common interests in specific circumstances, and can be based on common economic position, or on a common gender membership, but it is equally possible to form one based on a common interest in a leisure activity. Figurations are flexible and dynamic in that the interactions between individuals can change the initial state of the group and produce new specific manifestations. Such change cannot be predicted from knowing the formal rules of the group, or by having an abstract model of the power relations between members, and must be described and studied objectively instead. Being 'objective' here means paying due respect to the specifics of the group and its processes of formation, instead of trying to translate it immediately into some category derived from social theory – not seeing it as derived from an underlying **class** struggle or a struggle for power and domination between the **genders** or 'races', or seeing it in **functionalist** terms as the product of some shared values or trend towards consensus. I hope it is possible to see already that figurationalists claim to go beyond the usual debates in sociology between marxists and functionalists, feminists and their opponents, and it is this that has led to renewed interest in the approach.

Nothing could be read off in advance, since the actual patterns that the groups take on can emerge unpredictably. The dynamism is provided by a certain in-built tension between the possibilities we have described so far. Individuals feel they are subject to contradictory demands, both to act for their own interest, and to act in the interest of the group. The group can feel drawn towards either conflict or consensus, towards including all its members equally or towards introducing inequality. The actual pattern at any one particular time is thus the result of a balance of these tensions, and new movements and shifts can dissolve that particular balance and establish another one. One easy example to illustrate this is found in politics, where the parties and their members interact in complex ways. One of Elias's actual examples describes the different political allegiances between nobles and emerging middle-class groups found at the French court in medieval times (see Mennell, 1992). The French king was shrewd enough to realize that he often held the casting vote in the struggles between these groups, and would shift his allegiance to one side or the other in order to preserve his own interests, while different factions of the two groups would also be seeking to form alliances within their own parties and even with members of other parties to advance their interests.

It is clear that a figurational approach could have a very wide range of application indeed, and people have used it to analyse a number of different topics. However, it so happens that leisure groups are particularly suitable examples to demonstrate its power. Dunning, for example, actually uses the example of a football game as a figuration (in Elias and Dunning, 1986). The game is composed of individuals, but they are members of a group or team too, and, for that matter, they are all players in a particular game (Dunning argues that both teams form the figuration). As the game develops, particular patterns of interaction emerge among the players – one team attacks, while the other defends, play might be dominated by the contest between a particular forward and a particular defender, interactions with the spectators, managers or officials can also have definite effects, and so on. We cannot simply predict this pattern from knowing the rules of association football, or from trying to ascribe a particular power imbalance to the game – even when the top clubs play the minnows, the result is by no means guaranteed. Dunning suggests that the tensions between the players themselves, and between them and the spectators, are the source of the pleasure in the game: these tensions increase and decrease as the game progresses, until a pleasurable resolution is reached at the end. Indeed, Dunning goes on to describe a particular match precisely in terms of the tension balances which it displays – pleasure is increased when the teams are evenly balanced, where there is a rhythm and pace to the play, where particular events cause unpredictability and disequilibrium (such as a goal or a penalty), or where a satisfactory result enables the full discharge of tension for the spectators, who can talk about an exciting game even if their team has lost.

Football matches also happen to be excellent examples to illustrate how pleasurable tension is managed in our society. The spectators can enjoy the conflict, contact and aggression of the game without risking any harm to themselves. They can have their emotions heightened and then managed as the game follows its course. This is, in other words, a 'civilized' way in which to enjoy strong emotions (Dunning argues that football hooligans, unlike the 'normal fan' can enjoy those strong emotions in the relatively uncivilized form of actual fighting with other fans and the police). It is important that modern societies develop these civilized forms of enjoyment, since raw emotion and the open display of conflict and aggression threaten social disorder. Indeed, figurationalists describe the evolution of social life itself as a move towards 'civilization' – the relatively orderly management of emotion and tension. This analysis is often exemplified by comparing social life and leisure pursuits in the past. In medieval Europe, for example, it was much more acceptable to display open violence in one's conduct with others, to challenge rivals to a fight, or to indicate displeasure with one's spouse by beating her. Even polite society tolerated what would be regarded these days as appalling table manners as diners fell upon the food with obvious relish, tore pieces from joints of meat, and broke wind freely after a meal (Mennell, 1992, has some hilarious examples). Sporting contests similarly were aggressive and violent, often unregulated by codified rules or referees, and quite commonly ending in death for some of the players or spectators.

Substantial social changes have led towards civilization. A key factor is the emergence of the modern State which claims to monopolize violence and to forbid it in others. There is also a growing social interrelatedness among people. Social contact and the establishment of 'chains of dependency' in complex social systems mean that it is no longer possible to disregard the feelings of others. As soon as we begin to regulate our own excesses to spare the feelings of other people, we are becoming civilized. We develop self-restraint, think carefully of the effects of our behaviour, try not to disgust our companions with our behaviour at meal times, or get so carried away by our excitement in sports that we end up permanently damaging our neighbours. Institutions develop to enforce restraint, not only the police force, but also voluntary bodies which set out rules to limit the damage that can be inflicted on our opponents. Sometimes these rules are remarkably recent – Dunning tells us, for example, that the common practice of 'hacking' (kicking or raking the shins of your opponent) was only outlawed in soccer in 1865, and opponents of reform bewailed the consequent decline of 'manliness' (Elias and Dunning, 1986).

It is now possible to see that leisure is going to play a major role in the civilizing process. Strong emotions and tensions can never be regulated entirely or banished completely from social life. Indeed, over-regulation can produce monotony, a lack of interest, withdrawal of support, and even damage to mental health. What is needed instead is a safe form of managing emotion and tension. Ideally, such leisure forms should be 'mimetic', that is, offering an activity that people can identify with, that bears some relation to (or imitates) their lives. Football and other sports clearly do this, but so do films, plays and television programmes. This is such an important aspect of leisure, that it might be the defining characteristic itself – to paraphrase, what defines leisure in general, whatever form it takes, is that it produces this safe kind of emotional involvement and tension management. It is this quality, Elias argues (in Elias and Dunning, 1986) that really lies behind what is normally described as the differences between **work and leisure**.

The figurationalist approach has also become important as offering an explanation for football hooliganism. The civilization process is uneven, and affects those groups who are the most fully integrated into social life, those who have the longest chains of dependency, and those whose everyday life involves them in interaction with a wide range of other people. Certain social groups, and Dunning suggests that these are 'lower working-class groups' have much less integrated social lives, split between age cohorts and sexes, and offering only temporary alliances ('segments') instead of fully integrated social groups. It follows that the ability to restrain and regulate strong emotion and violent impulses is much reduced without strong social support. Indeed, we find that individuals can actually gain status by displaying strong emotion and expertise in violence in segmented groups in modern society, more or less as they once did in pre-modern societies. It is those groups who tend to form the bulk of football hooligans, Dunning argues (in Elias and Dunning, 1986). They find football matches are ideal venues to pursue their interest in violent behaviour, since opponents are conveniently delivered to a large arena, there is a large anonymous crowd with only a few policemen, and thus a low chance of having to exercise restraint.

Figurationalism has also produced a major study on the emergence of the modern diet (Mennell, 1985) (see **food**). We have already indicated how the approach might help to explain the shift towards modern notions of etiquette and table manners, and the idea of the modern meal as a social occasion which requires participants to exercise considerable restraint, sometimes to the extent of failing to satisfy their hunger altogether. Several other important social reactions to food and eating can also be explained, including the strange predilection among the British upper classes for nursery food, and the emergence of various eating disorders, Mennell argues. But there is also the issue of the make-up of the modern diet and how it has emerged from a complex process of social change, via a series of figurations which include chefs and laymen, elites from different European nations, the effects of the modern food industry, and the control of the supply of food. Once more, there is an insistence on complexity, as Mennell refuses to explain the modern diet exclusively in marxist terms (commodification resulting from the food industry), or, indeed in terms we encounter in the entry on **semiotics** (the symbolism of food arising from a deep structure of meaning of which few current individuals are aware).

As with all general approaches, figurationalism has its critics, of course. The emphasis on concrete detail and emergence could easily be seen as a refusal to identify the really effective factors at work, such as class or gender, or **cultural capital**, **disciplinary apparatuses**, or whatever are the alternative preferred concepts. There are methodological problems arising from the insistence on addressing objects with 'detachment', without preconceptions: Rojek (1986) has argued that this apparent detachment is best understood as a professional value commitment shared by the academic community. There are problems with the civilization approach as well, if it seems to be advocating a straightforward trend towards self-restraint and the regulation of violence: there is still a lot of violence about, and self-restraint among one group is often accompanied by violence towards another, as van Kreiken (1999) argues in the case of colonialism. The civilization process can be rather selective as a term to describe social trends, despite the injunction to study its actual emergence. Nevertheless, figurationalist work has enriched the work of other theorists, including Bourdieu (see Wacquant, 1995, on professional boxing and civilization), and, whatever its general claims, it has offered some excellent specific analyses of leisure groups in particular.

FURTHER READING

Figurational analysis is explained clearly and illustrated with reference to football and foxhunting in Dunning's chapter in Rojek (1989). Dunning and Waddington (2003) have a useful discussion on sport, nationalism, drugs, excitement and social policy. There is a collection of Elias's work online at SocioSite (2003), and another at the University of Sydney (2003). The University of Leicester (UK) has two excellent online sites: the Centre for Research into Sport and Society (2003) pursues more figurational approaches, while work on football hooliganism from a variety of approaches can be traced via the Sir Norman Chester Centre for Football Research (2003).

REFERENCES

Centre for Research into Sport and Society (2003) [online] http://www.le.ac.uk/crss/
Dunning, E. and Waddington, I. (2003) 'Sport as a Drug and Drugs in Sport', *International Review for the Sociology of Sport*, 38 (3): 351–68.
Elias, N. and Dunning, E. (1986) *Quest for Excitement: Sport and Leisure in the Civilising Process*, Oxford: Basil Blackwell Ltd.
Mennell, S. (1985) *All Manners of Food: Eating and Taste in England and France from the Middle Ages to the Present*, Oxford: Basil Blackwell.
Mennell, S. (1992) *Norbert Elias: An Introduction*, Oxford: Basil Blackwell.
Rojek, C. (1986) 'Problems of Involvement and Detachment in the writings of Norbert Elias', *British Journal of Sociology*, XXXVII, (4): 584–96.
Rojek, C. (ed.) (1989) *Leisure for Leisure*, London: Macmillan.
Sir Norman Chester Centre for Football Research (2003) [online] http://www.le.ac.uk/snccfr/
SocioSite (2003) [online] http://www2.fmg.uva.nl/sociosite/topics/sociologists.html#elias.
University of Sydney (2003) [online] http://www.usyd.edu.au/su/social/elias/elias.html
Van Kreiken, R. (1999) 'The Barbarism of Civilization: Cultural Genocide and the "Stolen Generation"', *British Journal of Sociology*, 50 (2): 297–315.
Wacquant, L. (1995) 'Pugs at Work: Bodily Capital and Bodily Labour Among Professional Boxers', *Body and Society*, 1 (1): 65–93.

The preparation and consumption of food have become a leisure activity (although food preparation is also work as well). The context for the consumption of food in particular helps us see the connections between leisure and important social and cultural processes.

Section Outline: *Food and culture: myths and meanings in structural anthropology. The food industry and commodification. Food, social class, cultural capital, gender and consumer politics: fast food. Postmodernism, food as 'disembedded', the collapse of cultural boundaries. The emergence of the modern diet. Eating disorders.*

At first sight, there seems to be little of interest for leisure studies in the preparation or consumption of food. It seems to be a straightforward matter of simply doing what is needed naturally, or responding to some physiological need. Like several other activities we have examined, however, closer examination shows that eating food is a highly cultural activity, replete with social meaning. This is easy to demonstrate if we consider special meals such as those eaten at family reunions, taking someone out to eat on a first date, a working breakfast, or the lunch that we are sometimes invited to consume at a job interview. The way you eat, how much you eat, how you handle your knife and fork, and the menu that you choose can all be of considerable social importance. Food and eating can also require the management of relations between different occupations, ethnic groups, **genders** or generations. As with other leisure activities, it is possible see how the preparation and eating of food have moved away from activities designed just to meet the basic necessities to become much more 'disembedded' (see Giddens, 1991), flexible and free-floating, as we would expect in societies that are approaching **postmodernism** or late modernity.

However, the preparation and eating of food were embedded in social life in pre-industrial societies as well. Lévi-Strauss has offered some classic **semiotic** analyses here, showing how food is something that people can think with, to use his phrase (see Leach, 1970, for a convenient summary of this approach). Foodstuffs come with a set of differences and similarities that can be used in cultural work. For example, they can be raw or cooked, and this happens to be a very useful difference to illustrate the way human beings relate to nature, and thence where human beings come from, when violence is necessary, and what people may or may not do with the natural order. It is also possible to subject foodstuffs to a process that is halfway between leaving them raw and cooking them fully – such as leaving them to partially rot (as we do with some cheese or game), smoking or curing them. Particular kinds of foodstuffs are actually found that way, and honey is an excellent example. It is not entirely raw, but nor is it fully cultural because insects produce it, not humans. These halfway foodstuffs can take on considerable symbolic importance as mediators between human beings and nature, and it is not surprising to find so many myths which feature them, according to Lévi-Strauss (see Glucksmann, 1974). Thus, a honey myth that relates the benefits and perils of particular ways of gathering honey, and then relates the mythical effects of consuming honey, contains moral lessons about the relationship between human beings and nature. The accidental, textural, and visual similarities between honey and equally ambiguous products like sperm (or menstrual blood) also permit meaning to be attributed to the use of honey, its effects on women, how it can be used to symbolize the relations of family life, and so on.

The ways in which food is cooked are also capable of expressing social meaning: to boil food, for example, preserves its qualities and also happens to be an efficient way of retaining the full value of the object in food terms. Roasting food is at the other extreme, and involves the loss of some of the substances and considerable transformation. It is not surprising to find that roast food is associated with important occasions and the display of wealth. This has persisted into European culture too, of course, as shown by the structure of an important symbolic meal such as Christmas dinner (see Finnegan, Block 1, in Open University, 1982). The classic menu offers a whole variety of raw food (the fruit or nuts at the end of the meal), a sequence of variously cooked food from (boiled) soup to the highlights of the roast poultry, and some ambiguous substances such as smoked or rotted cheese. Of course, additional delights are produced by remembering how mother used to cook parsnips, being able to display partners or offspring to families of origin, and to engage in an obvious bonding ritual based on one of the most fundamental social practices, which is sharing food with others. Turner (1996) reminds us that the term 'companionship' contains a reference to sharing bread in its first and second syllables.

109

Food

It is clear that the preparation and consumption of food have drifted away from their immediate origins, and that the modern diet is testimony to the huge organizational power of the modern food industry. Any local supermarket will display fruit and vegetables from a wide variety of other countries, some of which are fairly recent additions to the British diet, such as the kiwi fruit or oriental vegetables. As usual, the substantial increases in choice result from a thoroughgoing commodification process, as cash crops are produced for sale in an increasing number of countries instead of subsistence crops for immediate consumption by the population. This in turn has involved the introduction of Western notions of land ownership and the rational industrialized production of foodstuffs to a set standard and quality. As with other examples, a politics of leisure is apparent. To take a particularly pointed example mentioned by Simmonds (in Tomlinson, 1990), much of the modern vegetarian diet depends on foodstuffs being grown in this industrialized way in much poorer countries. As a result, choosing your diet to make a point about the exploitation of animals can involve you unwittingly in the systematic exploitation of land and people in other countries.

There are other examples of how choosing food has become a political matter, and recent consumer campaigns illustrate this particularly well. Nava (1991) thinks these are a very effective way to exercise power, probably more important than voting or trade union protest. Boycott campaigns of a variety of substances such as tuna, South African products (in the time of apartheid), grapes sold by United Fruit (once notorious for its dreadful industrial relations), or fur coats all illustrate the power of organized consumers. Recent campaigns against genetically modified food also seem to have been effective, in Britain at least, in persuading supermarkets not to stock the products. There have also been more positive campaigns for things like 'real ale' or traditionally baked bread.

There is a gender-based politics here as well, in that it still tends to be women who prepare food, except in the most highly paid and high status cases, where male chefs predominate. No doubt a fan of Lévi-Strauss would be able to explain the deep cultural roots of this practice, by pointing to the common tendency to elide together the female and the natural – the more cultural food preparation becomes, as in artistic haute cuisine, the more that men tend to dominate. More prosaically, it is clear that the purchase, preparation, and cooking of food for the family are one of the major tasks in the schedule of unpaid domestic labour which takes up so much of 'free time' and thus displaces other kinds of leisure.

Preparation and cooking have pleasures as well: to refer to some of those mentioned in the entry on **pleasures**, accurately following a recipe must offer the same pleasures as following a narrative to a successful conclusion, while being able to improvise offers pleasures which might be described as 'jouissance'. Some culinary tasks must also yield the experience of 'flow', or permit pleasurable fantasies, but one would expect these to be found in the more culturally refined cooking activities rather than the mundane business of preparing the family meal, or in the activities of elite chefs rather than kitchen hands.

Many meals are routinely produced under conditions that more closely resemble work, with its characteristic discipline, and conventional set of relationships between the genders and the generations. Meals also clearly reveal different 'aesthetics' rooted in social class, cultural capital, and the process of distantiation. We discuss these possibilities through the work of Bourdieu in the entry on **social class**, and examine how he can explain quite specific food tastes, such as preferences for heavy, fatty and 'satisfying' foods for working-class males. We have already mentioned some examples of the practical distanciation and differentiation tasks that can be accomplished during a meal – we can tell who is really at ease with a variety of exotic cutlery and dishes, who knows their way around a menu in French, or who can manage conversations in the appropriate sequence with fellow dinner guests, and so on. Food can feature as a component in a selection process, as in the famed 'knife and fork test' to select those destined for high rank in the British Civil Service – it was necessary to display the effortless deployment of **cultural capital** at the table in order to pass the test and be selected. This social process of selection and distinction can be put opposite the more companionable qualities of shared meals with which we began.

The process of disembeddedness progresses much further in postmodernism, for some critics, and we may now be seeing postmodern cuisine. It is easy enough to choose from a variety of national cuisines in any large city, purely for pleasure, and these opportunities often offer a major attraction to the tourist, as in Melbourne, for example. Sometimes food comes ready mixed, culturally speaking. At the more popular end of the market, one could suggest dishes such as the chicken tikka pizza as a candidate. The favourite British meal – a curry – also contains interesting cultural mixes, since the classic curry tends to represent what the British think Indian food might be like, even though it is often cooked by (Anglo-) Pakistanis and Bengalis. At the more esoteric end, Miles (1993) mentions the work of a fashionable American chef who has combined Thai and French cooking. To contrast with this cultural variety, we might also mention the spread of standardized fast food, which we discuss in the entry on **McDonaldization**, or note that 'something like three quarters of eating places in Britain operate principally by reheating industrially prepared products [in microwave ovens]' (Mennell et al., 1992: 87).

There is also a famous study which involves a **figurational** approach. Mennell (1985) begins in the classic manner by reviewing semiotic and marxist approaches, and concludes that these general approaches only work by sacrificing a tremendous amount of detail and process. His book goes on to supply some of that detail using detailed historical analysis of the emergent history of food. The European diet used to be much more closely tied to the satisfaction of basic necessities, which is partly responsible for some of the curiosities which we can still read about, such as the seasonal feasts at harvest time followed by periods of involuntary diet in times of shortage. Animals would be slaughtered to save having to feed them over the winter, and fruit would be picked and preserved by pickling or bottling – hence the custom of autumnal feasting on veal or poultry, and cooking preserved fruit in the form of pies and puddings. As he points out, the ability to grow sufficient surplus and to store food is fairly recent, but once that technology had been achieved, some of those traditional practices were able to change (some remain too, of course, as in the various 'goose fairs' that still take place at the start of winter in areas of the UK).

Tastes for food also changed, though, as ideas and then recipes were exchanged between the aristocracy in different European countries (especially France and Italy). Cooking practices were also exchanged. These tastes diffused downward to other social classes, but there was also genuine pressure from below to expand choice. More recently, the 'lower orders' have been able to travel as well, and have brought back from holiday dishes such as spaghetti bolognese or paella. We have also already hinted at the effects of British colonialism, and then of Asian immigration, on the British taste for 'Indian' food. As we discuss in the relevant entry, **figurationalist** analysis has also used the changes in table manners as a classic example of 'the civilization process', a move towards internal self-restraint and consideration for others, based on a growing inter-dependency and contact between people. Gradually, as the possibly distasteful fate of domestic animals entered consideration, it became less common to display the actual corpses on the dinner table, and to use instead various euphemisms such as 'steak'. Indeed, it is possible to suggest that matters have now become so refined that the point of a meal is not really to satisfy any kind of hunger or desires at all, but to use food, crockery, and cutlery as a set of props for polite intercourse.

Mennell (1985) ends his account by discussing the historical origin of various food disorders, including anorexia and bulimia. This is a large area, and one that again reveals the close connection between eating and culture. Food disorders provoke much social, psychological and popular discussion, and it is common to connect anorexia especially with a variety of cultural trends, including the current fashion for thin women, or the inability to separate what Goffman (1968) once called 'virtual' and 'actual' selves. Mennell et al. (1992) show how these factors impact especially on young white affluent women in industrial societies. They also add to this list the development of a set of cultural and historical distinctions based on fat and thin people. In medieval times when food was often short, it was the sheer quantity of consumption that marked the affluent and the elite, and it was socially valued to be plump. Dieting actually began among the elite who were worried about obesity and health. When food became more plentiful, thinness becomes a mark of social distinction instead.

FURTHER READING

Bourdieu (1986) has a detailed analysis of (French) tastes. Mennell (1985) and Mennell et al. (1992) are packed with examples. Miles's work (1993) actually contains a recipe.

REFERENCES

Bourdieu, P. (1986) *Distinction: A Social Critique of the Judgement of Taste*, London: Routledge.

Giddens, A. (1991) *Modernity and Self-Identity: Self and Society in the Late Modern Age*, Cambridge: Polity Press.

Glucksmann, M. (1974) *Structuralist Analysis in Contemporary Thought: A Comparison of the Theories of Claude Lévi-Strauss and Louis Althusser*, London: Routledge and Kegan Paul.

Goffman, E. (1968) *Stigma: Notes on the Management of Spoiled Identity*, Harmondsworth: Pelican Books.

Leach, E. (1970) *Lévi-Strauss*, London: Collins.

Mennell, S. (1985) *All Manners of Food: Eating and Taste in England and France from the Middle Ages to the Present*, Oxford: Basil Blackwell.

Mennell, S., Murcott, A. and van Otterloo, A. (1992) *The Sociology of Food: Eating, Diet and Culture*, London: Sage.

Miles, E. (1993) 'Adventures in the Postmodern Kitchen', *Journal of Popular Culture*, 27 (3).

Nava, M. (1991) 'Consumerism Reconsidered: Buying and Power', *Cultural Studies*, 5 (2): 157–74.

Open University (1982) *Popular Culture (U203)*, Milton Keynes: Open University Press.

Tomlinson, A. (ed.) (1990) *Consumption, Identity and Style*, London: Comedia and Routledge.

Turner, B. (1996) *The Body and Society: Explorations in Social Theory*, London: Sage.

113

Functionalism

Functionalism is a general term describing a number of linked approaches in social theory which tend to be (excessively?) interested in the formation of social solidarities. This interest is commonly found among politicians and spokespersons stressing the socially integrative role of sports and leisure (but with less sophistication).

Section Outline: *Functionalism and its different manifestations in social theory. Durkheim and the functions of religion. Parker and the functions of leisure. Leisure and tourism, the generation of local solidarities and senses of the sacred: liminality, 'flow' and social commentary. Sport, leisure and social cohesion. Social conflict.*

Functionalist ideas belong not just to a specialism associated with social theory, but are widespread in social commentary more generally. Most people if asked to justify government spending on leisure will respond that leisure is not just an activity that rewards the individual participants but has a deeper and broader social purpose. Most of us know what these purposes might be – leisure refreshes us, permits us to recover from work, and offers opportunities to be ourselves. Particular leisure activities bring particular benefits of this kind, so we feel that going away on holiday helps us to prepare for the next bout of work, or playing a team game reinforces the respect for rules and for social order, or engaging in hazardous leisure activity helps us to appreciate the constraints and routines of normal life. Governments also commonly mention benefits such as helping to reduce crime in poor neighbourhoods, to integrate the marginalized back into social life, to help people cope with unemployment, and so on. This sort of claimed benefit is discussed further in the entry on **leisure policy**.

You might have already detected a value position in this sort of argument. To argue that something is functional is also to support it, to approve of or want to justify a particular activity. This is an important aspect of early functionalist analysis, especially in anthropology. Early

---

encounters with pre-industrial societies often led to explorers or colonial administrators dismissing cultural practices encountered there as 'primitive' or as morally backward and reprehensible. It was important to develop a vocabulary that moved beyond this obviously value-laden and usually Eurocentric position, and functionalist vocabulary helped develop a more technical stance by asking what social functions were achieved by even unpleasant rituals. Students might like to cut their teeth here on the famous discussion of the cultural significance of cock-fighting in Balinese society (Geertz, 1973). However, approval can be overdone: functionalist analysis is prone to approve of any social practice, at least in the limited sense that it is seen to fit particular ways of life. The matter becomes clearer, perhaps, when we consider modern societies – to search for the functions of modern culture, work or military endeavour is almost inevitably to apologize for them.

Some functionalist theorists quite explicitly embraced the programme of searching for common value systems to help to integrate society politically, and this helps explain the link with so much current policy. Functionalism can explain disorder by seeing it as 'deviant', a result of the breakdown of the integrating forces such as socialization processes found in 'normal' family life, or arising from temporary dislocations in social order as societies change. This terminology can easily demonize and devalue those who do not share the supposedly central values.

It can be quite difficult initially to consider ways in which the functions of leisure might be critically evaluated, however. The entry on **social class** in this collection, for example, argues that leisure activities are as dominated by class discrimination, difference and social distance as any other activity, which would obviously limit the functional aspects that many people claim to be present. The same kind of theme can be found in the entries on **gender** or **identity**; women may experience discrimination based on gender if they attend sporting events or attempt to engage in traditionally male leisure pursuits, while gays often cite attendance at sports or leisure functions as offering a particular example of an occasion where they are likely to experience prejudice. Functionalist analysis can overlook these half-hidden conflicts and social strains. Of course, approaches that stress conflict can be accused of the opposite omission, as with the work on **disciplinary apparatuses**, while still further approaches attempt to study the balances of consensus and conflict without prioritizing either tendency, as in the work on **figurationalism**. It is of course important to avoid attaching too simple a label to any particular theorist, since most of them are well aware of the background debates. Those choosing a functionalist analysis normally do so on balance, as a way into discussing some of the aspects of the debate.

I have in mind here particularly the work of Parker (1983) to whom we shall turn in the entry on **work–leisure relationships**. Parker does list a number of social and individual functions of leisure, such as helping 'people to learn how to play their part in society . . . to achieve societal or collective aims . . . and it helps to keep society together' (Parker, 1983: 33). He cites theorists such as Dumazedier who opts for three main functions 'relaxation, entertainment and personal development' (ibid.: 35) or Noe who combines individual and social functions to examine the role of leisure as 'work, recreational and cultural' (ibid.: 39). But Parker notes that there are important intervening variables such as 'the demands and satisfactions of the occupation . . . And the [differences among] sex and social class groups' (ibid.: 41). Indeed, the demands of the particular set of occupations in question is the main factor leading to the concrete findings of this classic study (that there are three basic patterns of connection between occupation and leisure – extension, opposition and neutrality – further explored in the entry on the work–leisure relationship).

For social theorists, it is important to move beyond the level of social commentary and utilitarian politics when discussing the functions of leisure. For one thing, there are different strands within functionalism, with American functionalism being dominated by the work of Parsons (see Rocher, 1974). This work developed into a rather technical attempt to classify different activities in terms of their underlying functions, organized as four general categories. Some activities were directed to mechanisms of adaptation as social change was experienced, others to the definition of social goals, still others to mechanisms of system integration, and the last ones to a process that Parsons called 'latency', the ways in which social values became embedded in cultural systems. A latency effect would be achieved if leisure pursuits were successful in inculcating deep cultural roots and values. This claim often lies behind the view that playing team sports at school is supposed to provide a set of values (sportsmanship, fair play, competitiveness) that will stand you in good stead for the rest of your life. One application of this idea is found in the classic work of Coleman (in Halsey et al., 1961) on the compensations on offer to US high school students who fail in the academic system – they can often gain status in the sporting subculture instead. The entry on **effects analysis** investigates some arguments that leisure in the form of modern media has also had undesirable cultural effects such as desensitization to violence, or the development of a 'mean world' syndrome. The notion of a 'behavioural script' (also discussed in that entry) would fit with an attempt to explain how latency occurs at the level of individual personality.

European functionalism developed along a different path, traced best, perhaps in French social theory. We examine this path at a rather later stage in the entries on **semiotics** or **postmodernism**, but here we might examine the work of a 'founding father', Durkheim. A summary of the overall approach embraced by Durkheim can be found in Ritzer (1996), and a particular argument for the relevance of Durkheim for cultural analysis, is found in Alexander (1988). Following Alexander, it might be best to examine Durkheim's work on religion, which is fundamental to his concerns. We can immediately pick up a clue about how this is going to work, by noting the very common religious metaphors and analogies used to understand leisure. There is Ritzer's (1999) notion of 'cathedrals of consumption' offering a kind of religious enchantment. Tourism frequently deploys metaphors such pilgrimage: in fact, Dann's (2002) collection of essays includes a number of terms that originate with Durkheim (tourism as a social fact, tourism as a modern myth, and so on). Anyone who knew Durkheim's work would also find a clear trace in MacCannell's (1989) argument that the tourists' search for authenticity, and their attempt to manage encounters with others, means that tourism itself stands for society.

Durkheim's analysis argues that religion is thoroughly social in origins, and in its consequences. The particular forms that religious beliefs take are produced by the ways of life of the believers, who symbolize social relations in the ways in which they think of the divine and its connections with social life. However, this original connection is soon transcended – cultural systems and classifications have a life of their own and develop relations among themselves which far exceed the original connections with immediate social life. Indeed, religious experience must gain this independence if it is to appear as other-worldly, as sacred, as binding upon normal social life in some way. Religious ceremonies reinforce social bonds between believers in the form of rituals, and in their **ecstatic** early forms, they produced a worship of the social, using social processes ('collective excitation'). Religion thus offers a sphere of common belief, a sacred realm which cannot be doubted, and which persists to bind people together despite their more mundane differences of gender, age, or social position. Durkheim was well aware that religions undergo change, and that the simple collective rituals of pre-industrial societies have to adapt to far more complex forms of social solidarity in industrial ones. Nevertheless, even industrial secular societies need religion, although it often takes the form of nationalism, or even the 'cult of the individual'. Durkheim also intervened actively in social policy, especially in educational policy, to attempt to preserve this common sacred realm for all French citizens, in the form of a national curriculum, for example.

This kind of analysis has clear implications for understanding leisure in modern societies. It is one of the realms where the sacred might emerge, unlike work, which is increasingly differentiated, divisive, competitive, specialized and hierarchical. Engaging in leisure with others offers quite different social relationships, such as the chance to play alongside the boss as an equal at a works football match, or the glorious sense of solidarity that emerges among sports fans when their team wins and they experience considerable collective excitation and a sense that they have witnessed something sacred and pure. Visiting a heritage site can be an occasion for important social bonds to develop as members of the same family negotiate common interpretations and reinforce their intergenerational solidarity. Whole symbolic systems to manage togetherness and otherness can be grounded in tourism and travel. Wallace and Hartley (in Alexander, 1988) argue that the most satisfying of social relationships, including friendship, undergo a ritualized path towards setting aside the relationship as something special or sacred (and I am reminded of the ritual processes involved in becoming a member of a creative subculture). Percy and Taylor (1997) explore the marked similarities between the symbolic meanings, rituals and collective effects at a football match and those offered by new religious movements.

The cultural and symbolic pay-off explains the deep personal impact of leisure experiences on people. Just looking for immediate utilitarian pay-offs can never explain the commitment and the pleasure of leisure pursuits (and nor can the use of psychological arguments that involve terms like 'addiction'). The experience of being absorbed in leisure, in experiencing 'flow' is a religious experience for Durkheimians. Alexander (1988) also points out that the sense of being outside of normal life during rituals, of being 'liminal' while doing something important, can also explain the creative thinking about society or self that can take place in leisure, as we suggested above.

We have already mentioned the tendency of functionalist theory to minimize social conflict and division. Yet this is implicit in some of the examples we have examined – the tremendous solidarity generated among sports fans supporting one team can very easily turn into aggression and violence towards the other team and their supporters. It might be possible to risk the generalization that every form of solidarity is a form of exclusion as well. Whether or not genuinely sacred values can emerge to unite the different factions and groups (a strong belief in the value of the game, irrespective of the result, for example) remains to be seen: certainly, modern Durkheimians themselves seem prepared to minimize the emphasis on overall social solidarity in favour of more local examples. This selectivity is not uncommon, and functionalist theorists have also generated additional concepts to guide analysis, such as the difference between 'latent' and 'manifest' functions (roughly, those that are at work beneath the surface, and those that are immediately apparent to the groups concerned). Modern theorists are rarely found in a 'pure' state, of course, and it is common to incorporate concepts and arguments from other traditions. Thus, Merton (see Harris, 2003, for a discussion) is particularly aware of the possibility of unintended consequences and dysfunctions arising from structural strains and tensions in society itself.

See also: *authenticity, posts, semiotics, social class.*

FURTHER READING

Dann (2002) and Percy and Taylor (1997) are worth following up for some modern applications. Coleman (in Halsey et al., 1961) feels astonishingly contemporary and has been influential. The British Government currently stresses social inclusion as among the key functions to be provided by sport and leisure, see the online report on PAT 10 (2003).

REFERENCES

Alexander, J. (ed.) (1988) *Durkheimian Sociology: Cultural Studies*, Cambridge: Cambridge University Press.
Dann, G. (ed.) (2002) *The Tourist as a Metaphor of the Social World*, New York: CABI Publishing.
Geertz, C. (1973) *The Interpretation of Cultures*, New York: Basic Books.
Halsey, A., Floud, J. and Anderson, C. (eds) (1961) *Education, Economy and Society*, London: Collier-Macmillan Limited.
Harris, D. (2003) *Teaching Yourself Social Theory*, London: Sage.
MacCannell, D. (1989) *The Tourist: A New Theory of the Leisure Class*, revised edn, New York: Schocken Books.
Parker, S. (1983) *Leisure and Work*, London: George Allen and Unwin.
PAT 10 (2003) [online] http://www.culture.gov.uk/
Percy, M. and Taylor, R. (1997) 'Something for the Weekend, Sir? Leisure, Ecstasy and Identity in Football and Contemporary Religion', *Leisure Studies*, 16: 37–49.
Ritzer, G. (1996) *Sociological Theory*, 4th edn, Singapore: McGraw-Hill.
Ritzer, G. (1999) *Enchanting a Disenchanted World: Revolutionizing the Means of Consumption*, Thousand Oaks, CA: Pine Forge Press.
Rocher, G. (1974) *Talcott Parsons and American Sociology*, Ontario: Nelson.

Functionalism

> To gaze at something means to look at it in a particularly careful or systematic way, and this notion of a systematic, organized look at things has been used to explain the way a number of images are formed in order to capture our attention. To gaze at somebody carefully can also be a prelude to an attempt to discipline or control them (during their leisure activities in this case): similarly, to feel that you are constantly at risk of being gazed at can lead to a kind of constant self-discipline, a feeling of always being 'on show'.

Section Outline: *The 'male gaze' in feminist film theory: the representations of women and voyeurism. 'Dominant white gazes' and the depiction of 'race' in the media. Tourist gazes. Sources of resistance to the gaze. Optical and the other senses in the pleasures of tourism.*

We can begin to explore more systematically by considering a famous piece on how women are represented in the cinema. Mulvey (1975) has suggested that women are subject to a 'male gaze'. The representations of women that we see on the screen, the particular ways in which the camera looks at them, and the special ways in which they are located in **narratives** all represent dominant male values. It is certainly the case that the visuals we see on screen are usually extremely carefully constructed and organized. The process usually starts with the careful casting of people who are chosen to represent in a visual way a particular character or role in a story. It is certainly no accident that blonde women appear frequently on screen in particular roles, for example, because blonde hair is associated with devastating sexual attraction ('blonde bombshells'), assertiveness ('brassy blondes'), naïvety ('dumb blondes'), or sexy girlishness ('dizzy blondes'). There is no need to supply extensive scripting if you can convey a number of these meanings instantly, by having an attractive blonde move next door to a married couple, open a saloon in town, or take a job as a secretary. Great attention is paid to the framing and composition of the shots, the lighting, costume, make-up and the way in which people move. Classic Hollywood narratives place women symbolically in crucial scenes: maternal women represent home and community, attractive young women represent threat and disruption, nuns and bar girls represent a common range of sexual and emotional behaviour, and so on.

However, Mulvey (1975) has pointed to unconscious mechanisms at work as well. Gazing at women may have its origins in, and reproduce the pleasures of, a psychological fetish described by Freud as 'scopophilia'. This is the activity in which voyeurs or peepers engage, and it provides pleasure not only by revealing what is normally kept hidden, but by offering the voyeur a sense of power and control over the unknowing victim. The cinema is a particularly potent location for unlocking unconscious desires and permitting them to inform the fantasies of the viewer, and it seems to provide us with a private world where other people appear on the screen apparently unaware of our presence, so it is not surprising to find a great deal of voyeuristic pleasure for the male viewer as the camera spies on unsuspecting women, or offers particularly revealing views of them, for example. The very structure of direction and camera movement which so involves viewers, such as the 'point-of-view shot', where the camera presents us with the views of one of the participants so that we feel we are that participant, engages us in gazing in this sexually controlling way at the female actors. The dominant look is available to female viewers too, and they are almost obliged to internalize the male gaze in order to understand the narrative structure of the film, Mulvey suggests, although her later work (Mulvey, 1985) points to occasions where the male gaze leaves a brief viewing space for genuine female identification.

We suggest in the entry on **'race' and leisure** that the notion of an organized gaze can help to explain the ways in which people of colour are represented on the screen as well. Hall (in Alvarado and Thompson, 1990), has pointed to the possible existence of a 'dominant white gaze' in mainstream film, television, and, later, photography (Bailey and Hall, 1994). Hall argues that the media structure discussions of 'race' and ethnicity around a focus on the relations of subordination and domination; a notion of superior and inferior species; an attempt to displace issues from history into nature. Together, 'racial' differences emerge as signs of inferiority, arising from breeding or natural ranking. These effects show the influence of an 'absent but imperialising "white eye"' (Alvarado and Thompson, 1990: 14), which lies outside of the frame, but which sees and positions, offering history through the eyes of the imperialists. This can be seen in those films about the Raj, which acted as early documentaries, and offered popular images of India, or in the genre of the 'empire novel', where 'adventure' comes to mean colonizing. The argument is that black people are eventually permitted to appear more centrally in visual representations, but in ways that reflect dominant white values of them as dangerous outsiders, savages, noble savages, clowns, or possessed of some special connection to the natural and biological (which makes them highly emotional, natural athletes, sportsmen, dancers or sexual performers).

The entry on 'race' and leisure also refers to the ability of ethnic minority members to resist the dominant gaze as well, however. Thus bell hooks (who always spells her name without capital letters) points out that black women have never comfortably occupied the viewing position that invites identification with the white male gaze, but tend to be able to bring their own 'readings' to mainstream Hollywood movies (in Thornham, 1999). Signs of resistance to the 'white eye' among black British television viewers have also been detected by McCarthy et al. (2003). Some feminists have pointed to the alternative readings which women of dominant ethnic groups can also supply, including 'redemptive' readings of classic genres such as melodrama. Gledhill (1987), for example, points out that melodramas can be read as a triumph for the emotional skills of the women involved, who often have to tame and domesticate 'wild' men as the story unfolds. We might expect that challenges to dominant gazes are more likely where there is weaker institutional or organizational support for dominant views, in societies where racism and sexism are under challenge, or in the less controlled circumstances of watching television rather than the cinema.

The notion of the gaze has also been introduced into tourism studies via the work of Urry (1990). Urry refers to a 'tourist gaze', a systematic way of looking at tourist sights which involves the same kind of attempts to structure the view by employing sets of values to regulate the experience of otherness. There is no institutional base here (as in prisons), and no equivalent mechanism to focus viewing (as in the cinema), but tour companies themselves make considerable efforts to regulate the gaze of the tourists they accompany, perhaps following filmic devices of framing and composition. The heavily organized accompanied package tour seems to offer the best prospects, but organizing the gaze persists even after the heyday of the package. The process takes place as societies move towards the free-floating meanings associated with **postmodernism** and **hyperreality**: in these circumstances, both tourists and tour companies have to read and fix meanings, to become semioticians. Tourist brochures, for example, emphasize particular views (in both senses) of tourist resorts, as work like Selwyn (1996) indicates: thus themes of 'unspoiled nature', or 'getting away from it all', or 'feeling at home', or being able to avoid the natives if required, are all represented in both text and photographs. Promotional videos could also be analysed in this way, directing the gaze of the tourists towards the preferred attractions of the city or area, and away from the less desirable undersides (although Rojek, 1993, suggests that such 'sites of disorder' can actually be the focus of specialist tours). Sometimes, considerable licence is given to represent the 'reality' of the experience, of course – a video promoting Melbourne as a tourist destination links together the city, a scenic coastal road at least 70 miles away, and a ski resort an equal distance away in the other direction, and displays these as if they were side-by-side. A Disney promotional video uses the same technique to display widely separated sites in Florida, some of which are actually owned by rival companies. On the actual tourist site itself, preferred routes are signposted, and particularly good spots are designated from which to take conventional photographs.

The tourist gaze can be evaded by determined tourists, who deliberately stray off the beaten track in order to organize their own views and encounters. However, as usual, it is not that easy to **escape**. Tourists bring with them images and narratives gained from exposure to countless television programmes or texts of other kinds, which can still have an organizing effect. Rojek's (1993) example of 'literary landscapes' offers the example of literary texts or TV reconstructions being used to structure actual visits to 'Brontë Country', or 'Hardy's Wessex'. Tour companies are also quite willing to offer a kind of licensed deviation: the 'romantic gaze', usually deployed by isolated individuals or couples gazing at landscapes, can easily be accommodated within the tour. It probably takes some determination, and perhaps a certain amount of **cultural capital** to insist on seeing the industrial landscape near the Eden Centre in Cornwall, or the desert behind the suburbs of Cairo: intellectuals are able to develop best the romantic gaze, suggests Urry (1990).

Another kind of criticism suggests that the notion of 'the gaze' simply continues to uphold the importance of the optical in much Western philosophy and social science. At the most general level, using the sense of sight to gain information is a classic male aristocratic technique, which avoids interaction or any kind of emotional or bodily engagement, as in the activity of the *flâneur*. Detached analysis of what can be seen is a characteristic of rational modernity. Usually, the data provided by other senses are ignored, even though they can be extremely important. Sound, for example, plays a major role in providing an aural background for visual perception, and this background undoubtedly affects us in powerful ways:

Gazes

this point is made variously by reflecting on dance music (see **ecstasy**), or the importance of having a private soundscape that lies behind the popularity of personal stereos (see **adding leisure values**). Dann and Jacobsen (in Dann, 2002) have also highlighted the neglect of odour and the sense of smell, and the importance of tactile stimuli 'such as heat or the sensation of cool sea water on the skin' (ibid.: 210). For Dann and Jacobsen 'Aromas . . . can evoke memories of place, help retain a sense of locale, and '"play a major role reconstructing and sustaining major distinctions of social taste" [quoting Lefebvre]' (ibid.: 211). It is certainly true that an increasing number of tourist or heritage sites now pay attention to providing matching odours – the smell of Elizabethan streets at the Plymouth Dome, for example, or of mud and military uniforms at the Great War exhibition at the Imperial War Museum. Even the tourist sniff is being organized!

See also: *authenticity, visitor interpretation.*

FURTHER READING

There are 'reading guides' to Foucault, Hall and Mulvey on my website (Harris, 2003) – specifically via http://www.arasite.org/sagelist.html. Dann and Jacobsen (Dann, 2002), and McCarthy et al. (2003) should be followed up.

REFERENCES

Alvarado, M. and Thompson, J. (eds) (1990) *The Media Reader*, London: BFI Publications.
Bailey, D. and Hall, S. (1994) 'The Vertigo of Displacement', *Ten.8*, 2 (3): 15–23.
Dann, G. (ed.) (2002) *The Tourist as a Metaphor of the Social World*, New York: CABI Publishing.
Gledhill, C. (ed.) (1987) *Home Is Where the Heart Is: Studies in Melodrama and the Woman's Film*, London: BFI Publishing.
Harris, D. (2003) 'Dave Harris (and Colleagues): Essays, Papers and Courses' [online] http://www.arasite.org/
McCarthy, D., Jones, R. and Potrac, P. (2003) 'Constructing Images and Interpreting Realities', *International Review for the Sociology of Sport*, 38, (2): 217–38.
Mulvey, L. (1975) 'Visual Pleasure and Narrative Cinema', *Screen*, 16 (3).
Mulvey, L. (1985) 'Changes', *Discourse*, Fall: 11–30.
Rojek, C. (1993) *Ways of Escape*, Basingstoke: Macmillan.
Selwyn, T. (ed.) (1996) *The Tourist Image: Myths and Myth-Making in Tourism*, New York: John Wiley and Sons.
Thornham, S. (ed.) (1999) *Feminist Film Theory: A Reader*, Edinburgh: Edinburgh University Press.
Urry, J. (1990) *The Tourist Gaze: Leisure and Travel in Contemporary Societies*, London: Sage.

124

Gazes

Gender

Gender is usually defined as the cultural and social aspect of sexuality. As such, there may be more genders than there are biological sexes. Gender differences are important at the level of personal identity, and more broadly as a base of social classification and differentiation, so it is not surprising to find them affecting leisure as well.

Section Outline: *Reviews of some early feminist arguments that gender had been neglected in studies of leisure as an option and as an important organizing principle. Feminist work: youth subcultures, discos, bedroom culture, unpaid domestic labour, theoretical and methodological debates. Masculinity as a construction, especially in sport. Gay leisure: the hidden influences and preferences.*

Much of the early work prioritizing gender was undertaken by feminists and this can produce a slight problem for teachers. I find that feminism has an unpopular image among students, both male and female, and this can induce some reluctance and resistance when studying the topic of gender – students often expect to encounter solemn preaching about the need to treat the genders equally. I want to suggest that there is a challenge for students here in trying to be objective about this topic, to see what is of value, while suspending their initial judgements and reservations.

Early feminist work took two main forms, we can argue. First, feminists found that the position of women had just been completely ignored in much of the conventional research. This omission covered a great deal of the work of social scientists, not just those in leisure. To take one classic example, McRobbie (in Hall and Jefferson, 1976, and in Bennett et al., 1981) argued that the early work on **youth subcultures** focused almost exclusively on males. Her argument is not so much that women simply deserve to be studied as well, but that omitting them led to some serious misunderstanding. Much of the rebellious nature of these youth subcultures stemmed from a reaction to female norms in social life provided by families and mothers (McRobbie, in Bennett et al., 1981), while male theorists had attributed rebelliousness almost exclusively to a reaction against social authority (teachers, the police, and so on). Willis (1977) did something to restore the missing dimension of gender politics to his study of working-class 'lads' and their symbolic rejection of middle-class authority (see **ethnography**) when he noted that the same emphasis on masculinity led to a deep sexism in those subcultures as well, since women also commonly failed to live up to the norms of rugged self-reliance, an ability to endure manual labour, and so on.

Willis could still be accused of assigning sexism a rather secondary place in favour of seeing a form of class struggle as the dominant shaping factor. The same could be said of other earlier marxist analyses, including the work of Clarke and Critcher (1985) that we summarize when discussing **social class**. They certainly mention gender as an important aspect of the underlying struggle for control that shapes the pattern of leisure provision. They are not exactly clear how this fits with class struggle as such, however.

Feminist writers did much to suggest that gender struggles were not only important in their own right, but were dominant in the conflicts that beset social life, including leisure. Indeed, for some, struggles over gender were more fundamental than struggles over class, and there is certainly a wealth of anthropological material that suggests that males tend to dominate females in virtually all societies (Walby, 1990; Women's Study Group, 1978). There are theoretical explanations for this, notably one provided by the French anthropologist Claude Lévi-Strauss, who has argued that the avoidance of incest is the main principle of social life, and that in every society this takes the form of controlling access to women in various ways (such as by marrying off sisters to other men). An equally powerful social theory based on Freudian psychology argues that women find themselves in a subordinate position from a very early stage in the formation of social life, since the structure of language itself is associated with male power to name and classify things (the symbolic power of the father) (see Moi, 1986). These are complex areas, but they have informed analysis of family and social life generally, as well as having a powerful effect in analysing the inherent sexism in popular culture, especially in the movies, where they have informed work on one of the famous organizing **gazes**.

Feminist writers have also been engaged in theoretical debates which have led to some extremely interesting conclusions more generally. We can only summarize them very briefly here, but they consist of feminist critiques designed to show that even the best theorists, such as Foucault or Habermas, have reproduced assumptions based on the universality of the male experience (see Harris, 2003). Feminists have also been in the forefront of debate about 'foundationalism', the arguments that turn on whether there are particularly important central concepts which are essential to social theory. In this case, feminists offered searching debate about whether the concept 'woman' is an essential or universal one, or whether women should be studied in all their ('surface') diversity and complexity (see Ramazanoglu, 1993). More specifically, we find Deem (1999) thinking aloud about whether gender differences are crucial to all studies of leisure, or whether they happen to be particularly significant in studying just some.

If this first stage was necessary to assert the importance of analyses of gender, the second stage involved more concrete studies of the leisure activities of women specifically. There is rather a lot of work here, but we can choose some classic examples. On the one hand there is the work of McRobbie and Nava (1984) who have examined the pleasures for females of the disco (being able to enjoy dancing in female company without too much interference from predatory males). McRobbie (in Bennett et al., 1981) did much to raise awareness of what she calls 'bedroom culture', which went on not in public as with spectacular male subcultures, but among small groups of girls in the privacy of their bedrooms. Hobson found rather similar results in her study of housewives and their leisure activities (see Hall et al., 1980). Much of this work introduced for the first time the idea of home-based leisure, especially involving the role of the mass media, and issues such as shopping as a leisure activity. Some of this inspired new research on male counterparts as well, such as the 'bedroom culture' of male adolescents which is one of their main ways of getting involved with popular music (Frith et al., 1993).

On another tack, a famous study by Deem (1986) attempted to develop more empirical study of the leisure of women, and this sparked off a whole argument about participation and methodology. Briefly, women respondents tended to suggest that they had no leisure at all, or if they did, that it was closely related to the pressures of family life and the views of their husbands. Leisure theorists encountered the concept of 'unpaid domestic labour' and considered it along with the more familiar issue of the relation between leisure and paid work. There are other implications too – the concept of 'leisure' had tended to be shaped by male patterns of leisure, something done in 'free time'. Research instruments which tried to apply this concept would not really tap the experience of women. Women's experience in leisure needed to be seen as part of a much broader organization of their time, and as part of a broader relation to family members. This has shaped the pattern of much actual research on women's participation ever since, as classics such as Green et al. (in Critcher et al., 1995), or Coalter's (1999) study suggest.

There are implications here for the study of male leisure too. Once we cease to see male identity and preferences as some unquestioned natural norm, we can start to ask questions about how male options might be formed. Studies of the construction of male identities in sport soon followed, such as Nauright and Chandler (1996) or Light and Kirk (2000), both of which examine rugby football for signs of 'hegemonic masculinity'. Whannel (1999) offers an analysis of how the media comment upon and manage threats to traditional ideas of masculinity in their coverage of sporting events. This work implies that males are as restricted by patriarchy as females and that 'masculinity' constrains them as well. Useful as these studies are, there is a slight danger that they will dominate studies of gender again, as some people like Deem (1999) fear.

Finally, the discussion on the interactions between gays and leisure could belong to discussions of gender as here or to those of **identity**, depending on how you want to construe gayness (for example, whether you see gays as being 'born' or 'made', relatively culturally fixed or more flexible in their identities). Studying the leisure choices of gay people does provide some general insights into leisure itself though. For example, Kivell and Kleiber (2000), in their interviews with young gay people, reveal just how gendered leisure activities can appear to them. Even the choice of an instrument to play in the school band, for example, was seen as revealing clues about sexual identities: one student 'chose to play . . . the trumpet, in order to convey the social identity of a heterosexual male' (ibid.: 225). Dyer (2002) describes the particular fix on culture that can be taken by traditional male gays, and some of the impact that gay culture has had, almost without any straight people realizing it. For example, gay magazines seem to over-represent interest in classical records, ballet and cabaret: this does not indicate that male gays are predominantly middle class, but reflects their view that these cultural activities offered areas of **escape**, and represented a more liberal and tolerant stance towards them. Cabaret was much admired for its celebration of artifice and camp. Disco culture also celebrated 'theatricalism, sensuality and fun' (Dyer, 2002: 20) and was deeply influenced all along by 'an aesthetic that is unthinkable apart from notions of gay culture' (ibid.: 28). The general 'aestheticization' of life associated with **postmodernism** helped gays think of themselves as positively different, and offered an outlet for what they regarded as their repressed expressive and affective (emotional) aspects: the same point is made by Visser (2002) in his discussion of the contribution that male gay aesthetics has made to the gentrification processes in some cities, especially since gay communities happen to be geographically clustered in particular city areas.

A gay identity is particularly difficult to manage for adolescents especially, but it offers a challenge to everyone in a society that tends to ridicule sexual difference and to strongly promote conventional gendering. Plummer (in Seidman, 1996) talks about the necessary process of 'self-initiated learning' involved. Gays, rather like the disabled people that we examined in the entry on **bodies**, often go through different stages, involving gaining knowledge and information about themselves, realizing that they have a collective identity, becoming more confident and assertive in making the identity public and social, and then attempting to 'stabilize' the identity. The same kind of picture emerges from the work of Kivell and Kleiber (2000): the gay adolescents they interviewed reacted to leisure opportunities in a highly personal way, possibly because they had not reached the stage of wanting to go public. Thus, reading material and film watching could provide significant support, often because the characters were not actually gay, but because they were strong, resilient, and independent. Similarly, leisure activities were carefully considered for personal implications and opportunities. Some male gay people would avoid particular activities in sport and leisure that seemed aggressively masculine and heterosexual and they feared exposure (sometimes this was described as not revealing an aggressive or competitive personality). Gay women also avoided some activities, such as cheerleading, because these came with strong heterosexual assumptions and symbols. At the same time, gay women seemed particularly able to appreciate that sports and leisure activities offered the usual benefits of meeting more people like them, and would choose to participate on that basis. However, this sort of involvement was always limited, partial and instrumental, and, Kivell and Kleiber (2000) point out, it is still almost impossible to develop a public persona as a gay person in sports and leisure activities. There are, of course, always exceptions, such as openly gay male rugby clubs (see the list of international gay rugby clubs at Igrab, 2003).

FURTHER READING

Apart from following up pieces mentioned in the text above, Aitchinson (2001) has a good review of relevant feminist theory and some data on women and leisure management. Volume 18 (1999) of *Leisure Studies* is a 'special' on gender, and includes Mason's feminist critique of leisure ethics. Gay leisure tastes can be examined online (Pink Links, 2003) and there is an excellent online bibliography on gay and lesbian leisure (Web-

Sexuality/gay & lesbian, 2003). A useful website for references to works on gender and masculinity is The Theory.org.uk Directory (2003).

REFERENCES

Aitchinson, C. (2001) 'Gender and Leisure Research: The "Codification of Knowledge"', *Leisure Sciences*, 23 (1): 1–19.

Bennett, T., Boyd-Bowman, S., Mercer, C. and Woollacott, J. (eds) (1981) *Popular Television and Film*, London: BFI Publishing in association with the Open University Press.

Clarke, J. and Critcher, C. (1985) *The Devil Makes Work . . . Leisure in Capitalist Britain*, London: Macmillan.

Coalter, F. (1999) 'Sport and Recreation in the United Kingdom: Flow with the Flow or Buck the Trends?', *Managing Leisure*, 4: 24–39.

Critcher, C., Bramham, P. and Tomlinson, A. (eds) (1995) *Sociology of Leisure: A Reader*, London: E. & F. N. Spon.

Deem, R. (1986) *All Work and No Play*, Milton Keynes: Open University Press.

Deem, R. (1999) 'How Do We Get out of the Ghetto? Strategies for Research on Gender and Leisure for the 21st Century', *Leisure Studies*, 18 (3): 161–77.

Dyer, R. (2002) *The Culture of Queers*, London and New York: Routledge.

Frith, S., Goodwin, A. and Grossberg, L. (eds) (1993) *Sound and Vision: The Music Video Reader*, London: Routledge.

Hall, S., Hobson, D., Lowe, A. and Willis, P. (eds) (1980) *Culture, Media and Language*, London: Hutchinson.

Hall, S. and Jefferson, T. (eds) (1976) *Resistance Through Rituals*, London: Hutchinson.

Harris, D. (2003) *Teaching Yourself Social Theory*, London: Sage.

Igrab (2003) [online] http://www.igrab.net/

Kivell, P. and Kleiber, D. (2000) 'Leisure in the Identity Formation of Lesbian/Gay Youth: Personal, but Not Social', *Leisure Sciences*, 22: 215–32.

Light, R. and Kirk, D. (2000) 'High School Rugby, the Body and the Reproduction of Hegemonic Masculinity', *Sport, Education and Society*, 5 (2): 163–76.

McRobbie, A. and Nava, M. (eds) (1984) *Gender and Generation*, London: Macmillan.

Moi, T. (ed.) (1986) *The Kristeva Reader*, Oxford: Basil Blackwell.

Nauright, J. and Chandler, T. (eds) (1996) *Making Men: Rugby and Masculine Identity*, London: Frank Cass and Co. Ltd.

Pink Links (2003) [online] http://www.pinklinks.co.uk/Leisure_Lifestyle/

Ramazanoglu, C. (ed.) (1993) *Up Against Foucault: Explorations of Some Tensions Between Foucault and Feminism*, London: Routledge.

Seidman. S. (ed.) (1996) *Queer Theory/ Sociology*, Oxford: Basil Blackwell.

The Theory.org.uk Directory (2003) [online] http://www.theory.org.uk/directory.htm

Visser, G. (2002) 'Identity-Based Consumption and Urban Transformation', [online] http://www.uovs.ac.za/faculties/nat/geog/geohome/gustavissercv.html

Walby, S. (1990) *Theorising Patriarchy*, Oxford: Basil Blackwell.

Web-Sexuality/gay & lesbian (2003) [online] http://www.unc.edu/depts/recreate/women/sexuality.htm

Whannel, G. (1999) 'Sports Stars, Narrativization and Masculinities', *Leisure Studies*, 18 (3): 249–65.

Willis, P. (1977) *Learning to Labour: How Working-Class Kids Get Working-Class Jobs*, Farnborough: Saxon House.

Women's Study Group (1978) *Women Take Issue*, London: Hutchinson.

Gramscianism

Gramscianism is a rather clumsy word used to describe a particular approach, found most prominently in British Cultural Studies, and based on the work of Antonio Gramsci. Since Gramsci's work was ambiguous and incomplete, it has had to be interpreted and applied to modern conditions. The Centre for Contemporary Cultural Studies at the University of Birmingham UK and, later, the Popular Culture Group at the UK Open University used selections from Gramsci's work to radicalize and process certain themes and traditions in British social science.

Section Outline: *Gramsci's context and the development of British Cultural Studies. 'Hegemony' as an organizing concept. Revolutionary and cultural politics. A case study – gramscian analysis of the hegemonic representation of black sportsmen on (British) TV. Problems and criticisms: circularity and banality.*

Antonio Gramsci was a marxist writer and militant active in Italy in the 1920s and 1930s. His work took on particular significance for several reasons. He was working to develop marxism in the new era after the decline of classical marxism and the triumph of Bolshevism in Russia. Western versions of marxism had largely been discredited for a number of reasons, not the least of which was that during the First World War the working classes of the major European nations had fought each other instead of turning on their ruling classes to bring about socialism. Gramsci wanted to develop a view of marxism that might fit modern Europe, especially modern Italy, which offered a complex political and social situation (the urban industrialized North contrasting with the still largely agricultural and Catholic-dominated South, for example). He had decided to attempt to blend marxism with a range of other philosophical positions, and also to develop a suitable modern version of marxist politics: the Russian model that had been so successful in 1917 did not seem suitable for more stable Western European societies. Above all,

131

Gramsci had a pressing and novel political problem on his hands in the rise of Italian fascism: he struggled desperately to organize the newly-formed Italian Communist Party to resist, but was himself arrested and jailed by a triumphant Mussolini.

In prison, Gramsci was denied the use of a library, had his work censored and had to smuggle it out in the form of notes on various topics. Gramsci's academic legacy is one of highly promising and suggestive analyses of modern conditions, but one delivered in an ambiguous and unsystematic way, at least by modern scholarly standards.

I have given a fuller account of how this developed into a modern academic programme in Harris (1992). Briefly, Gramsci's work became important in Britain in the 1970s, as part of a general attempt to revive marxist theory by examining the work of European theorists. Gramsci seemed particularly suitable as a starting point to analyse the position of modern politics, especially cultural politics, in Britain. His work seemed to reject orthodox marxist views that saw the economy as the main mechanism of change, and the industrial working class as its main agent. Gramsci seemed far more interested in the role and importance of cultural matters. He had also offered an analysis which suggested that modern European states did not simply represent the ruling class, but had to work to manage public opinion, to which they were periodically answerable, and thus to enlist support from a number of other important cultural and political groups. States had constructed an outer ring of defences in the form of state agencies and organizations of various kinds, that were semi-independent (the modern term for them would be quangos or NGOs), or even 'private'.

This work seemed to offer a number of possibilities for those wishing to analyse cultural events in Britain in marxist terms, seeing them as partially but not fully independent of a wider political struggle for control, and also as a field or arena for competing definitions. I personally think that an academic agenda drove analysts to Gramsci as well, since the work seemed to offer a way of bringing together a number of options in conventional social sciences – between marxist and non-marxist analyses, and between subjective and objective forms of analysis. In the end, I think much of the political impetus of Gramsci's work was lost as a result, so that gramscianism developed as a particularly safe, British, and academic form of cultural commentary.

We can see examples of gramscian analysis at work in other sections in this book – in the discussion of **articulation**, in the entry on **ideology**, in the work of Clarke and Critcher in the entry on **social class**, or in the work on **youth subcultures**. These feature particular concepts derived from the work of Gramsci, but much developed since. The major underlying themes are revealed by considering the concept of hegemony.

Hegemony is used in a number of historical and political analyses to refer to a form of control exercised over a group, usually a nation-state. This control is not exercised just by the use of military force, but by the use of culture as well. For example, when Britain colonized India, she introduced a whole system of law, commerce, taxes, regulation, religious beliefs, customs and ways of behaving that derived from Britain and represented Britain as the source of cultural and legal dominance as well; English became the language used by dominant groups too. Successful colonization installs or institutionalizes these practices and organizations, so that they become naturalized, a way of life, the obvious way to do things. Of course, considerable cultural work has to be done in order to maintain this view of the social order. New events, political movements, or cultural developments may arise and these have to be interpreted in the light of the overall hegemonic system. There was, for example, a considerable struggle by the British to reinterpret the rise of Indian liberation movements such as the one led by Gandhi. British hegemony attempted to represent those movements as misguided, following special interests, backward and religious, criminal, and so on. One final point to notice is that it is not just the agents of the British State who are involved in such political and cultural, or even legal work – a number of other organizations and individuals also take part, exercising their full independence and autonomy from the State, and yet working in concert with it, upholding shared beliefs and frameworks. A major role is played by the mass media, for example.

This is the way in which modern European states were thought to work in dealing with class struggle and the tensions of capitalism as well. The resistance of oppressed groups, inside or outside the nation, could not be dealt with simply by banning them and trying to crush them with military force. People had to be persuaded and opinion formed by a number of agents as well as just the government. The force of those class resistance movements could even be incorporated or deflected, as the example of rational recreation indicates (see **social class**) – the genuine interest in sporting contests could be preserved but rendered safe and respectable by making the working classes play organized football and not mob football. This could never be entirely successful, both because societies were so dynamic and changing, and because marxist analysts always had to believe that there was resistance and countervailing force somewhere. The very experience of oppression, the long-established cultures of resistance, and the occasional need to revert to forcible

Gramscianism

oppression guaranteed resistance. Thus, hegemony was seen in gramscian work as much more dynamic, never completed, always showing an active process of negotiation, settlement, the outbreak of new tensions and contradictions, and so on. As we have indicated already, struggles over popular culture feature in this wider struggle for hegemony: a new youth culture seems to threaten the central values of the old order, so it has to be regulated, public opinion has to be marshalled against it, and commercial versions attempt to incorporate it back into the mainstream, and so on.

Perhaps Britain seems rather an unpromising example to choose for this kind of marxist analysis. One common view is that it is a particularly conservative country, for example, with no real tradition of revolutionary politics. In fact, that view of history is highly debatable, as a founding father of British Cultural Studies argued (Thompson, 1968). Nor had large tracts of the urban working class simply absorbed middle-class values, as a number of studies of working-class culture argued, including a piece by another founding father (Hoggart, 1981). In the 1960s, considerable cultural upheaval was apparent, especially when expressed in the so-called 'student revolt' (large anti-Vietnam War demonstrations, strikes, protests and civil disorder in a number of European capitals, including London, allegedly led by students). In the 1970s, there had seemed to be a growing wave of industrial militancy taking the form of strikes and walk-outs, often unofficial ones led by members on the shop floor themselves. Amidst all this promise, however, one striking fact about Britain remained – it lacked a large and well-organized Communist Party. Gramsci had helped to found the Communist Party in Italy after some years of dispute inside the Socialist Party, and his agitational work included an intriguing experiment to run seminars and workshops for factory workers in order to encourage socialist theory and practice. In Britain, there was the much less militant Labour Party, and a significantly different tradition of socialist intellectuals contacting workers through the more restricted medium of adult education courses.

It is perhaps not that surprising that gramscian analysis took the form of an intellectualized interest in popular culture rather than in popular politics directly. Indeed, the belief in the urban working class as the vanguard of the revolution soon declined, especially with the onset of 'Thatcherism' in the 1980s, and the gramscians searched instead for vanguards among other political protest movements – feminists, black activists, ecologists, anti-racists, and, finally, even in the crowd who had gathered to mourn Princess Diana. Cultural politics became the only focus of revolutionary politics. Cultural vanguards were to be contacted through the publication of the politicized lifestyle magazine *Marxism Today*.

The old route of contact with ordinary members of the population survived only in the highly flawed radicalism of the UK Open University and its courses. The OU Popular Culture Group constructed an excellent Open University course (code-named U203 – Open University, 1982) which systematized, codified, and academicized popular culture in Britain in a highly influential way, but never really illuminated wider struggles. That course has been much echoed since in a variety of similar ones in many universities in the UK. The colonizing tendencies of this version of cultural studies are also well known, and the approach has deeply penetrated sociology and media studies. At one time it looked as if it would colonize leisure studies too (see Tomlinson, 1989).

The Centre for Contemporary Cultural Studies (CCCS) had been established earlier at Birmingham University, and it had produced a number of highly successful books and also cheaply produced 'working papers'. These focused on a very wide range of topics such as working-class culture, social theory and, famously, youth subcultures. The position of women and black people were studied extensively in special collections (Women's Study Group, 1978; CCCS, 1982). Influential books included one analysing the 'moral panic' that had arisen in the 1970s about criminal black youth, and the authors studied the ways in which the press had managed and discussed this issue (Hall et al., 1978). In the spirit of the concept of hegemony, the press were seen to be following their own professional values of neutrality and objectivity, but also supporting the wider social and political system which saw black people as a threat to British values, as representing unwelcome social change, and so on.

The famous Open University course applied the same kind of analysis, sometimes with rather ambiguous interpretations of the concept of hegemony, however, to a range of cultural objects and practices, including film, radio and television output (especially the James Bond film, for example, or the coverage of football on television), popular music, music hall, seaside holidays and other Victorian pastimes, and popular public rituals such as the celebration of Christmas (see Harris, 1992). All alike were analysed as a kind of symbolic or coded politics, as offering not only entertainment and pleasure but signs of hegemonic struggle as well.

The main writers associated with the Popular Culture Group went on to produce a rich collection of other publications, including an analysis of 'Thatcherism' (Hall, 1988). The public appeal of Conservative politics offered an obvious puzzle to marxist theorists, which was resolved by understanding Thatcherism as an attempt to **articulate** a number of specific concerns, some of them genuinely popular, such as resentment of the bureaucratic state, with a number of classic Conservative values, including nationalism, anti-modernism and racism. This offered a classic modern example of how hegemonic blocs were built from a number of highly diverse cultural and political currents.

The Birmingham Centre and the OU Popular Culture Group also had a firm academic agenda as well. They wanted to operate with a kind of academic hegemony of their own, reading and appreciating a number of alternative theoretical resources, yet quietly weaving them into preferred systems. Gramsci, or rather the particular interpretation of Gramsci adopted at the time, turned out to be the master discourse, superior to all the others. Thus, the particular approach of academic historians towards popular culture had to be radicalized and placed in the context of wider class struggle. Conversely, abstract marxism of the kind Althusser and his followers embraced had to be made more concrete and specific. Some traditions in sociology could be borrowed, especially **ethnographic** research, while others had to be rejected for being insufficiently deep in their perception (the opening chapters by Clarke and Critcher (1985) criticizing functionalist and pluralist work in leisure studies offer an excellent example). In my view, this 'theoretical mapping' took precedence over the more specific political analyses, especially since the great success of the academic endeavours to systematize work on popular culture became apparent in the form of research programmes, publications, university courses and academic positions, while that on political radicalism seemed to be decreasing.

As an example of the kind of analysis that still persists based on this tradition, I have chosen a fairly recent piece analysing the ways in which black people are represented in television programmes about football (McCarthy et al., 2003). In order to make my criticisms clear I have been rather scathing about this piece, although I bear it no particular ill will. I even commend it in the entry on the **gazes** and **'race' and leisure**. I hope I can use it to offer a brief account of the strengths and weaknesses of gramscian approaches.

McCarthy et al. (2003) set out to analyse football commentaries made as part of the broadcasting of soccer on British TV. Their argument involves a substantial empirical study in which they recorded, then analysed, a large amount of television commentary. Commentaries were coded in terms of being supportive of performance, referring to physical characteristics, and making statements about the 'inner emotional state or personality characteristics of players' (ibid.: 222). The authors tried to see if these statements were allocated differently to players of different 'races'.

Then three black and three white focus groups were convened, each consisting of three members, made up of male students who were interested in soccer. All members self-identified as either white or black, and the fact that they knew each other (they were all students on the same Sports Studies courses) helped put them at their ease. The moderators of each group were from the same 'race' as the participants, and followed a semi-structured interview approach. Actual interactions were analysed from the video tapes taken at each group discussion, and views were recorded and their content analysed.

However, this was by no means a straightforward empirical study and not all the empirical data were used in this particular article. Furthermore, those data that were used had to be interpreted, and placed in the context of more general accounts of the politics of television representation. The team is interested in seeing the media as having 'the capacity to mould and create the "pictures in our heads", with all the resultant implications' (ibid.: 219). Sports are seen as a particularly powerful 'agency in the depiction of racial groups, and the consequent creation and reaffirmation of stereotypes' (ibid.: 219), and the key to these stereotypes lies in assumptions that black people are somehow naturally more physical, and thus biologically different from white people. Recent studies of 'race' in Cultural Studies have also emphasized the role of language and representations of the 'non-European "other"' (ibid.: 220). In order to address this issue, McCarthy et al. used some classic work in gramscian Cultural Studies – a discussion of coding and encoding (see Hall, in Hall et al., 1980), the need for active interpretation by readers, tracing the effect of cultural contexts which viewers occupy, and so on.

To be brief and partial, this work represents a characteristic gramscian borrowing from **semiotics**, in this case, the work of Barthes. Political values from dominant groups have to be coded, and this takes place through the apparently neutral conventions of television. In this way, culture is politicized, and the hegemonic project goes its cunning way. However, there must also be resistance, for political as much as theoretical reasons, and so some viewers at least must be able to decode television in a way which does not reflect the dominant or preferred reading. Apart from anything else, it would be a deep insult to suggest that oppressed groups cannot recognize the ways in which they are being adversely represented. I think these political preferences are easily detected in the analysis which appears in McCarthy et al.

For example, the original analysis of television commentary failed to supply very much conclusive evidence of racism. The authors themselves suggest that television commentary has become much more 'guarded' these days (it cannot be a genuine rejection of racism that is being witnessed, since television must be part of a general hegemonic project to oppress people). The authors do not wish to accuse commentators of open racism, though, since they are probably 'voicing subconscious assumptions and understandings of race and racial difference' (McCarthy et al., 2003: 227), as in the general thesis about how professional values support deeper hegemonic ones in Hall et al. (1978). However, this tendency merely to voice subconscious assumptions is found only among TV commentators: black students express accurate, conscious and authentic comments representing the black experience, while white students merely reproduce a widespread strategy of denial, preventing much explicit comment at all. The researchers can find evidence to support their view that black footballers are treated differently from white ones, however, since it seems that *positive* (my emphasis) comments about the physicality of black players are more frequent than those addressed to white players. The data also indicate that, overall, white players receive more comments about their physicality than do black ones, but again this cannot be interpreted literally and at face value, perhaps (because gramscian analysis rejects the adequacy of empirical data which operates only 'at the surface' and fails to show deep hegemonic structures, at least before interpretation).

Turning to the analysis of the focus groups, the authors suggest that the black people in discussion groups did perceive considerable inequality expressed in the commentary. This fits with studies of beliefs among other black people that they are experiencing unfair treatment, or that they have to overachieve in competition with white players. It seems that other black viewers are also 'very sensitive to media definition' (citing another study, McCarthy et al., 2003: 228). As a result, 'a discourse of resistance was seen to emerge as a direct reaction', although, again, other authors are cited to illustrate this tendency. Some brief examples of actual comments finally appear which seem to confirm this view, and this is held to support the 'well documented traditional stereotype . . . [that black athletes are] . . . quick, instinctive, physically strong, yet lacking in intelligence' (ibid.: 229), although none of the respondents in the study seemed to have used these actual terms. Black respondents refused to accept the stereotyped views of the commentary, which apparently illustrates a view that black males feel empowered by such resistance. There are some interesting summaries of other studies that show how black players can overachieve on the sports field in order to assert their identity against hostile and racist spectators, but no actual evidence of that on this occasion. Taking sports science courses enabled these particular students

Gramscianism

to resist dominant readings, although such courses do not seem to have challenged the views of white students.

The white focus groups read the commentaries differently, in a way that did not pick up on racial stereotypes. Some seem to have noticed the tendency for commentators to refer to physical characteristics of black people, but denied any lasting significance. The authors interpret this as 'white denial' (ibid.: 231). This leads to a discussion of whiteness being taken as normal and thus invisible or natural in our society. There were also views expressed that contemporary societies have overcome racism, and this led some white respondents to deny, or to excuse, the use of physical descriptions by commentators: it was not racism, but simply related to the individual characteristics of the player. It follows that anyone seeing such remarks as racist was being over-sensitive. This is part of a more general tendency for white people to distance themselves from noticing the impact of such practices on their everyday lives, even though they recognize racism and theories about it at the intellectual level. Some more examples of the comments of white respondents indicate that whiteness is taken as normal, a classic 'unconscious defence against accusations of racism' (ibid.: 233). Racialized discourse can be invisible to a white audience, especially if they see racism in terms of individual acts of aggression confined to an insignificant minority, and this helps denial. Here, however, the views of white respondents, unlike those of black respondents, are treated not as data but as a series of symptoms requiring interpretation before they make sense. To be fair, the authors explain this by arguing that definite cultural competences are needed to identify collective and unconscious racism. Black students had much more experience of stereotyping, while the white ones could only acknowledge the existence of stereotypes more abstractly. Again, support is found in other work too. Overall, it is the 'racist vernacular and discourse which permeates all levels and aspects of the game' that is really responsible, and McCarthy et al. expect their readers to know what this means and to agree. The mass media bear a particular responsibility for popularizing this discourse.

I hope I have indicated that a major problem with gramscianism is that it provides enough theoretical resources to argue for almost any sort of conclusion that you wish to find. Hegemony involves processes that both defend the status quo and represent opposition to it. Political discourses embodied in cultural events such as television broadcasts have to be both encoded and decoded. Oppressed groups have to have their oppression explained in terms of the massive controls exercised over them, and yet they must also be capable of having enough experience to see through the cultural masks that conceal the power relations. Empirical studies can demonstrate these power relations, yet they can never be decisive because they operate only at the surface. In this way, gramscianism can never be refuted. This is an excellent characteristic of a powerful academic system that can offer to reinterpret academic developments and arguments in ways which only strengthen the original, and thus generate substantial research programmes.

It also lends gramscianism a definite 'banal' quality, to quote Morris (1988). There is a kind of permanent circularity in it: first, discourses are analysed, and then reactions to them; controls on the audience and then resistance to those controls; subtle mechanisms to maintain the dominant order, and then appeals to the common-sense and everyday experience of the oppressed to resist them. This kind of circularity often involves a gross simplification, both of earlier academic analyses that are accused of neglecting one side or the other of the circle, and of the reactions of actual viewers and readers; these too have to be processed into familiar forms before they are allowed to appear. No gramscian analysis to my knowledge has ever allowed audience reactions to be genuinely complex, contradictory, uncertain, ill-formed, ambiguous or elusive. The real secret of its apparently powerful ability to explain everything is that it only ever explains the same thing, over and over again.

FURTHER READING

I have some 'reading guides' to major pieces by Hall and his colleagues, and to the CCCS 'specials' on gender and 'race' on my website (Harris, 2003), specifically obtainable from the page http://www.arasite.org/sagelist.html. Read McCarthy et al. (2003), not least to see if I have been unfair, and trace the references they use to support their arguments. Miller (1994) reviews the effects of the Popular Culture course during the Open University phase.

Morris (1988) is a useful commentary on Baudrillard as well as on gramscianism.

REFERENCES

CCCS (1982) *The Empire Strikes Back: Race and Racism in 70s Britain*, London: Hutchinson.

Clarke, J. and Critcher, C. (1985) *The Devil Makes Work . . . Leisure in Capitalist Britain*, London: Macmillan.

Hall, S. (1988) *The Hard Road to Renewal: Thatcherism and the Crisis of the Left*, London: Verso.

Gramscianism

Hall, S., Critcher, C., Jefferson, T., Clarke, J. and Roberts, B. (1978) *Policing the Crisis: Mugging, the State, and Law and Order*, London: Macmillan.

Hall, S., Hobson, D., Lowe, A. and Willis, P. (eds) (1980) *Culture Media and Language*, London: Hutchinson.

Harris, D. (1992) *From Class Struggle to the Politics of Pleasure: The Effects of Gramscianism on Cultural Studies*, London: Routledge.

Harris, D. (2003) 'Dave Harris (and Colleagues): Essays, Papers and Courses' [online] http://www.arasite.org/

Hoggart, R. (1981) *The Uses of Literacy*, Harmondsworth: Penguin.

McCarthy, D., Jones, R. and Potrac, P. (2003) 'Constructing Images and Interpreting Realities', *International Review for the Sociology of Sport*, 38 (2): 217–38.

Miller, R. (1994) '"A Moment of Profound Danger": British Cultural Studies Away From the Centre', *Cultural Studies*, 8 (3): 417–37.

Morris, M. (1988) 'Banality in Cultural Studies', *Discourse*, X (2): 3–29.

Open University (1982) *Popular Culture (U203)*, Milton Keynes: Open University Press.

Thompson, E. (1968) *The Making of the English Working Class*, London: Pelican.

Tomlinson, A. (1989) 'Whose Side Are They On? Leisure Studies and Cultural Studies in Britain', *Leisure Studies* 8: 97–106.

Women's Study Group (1978) *Women Take Issue*, London: Hutchinson.

Heritage

'Heritage' can refer to anything of cultural significance that is left over from the past. As usual, the choice of what is significant tends to depend on who has the power to decide. One particular trend associates the values of the past with current commercial and political emphases – the 'heritage industry'. Other approaches try to break this association and develop new emphases for educational or critical purposes.

141

Section Outline: The rise of the heritage industry: commercial and political motives. Heritage as ideological distortion of the past. Thatcherite and New Labour variants: the Millennium Dome. Postmodernist and marxist alternatives. Problems with critical accounts and alternatives. Professional perspectives and links with visitor interpretation.

Heritage has become big business not only in the UK, but globally. Its economic exploitation provided a major source of growth in the 1980s and 1990s in Britain, so much so that heritage sites are pretty well everywhere. I have Australian friends who claim they now navigate their way around the UK using the distinctive brown road signs pointing to various heritage sites – their own country is becoming replete with them too, though.

Most heritage sites feature some sort of 'authentic' artefact on which to base the development – old buildings offer the classic examples, and UK sites have been created around formerly busy ports, the remains of castles and medieval churches, monasteries or hostels (like the one in Winchester which once treated some wounded Crusaders). The latter, predictably, offers the visitor a 'Crusader experience', complete with images of faces cleverly projected on to wooden dummies, and a rather creaky reconstruction of the siege of Acre. Other sites are 'absolute fakes', to use Eco's (1987) terminology, such as Frontierland in Disney World, or the Land's End Experience in Cornwall. Rojek (1993) offers a classification of his own and provides detailed descriptions of many examples.

British heritage was entrusted to the care of companies such as English Heritage in the 1980s, and subsidies were either withdrawn or limited, while the right to charge visitors was granted. Local authorities tended to invest heavily in heritage as well, as part of a project to increase tourism in their local areas. The State also invests, directly and through funds provided by the UK National Lottery. The funds do far more than just preserve the sites, but popularize and commercialize them too. We can therefore start to understand the provision of heritage as an industry, operating in the familiar way as a combination of big business techniques, revenue-raising, technologically advanced transformations of traditional cultural artifacts and practices, and customer surveys, all intended to package and **add leisure values** for the customers.

This has proved controversial. Hewison (1987) has probably written the classic book, at a timely moment relatively early in the growth of the heritage industry when the government's neo-conservative policies ('Thatcherism') were becoming unpopular. He has also produced additional commentaries, such as the ones in Corner and Harvey (1991), or in Uzzell (1989). These works can still deliver a fresh critical view of much of what we now accept as normal.

Generally, Hewison argues that heritage sites offer a dubious version of the past which is commercialized, trivialized and deeply 'ideological'. Although he does not explicitly adopt a **gramscian** perspective himself (and his support for Jameson – see below – indicates an allegiance to a different sort of marxist theory), it is quite possible to see his work as offering a similar account of 'hegemony'. There are also clear parallels with the criticisms of **Disneyfication**, and the work on **authenticity**. Thus, Hewison (1987) suggests that the products of the heritage industry are often sentimental, nostalgic and patronising, for example, with depictions of life in pastoral 'Merrie England' or in the 'good old days'. Any of the examples cited above would easily illustrate this critique. Minorities and political dissidents are absent, denied a voice or sentimentalized, and there is little understanding of the collective (especially class) struggles which produced the past. Morwhellam seems full of happy artisans, and the journey into the copper mine is a ride, as if the miners entered merely to admire the rock formations. The Eureka Stockade Experience in Ballarat celebrates a period of industrial and political upheaval in the Australian gold-mining industry, but ends in a cheery, matey kind of reinforcement of Australian identity as locals salute their Irish forebears for being so feisty.

The past is gentrified, domesticated, and 'antiqued' (Hewison, 1987: 132). Thus, it becomes safe, a 'sedative' (ibid.: 140), no longer a source of critical contrast to the present or of understanding, no longer able to shock us. At the 'First World War Experience' in the Imperial War Museum, for example, the threats and terrors are mere effects, and no-one asks whether the real thing was ever worth it, whether the people who endured the real thing would be happy with what we have now, or why we fought those wars in the way we did. 'What really happened' is now strictly for 'intellectuals', who suffered particular public contempt in the Thatcherite era. The heritage industry is about nostalgia and selling, and all the unpleasant thoughts of death, suffering or sacrifice have to be repressed as bad for business.

There are no theories or **narratives** that might lead to understanding, but a mere 'collage' of impressions, joined together because they sell rather than because they make any sense. A visit to the on-site shop makes this point, as local heritage souvenirs compete with Beatrix Potter books, hand-made candles, watercolours of the landscape, camomile teabags, sensible travel rugs, maps, and little wooden acorns (I am describing any UK National Trust shop here). In Hewison's terms (actually Barthes' originally), this shows that 'heritage' is an 'empty signifier', capable of being attached to almost anything. To take an example, the UK National Lottery Heritage Fund officially celebrates the diversity of British heritage, and offers to fund 'important natural habitats and countryside, historic parks and gardens, museum collections, historic library collections and archives, historic buildings and sites, industrial, transport and maritime heritage' (National Lottery, 2004). In practice, this has led to quite a wide assemblage of projects getting funded, and almost certainly an equally wide range being rejected for funding: much depends on the (unevenly distributed) expertise available to back the bid.

According to Hewison (1987), the heritage industry suggests the present has just evolved out of the past (and the two are often compressed together anyway: coal or tin mines close and, only a few months later, re-open as a 'mine experience': the open-air industrial museum at Ironbridge in Staffordshire replaces the closed-down British steel industry, Liverpool's Albert Docks re-open but as a waterside recreational area). Somehow, the past and the present join in an image of 'the nation'. 'England' is a land of country houses (some now owned by the National Trust) and *Brideshead Revisited*, says Hewison (ibid.: 72), and there is collusion here with those sentimental critics who see Britain as based on 'agricultural simplicity' (ibid.: 69). There may have been a past when things were done differently, but we do not have to worry about it any more and can proceed to welcome the Thatcherite version of the new.

Hewison's analysis echoes some familiar arguments in the work we have seen in other entries. He likes pointing out that television representations merge with heritage representations to become 'more real than reality' (or **hyperreal**), and he uses terms like 'collage' or 'pastiche', or 'nostalgia' to describe the representations he loathes. This sounds like a **postmodern** approach, but Hewison ultimately wants to reject that approach and retain a more marxist critique. These tendencies are not just an artistic take on the real and its replacement by the hyperreal, but an ideological distortion, traceable to a basic capitalist system. That system prompts the combinations of commerce and ideology (a discredited 'foundational' approach for postmodernism). He chooses to argue this via the work of Jameson, a marxist theorist who claims to be able to explain everything the postmodernists describe in terms of an alternative account of 'late capitalism': '[which suggests]. . . that the [economic] base . . . generates its superstructures with a new kind of dynamic . . . [and which] . . . seems to obligate you in advance to talk about cultural phenomena at least in business terms if not in those of political economy' (Jameson, 1991: xxi).

Corner and Harvey (1991) pursue a similar line, although in more explicitly **gramscian** terms. Briefly, the heritage industry is an (ideological) response to one of those periodic crises in hegemony induced by capitalist modernization and globalization. Thatcherism has

144

to avert the crisis, and one obvious solution is to engage in cultural politics to gloss over the contradictions. Thus the socialist tradition of the past is repressed, and a reinterpretation is offered instead which glorifies 'the ideals of eighteenth century free-market capitalism' (Corner and Harvey, 1991: 14). Heavily positive implications are to be drawn for the present, of course. As the book title suggests, both 'heritage' and 'enterprise' are reinterpreted in this way, and there are some useful examples cited which combine both.

Hewison appears here too (Corner and Harvey, 1991: 173 ff.), this time discussing the growth of the (then) newly independent (commercial) museums, involving the production of the past as well as the consumption of it, as he puts it. He also refers to the growth of McJobs in tourism, and condemns the make-over of the (London) Victoria and Albert Museum, with redundancies for the old intellectuals and scholars, as part of a 'gentrification project', merging commerce and culture. That project created outrage at the time with its revealing advertising slogan referring to the famous building as a 'nice little caff [café] with a museum attached'.

It is interesting to compare the Thatcherite era with the more recent one of New Labour, who invested a great deal of financial and political capital in the construction of the Millennium Dome. Costs exceeded £500 million, and the building is still unsold. Although the project was initiated by the outgoing Conservative Government, New Labour confidently took over, and put Peter Mandelson, a major political figure, in charge. The exhibits varied, with some focusing on heritage, but others borrowing from recent advances in interactive displays to deal with scientific themes ('the Body'). There were also some quite characteristically English heavy-handed 'educational' exhibits, including one on the new education reforms, and one on various religious faiths.

My outstanding personal memory is the wince-making attempt by financiers in the City of London to invite visitors to play financial games like they do (with our money), and trying to impress us with a playful display of stacks of currency (the sort of bonus awarded to the modern executive, no doubt). Overall, the exhibits could be seen as celebrating some aspects of Britain's scientific, educational, cultural, and financial heritage, and there were connections with the concept of 'Cool Britannia' that New Labour wanted to embrace in its early stages. Celebrating the new millennium seemed an ideal opportunity to launch a new unifying cultural display.

The project soon encountered problems, however, beginning with a badly planned opening night which annoyed many members of the popular press. A number of elements began to coalesce into a tide of discontent – the unpopularity of Mandelson and his association with political 'spin', the suspicion that New Labour's vision of Britain was nebulous, rejection of the confident trendiness of the Labour-supporting elite, artistic disagreements and controversies, the massive costs. Questions began to emerge about some of the corporate sponsors of the exhibits. New Labour began to dissociate itself from the Dome and the building became an object of derision for many: its high public profile probably added to its problems. Despite all the modern arts of design and spin, many refused to accept the vision of Britain's image and heritage that had been manufactured for them: indeed, the press were able to construct quite a different interpretation of the whole project.

The heritage industry does not always get it right. Sometimes it can test its flexibility to destruction, with risky offerings such as the 'death tours' and 'black spots' described by Rojek (1993). The public can stir in protest, as shown in the American controversy over the Disney Company's plan for a heritage site on or near the US Civil War battlefield at Manassas. In Britain, heritage sites and developments have not always been commercially successful when initial Lottery funding ran out; the best of marketing and business expertise has not saved attractions as different as a museum of popular music in Sheffield or botanical gardens in Wales.

Critics of the heritage industry encounter problems of their own. There is often an assumption that marxist methods of analysis offer correct and valid access to the 'real' past, but we can expect some interpretation and selectivity and probably some circularity with them as well. To borrow and invert Fowler's critique (in Uzzell, 1989), marxist historians also face the dangers of an over-emotional involvement in the more excitingly revolutionary bits of the past, and can fall prey to the 'self-delusion' that they can easily empathize with past generations of gallant 'strugglers' and working-class heroes.

The approach also assumes that most visitors will be gullible and easily swayed by this ideological account of the past. Other entries in this book (like the one on **gender**) show that such passivity and dependence on the single text on offer are unlikely. Certainly the Australians I accompanied round the Eureka Stockade Experience were very active: they cheerfully mocked the displays and themselves, making bird calls during the dramatic pauses, and barracking the actors in period dress during their solemnly 'educational' speeches.

Finally, we are not really clear about what a suitable presentation of the past would look like for marxists: it should be critical, emphasize struggle, expose the working of the class system, and so on, and offer a more 'scholarly' and academic history, but what would that actually look like and how could it be made popular? The implicit alternative presentation sounds suspiciously like a kind of academic lecture, turning the heritage industry into a series of university seminars, but that is hardly likely to pull the crowds. Hewison (1987) supports the writers and broadcasters in Britain who offer more critical perspectives, but he knows the problems with making 'critical realism' popular. It is an old dilemma for marxists trying to turn the culture industry to their purposes. It is possible to produce serious marxist accounts which are critical, shocking or thought-provoking, but these tend to be watched only by a few of the already converted. Critical analysis can be disguised as entertainment, but that runs the risk of people engaging just with the entertaining elements and ignoring the political messages. The task which remains is to produce histories which are both critical and popular.

In my view, there is also a particular irony in university academics or writers posing as the bearers of objective, detached, 'pure' critique, unsullied somehow by the taint of popularity or commerce: one legacy of Thatcherism is that UK universities were also obliged to generate a financial surplus, and began to relate to commerce and big business evermore closely themselves. We could be equally critical about the Coca-Cola Chair at Edinburgh University, or the Rupert Murdoch Chair at Oxford. Universities are not above a little sentimental distortion of the past or the present themselves, as a quick glance at any promotional material will show. University professionals can see themselves as reluctantly having to manage the rival claims of autonomy and commerce in a heroic way that does not compromise their integrity, but they do not seem prepared to allow that heritage professionals (or media professionals) might react in the same way.

In the entry on **visitor interpretation**, a quite different approach to the heritage industry is revealed. To preview that approach, it is important to begin with some caution against over-generalizing: Frontierland might be absurd, but there is a point to adding values and cultures to historical sites, and telling popular and involving stories about them. Rumble defends English Heritage's activities like this, in Uzzell (1989), by arguing that it is obliged to conserve its old buildings, attract visitors and cater for all sorts of interests in the past, and to do so in competition with all sorts of much more compromised heritage sites. Professionals do their best, says Rumble, offering only a 'minimal orientation' for those visitors that want one, and providing the same sort of service as any educator – trying to be as objective as possible while remembering the sensitivities of visitors and the need to get the level of popularity and complexity right. Uzzell's own piece (Uzzell, 1989) is in the same vein, pointing to real difficulties in depicting the 'reality' of historical suffering. The more commercialized heritage sites usually do not handle this at all. The visitors themselves often shrink away from controversy, and defuse the suffering of the past, as we would expect from people seeking pleasurable moments in leisure: the trick is to offer real history at the optimal level of challenge.

FURTHER READING

Hewison (1987) and Corner and Harvey (1991) offer classic early commentaries (the latter contains some useful case studies including work on heritage films). Urry (1990) also has a good section on heritage, putting a more postmodernist case. Rojek (1993) describes and analyses a wide range of examples. Bennett (1998) offers a useful essay on museums and the ideological discourses apparent in them (not so much commercialism but Darwinism and subsequent accounts of the modern self). The case of the Millennium Dome can be explored via a record of a visit (Millennium Dome, 2003), and a useful archive of press articles about its construction and the subsequent controversies (Guardian Unlimited Special Report on The Millennium Dome, 2003). Hesmondhalgh (2002) updates the debates.

REFERENCES

Bennett, T. (1998) *Culture: A Reformer's Science*, London: Sage.
Corner, J. and Harvey, S. (eds) (1991) *Enterprise and Heritage: Crosscurrents of National Culture*, London: Routledge.
Eco, U. (1987) *Travels in Hyperreality*, London: Picador.
Guardian Unlimited Special Report on The Millennium Dome (2003) [online] http://www.guardian.co.uk/dome/archive/0,3332,223662,00.html
Hesmondhalgh, D. (2002) *The Cultural Industries*, London: Sage.
Hewison, R. (1987) *The Heritage Industry: Britain in a Climate of Decline*, London: Methuen.
Jameson, F. (1991) *Postmodernism, or, the Cultural Logic of Late Capitalism*, London: Verso.
Millennium Dome (2003) [online] http://www.czajkowski.co.uk/Dome/dome_review2.htm
National Lottery (2004) [online] www.lotterygoodcauses.org.uk/
Rojek, C. (1993) *Ways of Escape*, Basingstoke: Macmillan.
Urry, J. (1990) *The Tourist Gaze: Leisure and Travel in Contemporary Societies*, London: Sage.
Uzzell, D. (ed.) (1989) *Heritage Interpretations: The Natural and Built Environment* (vols 1 and 2), London: Belhaven Press.

Hyperreality *is a state of normal reality with cultural and social dimensions that have been added by modern communication and commentary. A variety of media interpretations offer additional meanings to our perceptions. Sometimes, these meanings lead to more complete understanding but they can also be manipulative, mutually cancelling or exhausting.*

Section Outline: *Hyperreality in Eco and Baudrillard and as a central term in postmodernist commentary. Examples in tourism and television coverage. Disneyland as reinforcing the reality of other cities. Cities as communication. Leisure in hyperreality:* flâneurie, *virtual* flâneurie, *mass apathy, adventure.*

'Reality' is a concept that has proved very elusive, although it is something that we rarely think about in everyday life. Anything that we have to deal with despite our wishes, that seems beyond our control, or that resists us in some way tends to be conceived as 'real', hence Dr Johnson's famous demonstration that there was a real world which involved kicking a stone and experiencing pain. Philosophers would not be convinced by such a simple demonstration, however. Relying on our senses, such as the sense of pain, or our detection of resistance, is not usually seen as a very reliable test, because we all know of occasions when the senses let us down, when we mishear something, or misperceive. The real world takes on a number of appearances which can mislead our senses. To quote a famous example (actually Descartes') a piece of wax presents quite different appearances according to whether it has solidified or melted. To follow the next stage of the argument, it is clear that something else is required, some thought, interpretation, concept or mental construct that tells us that it really is the same piece of wax despite its very different appearances.

This point appears in quite specific and much more modern terms in discussions found in other entries. The role played by **fantasy**, for example, is an important one in delivering our experiences and understandings of leisure activities, and fantasies indicate the constructive capabilities of consciousness. A successful fantasy, one might argue, imposes an interpretation on events irrespective of any fixed 'reality'. On another level, **ideologies** present us with ready-made conceptions of the world, which have a vital role to play in our understanding, perhaps even more that any particular sense data we may acquire from direct experience. No amount of experience can qualify the sort of thinking that ideological stereotypes develop: encountering a strong and clever woman will only convince the dedicated misogynist that she is not a 'real woman' at all. It is clear that our notion of reality depends at least as much on a set of interpretations, meanings, and images as it does on our direct attempts to use our senses to react to objects in the world.

On a more practical level, those who understand how television documentaries are assembled have long realized that cameras do much more than just record reality. They clearly interpret as well, and, arguably, actually construct reality. It is impossible to access reality otherwise, since all machines have their limitations and all technologies their conventions: what tends to be visually recorded is what 'looks good' on screen, for example, and you have a better chance of being heard if you have a 'good radio voice'. Avant-garde films have attempted to record reality with as little mediation as possible (one of Andy Warhol's films consisted of uninterrupted, unedited and unmoving video coverage of an office block), but these can have the paradoxical effect of not appearing real at all. We are simply used to reality appearing to us in a conventional way, with intelligible sound, conventionally framed images, unobtrusive editing, and guidance provided by **narratives**, in the form of commentary, witnesses, or the reconstruction of events on camera.

The notion of hyperreality offers a particularly acute recognition of the role played by these interpretations of the world. Eco (1987) uses the term to describe the sensation of being bombarded with interpretations, meanings, narratives, and **visitor interpretations** during his tour of California. Thanks to the development of the leisure and tourism industry, the visitor is never left alone with just their senses and the object of contemplation: instead, sites such as Hearst's castle offer many examples of frantic communication designed to fill out the meaning of the perceptions that the tourist may be trying to acquire. Every space communicates, every object has a label, and the visitor can never escape the mass of guide books or visitor interpretation devices. As a result, perceptions of reality have become saturated with meanings supplied by specialists. When we consider the role of the modern mass media, the problem becomes even more obvious. Television documentaries offer the viewer commentaries on famous tourist sites such as the pyramids near Cairo: TV archaeologists tell us about their construction, diagrams appear on screen to explain how the tombs are laid out inside, aerial shots provide vistas of the whole plateau, cranks are allowed to explain their favourite theories about the divine origin of the pyramids, tourists give accounts of their experiences, and travel programmes guide us. Even if by some miracle the visitor manages to avoid these commentaries, on site local guides are there ready to interpret what is being seen in ways which are hard to refuse. This sort of commentary not only amplifies our sense of reality, but radically improves on it, since no one actual visit could possibly cover so many vistas, perspectives or interpretations, especially the ones that involve reconstructions or virtual walk-throughs of electronically restored temples. Television documentary crews are able to pick the best times and positions for their visual coverage, and they recruit the best experts, whereas the actual visitor can find their particular visit spoiled by bad weather, a migraine, a transport delay, or an unscrupulous guide.

Hyperreality not only improves on reality, but gradually comes to replace the usual conceptions of it. Most of us can directly experience the effects of hyperreality: it is now practically impossible to remove images from your own head, to forget all those documentaries, to react with genuine surprise to, or to gain new knowledge from an actual visit. It is easy to see the implications for the debates about **authenticity** here. It is not just the 'staged authenticity' encountered on the actual site that threatens the genuine encounter with otherness, but the huge amount of prior strategic communication consumed by the visitor long before they actually arrive.

Communication saturates our awareness and our attempts to develop our own **semiotic** understanding. To take some of Baudrillard's (1983) most striking examples, television coverage of the Paris Air Show was available even in the cockpit of a plane that was about to crash, so the unfortunate pilots were already subject to commentary and interpretation about the meaning of their own impending deaths. Baudrillard is also notorious for arguing that the (first) Gulf War never happened (see Baudrillard, 1991, for a brief version). What he meant by this is that for most of us, television saturation coverage of those events provided the reality of the war as we perceived it. This is demonstrated best in some of those striking video scenes of smart bombs hitting their targets. Not only did those videos look exactly like a number of other videos, including training videos, but some of them actually turned out to be training videos. The effect, in supporting the military and persuading the public

Hyperreality

that the war had been a successful use of advanced technology, was the same regardless of the philosophical status of the 'reality' being depicted on screen (whether real reality or simulated reality). No doubt, television coverage and commentary played a major part in the understanding of those events for those who decided to launch the second Gulf War as well.

Baudrillard (1983) extends these remarks in arguing, for example, that simulation plays an important part in trying to defend a vanishing sense of what is real. Specifically, sites such as Disneyland offer such obvious and simple simulations of the world that we think that actual cities are real by comparison. They are not simply real, of course, since even normal cities are designed to communicate with us. The best example is Los Angeles, perhaps, with its buildings designed to be little more than display boards, with signs telling us that it is the sort of place where we are supposed to be playful and have fun. Far more workaday cities can also be 'read' in this sort of way too, as Bocock's useful summary indicates (in Bocock and Thompson, 1992). Thus Paris was deliberately redesigned in the 1860s to look like a fully modernist city, celebrating the ability to plan cities rationally, to convey cultural modernity through having wide-open spaces accommodating strolling crowds (and permitting rapid military action if necessary). The gentrification of inner cities deliberately suggests leisure values. Soja (1989) argues that a district of San Francisco attempted to reproduce some of the well-known features of **postmodernism** in its redesign exercises. At the other extreme, the centre of the English town of Basingstoke stands for Thatcherite values, according to Campbell (in Hall and Jacques, 1983), with its rather brutal functional concrete architecture, dominated by the blocks occupied by the new sunrise industries.

How do people react to the experience of being bombarded with constant persuasive communication, especially if specific communications contradict each other? The effects are discussed in a number of commentaries on modernity as well as postmodernity. One consequence might be the development of a new leisure activity, for example, as in the writings on *flâneurie* (Tester, 1994). The *flâneur* takes an objective, detached and amused stance towards the cultural variety and cosmopolitanism that he sees as he strolls around the city. This stance requires the sort of qualities that comprise the 'high aesthetic' in Bourdieu's discussion of **social class**, including a lack of involvement (the *flâneur* only looks and then moves on), or an interest in form and not content (the *flâneur* does not take sides, but can engage in poetical speculation, or classify and observe activities for his own amusement).

Hyperreality

There are clear signs of a version of *flâneurie* in the cultural commentary of the film critic, travel writer, or cultural studies ethnographer, writing about, but not necessarily involving himself in watching foreign films, eating at McDonald's or visiting a Disney site.

As a number of commentators including Wolff (1985) have pointed out, the classic *flâneur* is always male, because only males could wander unmolested and unremarked in the public spaces of cities such as nineteenth-century Paris. For these reasons, Wolff argues that there could never be a (female) *flâneuse*. However, in modern shopping malls or theme parks, female *flâneurie* is much more possible, since females can wander unmolested in these public spaces. With the advent of electronic technology, perhaps virtual *flâneurie* can take place by both sexes as well: the experience of browsing the Web must closely resemble the experience of actually wandering around in cities, and can even be undertaken with a male virtual identity if required (although eradicating every sign of female gender can be difficult, as we suggest in the discussion on **virtual leisure**). A search of my own soon revealed a number of weblogs and fotologs which might qualify as evidence for female *flâneurie*, including Flâneuse (2003).

Other options are available to those with different amounts and types of **cultural capital**. For what Baudrillard calls 'the masses', for example, weariness and disinterest can be the result of constantly being bombarded by anxious communicators on TV. As a result, apathy develops, and the masses become a 'black hole' into which communication simply disappears with no response. This kind of reaction often fills activist cultural commentators with despair, because they associate apathy with being manipulated. There is a view, for example, that postmodern playfulness in children's television will produce confusion, and make children vulnerable to the advertising people, or to peddlers of simple moral messages (see Kinder, 1991). However, Baudrillard identifies such apathy as a major future problem for commercialized capitalism, and sees it as almost a deliberate counter-strategy to preserve a private sphere (which links to much earlier work on defending the private sphere as a social response). In consequence, more and more effort is needed in advertising, customer surveys or promotional activities to yield any response at all. We may be already seeing signs of terminally deep apathy in reports of falling domestic consumption in the older generations (especially in the purchase of high-tech leisure goods such as mobile phones), or withdrawal from the political process (as in the recent reaction to excessive spin and news management). This is clearly depressing news for anyone interested in developing popular support for leisure policy, and we may already be seeing signs of apathetic responses to initiatives to combat obesity, avoid illegal drugs or play more team sports.

Yet there is a third option that takes a middle route, and involves an attempt to manage a controlled exposure to novelty and otherness through the medium of a modest adventure (which can include cultural adventures as well as risky journeys). We investigate in more depth in the entry on **escape**.

FURTHER READING

Eco (1987) and Baudrillard (1983) are classics well worth reading in more depth. The pessimistic remarks about apathy and black holes are also discussed in Gane (1991). Tester (1994) contains some classic writings on the *flâneur*.

REFERENCES

Baudrillard, J. (1983) *Simulations*, London: Semiotext(e).

Baudrillard, J. (1991) 'The Reality Gulf', *The Guardian*, 11 January 1991.

Bocock, R. and Thompson, K. (1992) *Social and Cultural Forms of Modernity*, Cambridge: Polity Press, in association with the Open University Press.

Eco, U. (1987) *Travels in Hyperreality*, London: Picador.

Flâneuse (2003) [online] http://www.fotolog.net/flaneuse/

Gane, M. (1991) *Baudrillard: Critical and Fatal Theory*, London: Routledge.

Hall, S. and Jacques, M. (eds) (1983) *The Politics of Thatcherism*, London: Lawrence and Wishart, and *Marxism Today*.

Kinder, M. (1991) *Playing with Power in Movies and Television: From Muppet Babies to Teenage Mutant Ninja Turtles*, Berkeley, CA: University of California Press.

Soja, E. (1989) *Postmodern Geographies: The Reassertion of Space in Critical Social Theory*, London: Verso.

Tester, K. (ed.) (1994) *The Flâneur*, London: Routledge.

Wolff, J. (1985) 'The Invisible Flâneuse: Women and the Literature of Modernity', *Theory, Culture and Society*, 2 (1): 37–48.

154

Identities

> An identity is a summary statement about who we are, a symbolic way to display important information about ourselves in an abbreviated manner – our tastes and choices in leisure (in this case) and the groups to which we belong. The term appears in the plural to accommodate the debate about how stable and fixed our identities are in modernity, whether we have just one main one, how many we can successfully develop, and how easily we can maintain them.

> **Section Outline:** The move from 'master' identities to more flexible options. Queer theory and sexual identities. Youth subcultures. Identity, belonging, the role of socially approved knowledge and acceptance. Consumerism, leisure and identity. Modernity: choice and novelty, or instability, narcissism and disillusion?

In the sociological work that informs much leisure studies, the notion of identity has a double aspect. We meet it in discussions of **social class**, **gender**, or **'race'**, for example. Social conditions produce particular outlooks, leisure choices, tastes and opportunities. We grow up wanting particular things because we are particular kinds of persons – we are working-class males, and therefore we support our local football team; or as middle-class women we develop a taste for domestic programmes on TV (as long as they do not interfere with our family responsibilities); or as descendants of immigrants from the Caribbean, we feel drawn towards particular kinds of music or lifestyle, and we express our sense of belonging through those. The social origins of identity are important, and for a long time, they were thought to provide us with 'master identities'. No matter what else we were, we were still always people located in particular categories of gender, ethnic group and social class, and traces of those social origins could still be detected, no matter what personal differences we had developed subsequently. This is sometimes expressed in a slightly more 'political' sense, such as in the view that women's gender is always a factor in their interactions, no matter what they achieve as individuals, or that people of colour always remain as 'outsiders', no matter what they do or how they dress.

However, some additional work suggests that identity is far more fluid a matter in modern or **postmodern** societies. That is so partly because the old social groups have lost some of their solidarity and cohesion, and thus their values have ceased to be held so firmly. The traditional working class has declined in Britain, it has been argued, as traditional occupations have changed, traditional neighbourhoods and communities have been broken up, and traditional religious or political bonds have weakened. Culture has become globalized: tourism and travel have increased in both directions, the global mass media saturate us with images of ways of life which are quite different to our own. For some theorists, culture has become free-floating, and independent of the traditional social ways of life (see Crook et al., 1992).

Examples that seem to fit this trend can be found readily in popular culture. For example, in the 1970s in Britain, the particular social problems faced by youth, especially male working-class youth, led them to adopt particular lifestyles that could be seen as symbolizing these problems. I am summarizing some work developed in collections such as Hall and Jefferson (1976), discussed in the entry on **youth subcultures**. Thus, bikers were acting out a drama that they were experiencing as the classical values of skilled working-class males were being threatened by globalization and industrial change, hence the strong values given to the traditional biker pursuit of tinkering with and customizing unreliable but charismatic old British bikes, while pouring scorn on the easier options offered by Japanese imports. 'Skinheads' represented an exaggeration of the traditional muscular male working-class values that were under threat in traditional British cities, hence the aggressive male haircuts, liking for violence, territoriality displayed at football matches, industrial clothing, resentment of outsiders, and so on.

However, it is clear that both biker and skinhead looks have developed into something more like a deliberately cultivated style. There are Japanese skinheads, for example, who like the look, and cannot really be seen as acting out any social tensions induced by change. The same goes for bikers, who find a much wider variety of pleasures and express a wider variety of values than the resistance to industrial change cited in the 1970s' case (see McDonald-Walker, 2000). To cite some examples recently encountered, there are now Bikers for Jesus or Dykes on Bikes as well as old-timers coaxing ancient British mounts. These days it is all far less serious, and people can even be self-mocking or ironic about the look they are currently displaying: what else explains the artificial furry ears applied to many contemporary biker helmets?

Identities

An excellent example of the point is found in that fairly recent tradition used to examine sexual identities known as 'queer theory' (see Seidman, 1996, for a collection of essays). Queer theory grew out of earlier work on conventional female and homosexual male identities to consider a much wider range of possibilities including transsexuals, drag, differences between butch and femme lesbians, and so on. Lurking behind this work is a central argument that gender is a performance, that people do not just release a gender identity but actually enact or express one. Marginal examples illustrate this well, as in Butler's analysis of drag (Butler, in Nicholson, 1990). Dyer also points out that more traditional identities such as male gay have long developed much more flexible possibilities: for him the term 'Queer', far from being just an old abusive term for male gays is now about ' something you are . . . rather than something you might do (have done), feel (have felt), mainly, sometimes, once, maybe' (2002: 3) (it is this new reclaimed and expanded notion that is indicated in Dyer's use of a capital letter for 'Queer').

To take concrete examples, one reading of a fairly typical piece of work such as Hurtes (2002) on the effects of gender on outdoor activity could be that the girls involved brought with them adolescent subcultural notions of themselves as girls who did not get sweaty or dress in unflattering clothing, and that this severely limited their participation in those activities: '[in these circumstances] . . . it is unlikely that . . . girls will truly experience leisure' (Hurtes, 2002: 109). Hurtes sees the girls almost as victims, as over-dependent on the valuations of others. However, it is also possible to read it differently and to see the girls' reactions as demonstrating 'proper femininity' as they saw it, to speculate that they were using the pretext of outdoor activity to deliver a skilled and self-aware performance as 'proper girls' (which included a need to show you knew how to be 'cool'). This sort of reading can be at the least a useful warning against 'sociologism' – the tendency to explain all social life as the product of mysterious deep social processes – which we discuss in the entry on **social class**.

It is now possible to acquire the market goods that can be used to display an identity, of course, instead of having it emerge from a way of life. Goods become signs used to emphasize similarities and differences among people, rather than being limited to their utilitarian value. Students learn how to buy the sort of clothes and other goods that make them look like students, for example, while a whole range of designer goods are used to signal membership of more specific (leisure-based) fractions within overall social groupings – sports student, surfer student, skater student, clubbing student, gay student, mature student, well-off student, overseas student, and so on. It becomes possible to change public identities quite rapidly as a result, as fashions change and new products appear on the market. We should add to this the great range of cultural materials we know about from a globalized mass media and the travel industry.

As with other demonstrations of the apparent universality of 'choice', we need to consider some reservations at this point. Some people clearly have far more opportunities than others to express themselves by purchasing symbolic goods. You need to have considerable economic and probably **cultural capital** to express yourself by buying antique furniture for your home. It may be quite true that even the poorest people are able to choose goods that express their identities to some extent, as Willis (1990) has argued in his discussion of 'common culture' – you do not need much money to achieve a 'retro' look from recycled second-hand clothes, or to decorate your rented accommodation with cheap posters. However, you are barred from the option of expressing your desire to return to nature by building a conservatory on the back of your house and stocking it with tropical plants. Similarly, the option to change your sex or appearance (even skin colour) by plastic surgery is technically available to all, but limited in practice to those who can afford it, even though much can be done with diet, body-building, cosmetics and exercise. The apparent universality of differentiation has been exaggerated by advocates of flexible identities and difference, possibly because they happen to come from social strata where there is much more flexibility and interest in difference in the first place.

There is also the problem that consumer goods arrive with meanings attached to them already. Companies employ specialist advertisers and marketers to tell plausible stories in which possession of their particular goods is embedded. Suzuki motorcycles already have an image of freedom, progress, modernism, and nature attached to them expressed in the slogan 'Ride the Winds of Change'. Trainers borrow the glamour and personality of the celebrities who endorse their use, as discussed in the entry on **adding leisure values**. Of course, consumers have long been able to add meanings of their own in creative moments. It is hardly surprising that leisure offers perhaps the best space for these creative and initially playful moments.

Assuming an identity is not always easy. There are rather esoteric aspects of youth cultures, each with their own distinctive clothing, musical tastes and argot (to summarize Brake, 1985). Knowledge of these peculiar meanings is quite important if you want to belong. As a biker in the 1960s and 1970s, I felt much more at ease once I knew that the much-mentioned E3134s were high-lift cams for Triumphs, and RRT2s

Identities

the close-ratio gearboxes fitted to BSA Gold Stars. I now risk serious embarrassment by not knowing whether the engine in the Honda Hornet is the same as the one in the Fireblade, or whether all Ducattis have desmodromic valve systems. As we would expect, these obscure matters have a social function in separating out levels of commitment to the core of the identity in question.

The successful maintenance of an identity also depends on the reactions of others. It is no good carefully choosing a look to express your particular identity of the moment if you make embarrassing mistakes over the fundamentals. I am reminded of the work on 'normalization' (see **illegal leisure**), and of classic work like Becker et al. (1961) on occupational socialization. We need to enter identities in stages and progress from peripheral to core membership: as our knowledge grows we feel far more at ease and far more committed to the core values of the group in question. The process can require a lot of detailed observation and hard work to adjust – a kind of popular **ethnography**. We need to know what is going on, and then to contribute with stories and actions of our own. Identities have to be learned, and I am not convinced that lifestyle guides are very efficient ways to learn the subtleties, nor that commerce can provide these in sufficient detail (but see Thornton, 1995, for a different view). Roberts (1997) tests out some options with some empirical data, and argues that leisure pursuits are too unstable to produce lasting identities.

Work in 'queer theory' has also noticed the risks, and Esterberg (in Seidman, 1996) describes the dilemmas faced by lesbians who have to negotiate a careful balance between being visible to other lesbians and risking being stereotyped. Goffman's classic work on stigma (1968) shows that the seriously stigmatized have to develop various, often ingenious, possible ways to relate to 'normals', and some are described in the entry on **bodies**. However, flexible identities may just not be capable of being brought off by an act of individual judgement and effort alone, and others may have more power to impose their views.

Indeed, some commentators have noted unhappiness and 'lack' in consumption-based identities (especially Rojek, 1993, 1995). Relying on goods that you purchase for a sense of identity binds you tightly to commercial capitalism. Given the restless drive towards novelty in commercial capitalism, the sense of insecurity increases, since a possession that reliably indicates core identity one year is replaced the next: we have only to note the weekly changes in what is deemed to be fashionable dress in any colour supplement. Finally, we know in our hearts that we can never be totally confident in ourselves simply by buying outward appearances, because these are not simply identified with us as people (to echo Roberts, 1997). We can fantasize that we look as cool as the models in the fashion shoots, but we can never actually become those models. This gap or 'lack' is an irresolvable problem for the consumer and is the source of the ever-present disillusion that accompanies consumerism. It is commercially very useful that this should be so, of course, because it keeps us buying.

There may even be risks of long-term damage. The gloomiest analysis is provided by Lasch (1982) who predicts the widespread occurrence of narcissism. This is a pathological condition where the self can only relate to others in a shallow and egocentric way. More frighteningly, narcissists are incapable of modifying their own behaviour, since they have a shallow relationship with themselves as well. Lasch thinks the condition is growing in the USA at least, blaming the spread of consumerism and the decline of the old social groups for eroding the basis of a strong normal personality. In contrast, Giddens's (1991) account of the kind of lifestyle found in modernity argues that individuals are still in control, still able to regulate their consumption, able to resolve their insecurity by a combination of acquiring lifestyle guides and gurus, and reflexively examining their own lives to avoid crisis.

FURTHER READING

McRobbie (1994) has a piece on the implications of flexible identities for feminist work, and the issue underlines much of the debate in Ramazanoglu (1993). David Gauntlett has provided an excellent online archive on gender and 'queer theory' (see The Theory.org.uk Directory, 2003), and there is another online archive at QT (2003). Butler's work is famous and worth exploring – the essay in Nicholson (1990) is a good introduction. Lasch (1982) is worth comparing with Giddens (1991). Roberts (1997) has some empirical data and a useful list of references (and there is a 'reading guide' to this piece on my website, specifically on www.arasite.org/kcroberts.html). Harris (1996) sets out my case for scepticism about flexible identities.

REFERENCES

Becker, H., Geer, B., Hughes, E. and Strauss, A. (1961) *Boys in White: Student Culture in Medical School*, Chicago: Chicago University Press.
Brake, M. (1985) *Comparative Youth Cultures*, London: Routledge and Kegan Paul.
Crook, S., Pakulski, J. and Waters, M. (1992) *Postmodernization: Change in Advanced Society*, London: Sage.

Dyer, R. (2002) *The Culture of Queers*, London and New York: Routledge.

Giddens, A. (1991) *Modernity and Self-Identity: Self and Society in the Late Modern Age*, Cambridge: Polity Press.

Goffman, E. (1968) *Stigma: Notes on the Management of Spoiled Identity*, Harmondsworth: Pelican Books.

Hall, S. and Jefferson, T. (eds) (1976) *Resistance Through Rituals*, London: Hutchinson.

Harris, D. (1996) *A Society of Signs?* London: Routledge.

Hurtes, K. (2002) 'Social Dependency: The Impact of Adolescent Female Culture', *Leisure Sciences*, 24: 109–121.

Lasch, C. (1982) *The Culture of Narcissism* London: Sphere.

McDonald-Walker, S. (2000) *Bikers: Culture, Politics and Power*, Oxford: Berg.

McRobbie, A. (1994) *Postmodernism and Popular Culture*, London: Routledge.

Nicholson, L. (ed.) (1990) *Feminism/Post-modernism*, New York: Routledge.

QT (2003) [online] http://www.queertheory.com/

Ramazanoglu, C. (ed.) (1993) *Up Against Foucault: Explorations of some Tensions between Foucault and Feminism*, London: Routledge.

Roberts, K. (1997) 'Same Activities, Different Meanings: British Youth Cultures in the 1990s', *Leisure Studies*, 16 (1): 1–16.

Rojek, C. (1993) *Ways of Escape*, London, The Macmillan Press.

Rojek, C. (1995) *Decentring Leisure: Rethinking Leisure Theory*, London: Sage.

Seidman. S. (ed.) (1996) *Queer Theory/Sociology*, Oxford: Basil Blackwell Ltd.

The Theory.org.uk Directory (2003) [online] http://www.theory.org.uk/directory.htm

Thornton, S. (1995) *Club Cultures: Music, Media and Subcultural Capital*, Cambridge: Polity Press.

Willis, P. (1990) *Common Culture*, Milton Keynes: Open University Press.

Ideology

In common usage, the term 'ideology' refers to a set of explicit beliefs, usually political in nature, to which people are committed. More specialist work in social theory sees ideologies as both beliefs and practices. Ideologies are connected with ways of life – they code the social lives of actors and they lend weight to seeing those ways of life as natural, inevitable, or desirable.

Section Outline: *Notions of ideology in Marx, Althusser, Hall and Adorno. Examples: 'vulgar' and 'scientific' ideologies, 'hailing', hegemony and 'ideological effects' in the media, the ambiguities of 'free time'. Clarke and Critcher on leisure in capitalism. Lacan and feminist film theory. Methodological and political critiques.*

To say that someone acts for ideological reasons implies an irrational commitment to a set of beliefs, a policy associated with a political party or religious group. In more specialist sociological discussions, the sense of an ideology as a set of beliefs is sometimes retained, although there are more dimensions and implications to discuss.

Ideologies are often connected to and somehow represent ways of life. This might seem strange at first because we tend to think of ideas as free-floating, to be adopted or rejected for their own sake, but a number of social theorists have argued that there are social factors involved. For example, the way you are brought up might affect your beliefs about what counts as a proper family, the correct relationship between the genders, what a successful marriage looks like, and so on. The term often used to describe this connection is 'socialization', but Bourdieu uses the term 'habitus' to describe the unconscious set of beliefs and values which people are taught, not only by speaking to their parents, but by interacting with them and living with them (see, for example, Bourdieu, 1977). We are not just talking about individuals here, but groups of people who have shared patterns of upbringing.

Functionalist perspectives on leisure include Durkheim's view that particular ways of life and social relations became 'coded' into a set of symbolic relations, and that religious beliefs took the shape they did from this original coding process, even though they developed a certain independence afterwards.

The ideas that people hold therefore reflect their ways of life. They can also express more direct interests. Thus, to take an example in Marx (1977), someone who became a small businessman them-selves might well hold a typical small businessman's view and set of opinions – they would see it as right and normal that the national economy should be run like a small business, that on the whole people should not borrow too much money, and that hard work and individual effort are the key to success. Weber develops a similar view here in his analysis of religious belief, suggesting that, for example, successful Protestant businessmen saw a particular value of translating

Protestant beliefs into the view that work was a calling and an ethical duty (see Turner, 1981).

It is marxist views that have had the greatest impact, perhaps. As the example above indicates, ideologies can have a social role as well, in 'reproducing' economic and social systems such as capitalism. The small businessman we referred to above would obviously want to support the major institutions of capitalism, such as the wage labour system, the belief in free enterprise or private property, the rights of owners and bosses to own any surpluses produced by the business, and so on. This direct connection between immediate interests and beliefs is sometimes called 'vulgar' ideology to distinguish it from another sense. Marx wanted to suggest that even social scientists and academics, the economists and philosophers of his day, allowed aspects of existing social reality to influence and limit their thoughts. This is 'scientific' ideology.

To give a brief example, the economic system of capitalism offers a very misleading surface appearance to any inquirer, and it is this that limits any scientific approach wanting to study it without being too critical or too philosophical. In particular, economists failed to understand that the movements of prices on the surface reflected a deeper notion of 'value' under the surface. Commodities looked like simple goods and services that were exchanged for money, but for Marx they were more complex than that and expressed two kinds of value (use value and exchange value). Labour looked like it was a simple commodity as well, but it had a unique use value in that it could add value in the production process to other commodities such as raw materials.

To take another quick example, it is common to call our political system a democratic one, because we are able to vote for our political leaders. For marxists, this is misleading, however, because we only get this ability to vote on one day every four or five years, so to call the whole system democratic just as a result of this one moment involves a very large abstraction and generalization. Calling this system 'democratic' is also to support it, of course. In reality, our political leaders do not have to respond to us once elected, and they have considerable power over us for all the rest of their time in power. However, what happens for most of the time is not used as a name for the entire system; 'Parliamentary dictatorship' might be more accurate, and, clearly, far less approving.

There is much more to understand in this analysis, and I have offered my own examples and further discussion in Harris (2003a), but I hope it is possible to see that even academic ideas can be limited by the appearance of the social reality they are trying to explain. A limited understanding helps the reproduction of capitalism as well, because it

163

makes it look like an automatic mechanism with its own laws, whereas beneath the surface, class struggle is the real mechanism and motor of development. I have only been able to offer a brief discussion of how ideas are embedded in social relations for marxists, and I offer a much longer discussion in Harris (1996).

We explore in another entry how the **gramscians** have interpreted this general critical work on economics and politics to see the modern state as involved in cultural struggle as well – masking class struggle, preserving a misleading surface appearance, and handling cultural contradictions and challenges in a constant struggle for hegemony. A particularly penetrating example is offered by Hall (in Curran et al., 1977), this time on the media (and drawing on the work of other theorists as much as on Gramsci). The media work with all sorts of ideas about British society and its unmistakable social divisions, but fail to grasp the real mechanisms behind inequality (provided by social class, remember). They deal with stories about social divisions such as those between the old and the young, the North and the South, the resident and the immigrant. Occasionally, hope is offered that these divisions can be healed, usually symbolically – at Christmas, in times of public grief, or on great sporting occasions (like the World Cup). This is a whole discourse about unity and division, conducted entirely in the wrong terms for marxists, but it has a useful political role in offering a way to explain society in a suitably conservative way: we will always have inevitable or 'natural' social divisions, the argument goes, but we can rise above them when we have to, without needing any radical political change.

Another marxist theorist, Althusser, helped to advance the theory of ideology by looking at the actual social mechanisms involved in more detail. We have seen how for an academic in nineteenth-century Britain observations of the economic system could mislead. What about ordinary people as they go about social life in the twenty-first century? Here, Althusser offers a sketch that has proved to be very rich in implications. He suggests that the key to modern notions of ideology is the root view that we are free autonomous individuals. How is this view conveyed to us and reinforced by our experience? For Althusser, (1977) it is a matter of 'hailing'. This is easy to explain with a simple example of someone being hailed in greeting by a friend in the street, perhaps by calling their name. The person so hailed turns round and recognizes himself or herself as the individual concerned, but this really depends on there being a hailing mechanism in the first place. Althusser uses a religious analogy as well – Christians know they are full individuals when they are hailed or called by God, but this clearly implies accepting the view that there is

Ideology

an all-powerful God in the first place with the ability to bestow individuality on us. By extension, our individuality is bestowed on us, not by God, but by the actions of particular powerful social institutions (ultimately by the State), and Althusser gives examples such as the media, the family and the school. Leisure organizations would also be ideal examples. The main function of these organizations is to create us as individuals, and to reinforce this misleading perception in practice. It is misleading, because the power relations are not recognized, and because the pleasing sense that we really can be free individuals in capitalism (when we play soccer or go shopping) lends the system legitimacy.

Althusserian analysis sparked off a tremendous debate in social theory, as did a similar-looking one by Lacan (whose essay is also found in Althusser, 1977). Lacan's view takes on a more 'psychological' appearance at first reading, since it discusses that stage in the developmental growth of an infant when they recognize themselves as an individual. Freud described this stage as the 'mirror phase': at that stage individual infants are mature enough literally to recognize themselves in actual mirrors as separate entities. Again, the broader implication is that we become individuals only when we enter a social system that 'mirrors' us, puts us in the social slot that other people have constructed for us, gives us a name they have thought of, and a conventional identity.

Let us now turn to some specific applications to leisure theory. We have seen in the discussion on **social class** that leisure relations can often present a misleading appearance, just as the economic system does. What appears to be a realm of freedom, individual choice, or **escape** from work is quite different when you look beneath the surface. Clarke and Critcher (1985) reveal the hidden influences at work, including the political regulation of leisure intended to stifle popular pursuits and channel them into safer and more commercial forms, or the hidden economic control of leisure activities by large leisure corporations. Such organizations offer a choice in a commercialized sense (a choice between one or other of their products) but not a choice to consume something completely outside their range. Indeed, corporations can close down rival companies and reduce choice if they manage to gain control of a market, a tendency seen clearly in the food and drink industries, for example. Similar analyses have been used to expose what looks like the free choice of consumerism as a clever commercial strategy to **add leisure values** to commodities.

Another marxist approach, which we do not mention in any depth at all here (but which is discussed in Harris, 2003a) is usually called 'critical theory'. It draws on a wide range of philosophical and sociological sources as well as marxism which produces a very deep critique of modern culture. Briefly, modern popular culture is seen as the product of a 'culture industry', thoroughly penetrated by capitalist mechanisms, seen best in the obvious commercialism of much of its products. As a modern and sophisticated industry, the culture industry is well aware that it needs to offer individualized products, or to cater for particular niches in the market. It is this that provides the major illusion of individual choice, and also the apparent direct connection to the real subjective needs and desires of the consumer. I have a series of 'reading guides' to these essays on the culture industry on my personal website (Harris, 2003b, specifically www.arasite.org/sagelist.html). Adorno's short essay on 'free time' (in Adorno, 1991) summarizes many of the themes: so-called free time can only be understood in connection with the demands of work as part of social totality, and much of what passes for leisure activity is actually work-like. Adorno gives examples such as do-it-yourself, having a hobby, cultivating a suntan, enjoying trivial entertainment, and doing sport. His analysis looks rather like the one we discuss in the entry on **disciplinary apparatuses**, although it is based on different theoretical resources.

Althusserian notions of ideology have been applied in analysing the mass media and their effects in 'hailing' people, with the same consequence – a sense of individuality has been gained, but only by submitting to commercial and political interests. Cinema in particular 'hails' us effectively, and we explore the role of a particular kind of 'realist narrative' in doing this (see **narratives**). Realist narratives work to deliver a sense of insight to the viewer, so we feel that we are indeed knowledgeable individuals, but only because we have submitted to and obediently followed the narrative in the first place. We explore some more implications in the entry on **gazes**.

The Lacanian mechanism has provided much insight into the construction of gender hierarchies, and thus has been extremely influential in the development of some feminist analysis. We can begin to see how this might work, when we remember that the role of the Father is crucial at the moment of the mirror phase. The Father, spelt with a capital letter, is a symbolic role, representing culture and the social order into which the infant is being inducted. In this way, is possible to argue that culture and the social world are inherently patriarchal, and this has led to much feminist criticism in both of those spheres (for developments in feminist film theory, see Williamson, 1987).

Even these brief examples serve to illustrate the power of the concept of ideology in marxist hands. We must attempt our normal assessment and criticism, though, and I want to begin with a common objection to marxist analysis, namely that it is an ideology itself. It is clear that marxist analysis usually involve strong political commitment and belief in an alternative system, and this raises the suspicion that marxist concepts may themselves be ideological, either in a vulgar or a scientific sense. However, the usual counter-claim is that marxist analysis offers an unusually systematic and rigorous scientific approach and methodology which represents no one social class, and this prevents it from being merely ideological. This follows from the discussion above, which referred to other approaches being 'misled' either by the (class) interests of the analyst, or by the failure to penetrate misleadingly simple surface appearances. Much debate has gone on about Marx's own method, and whether it can offer a more rigorous and systematic form of analysis (see Sayer, 1991). Much of Althusser's work is actually devoted to attempting to discover Marx's scientific methods. Once we realize this, we can also start to explain the widespread disillusionment with marxism that affected many social, media, and leisure theorists in the 1990s and since. Some commentators point to the collapse of the Soviet system and the apparent triumph of 'the West' in the Cold War, but while this may have disillusioned many supporters of Soviet communism, academic and intellectual marxists were probably affected more by the substantial scepticism directed at Marx's methods. This scepticism is discussed briefly in the entry on **posts**.

FURTHER READING

You might want to begin with some of the 'reading guides' (notes) I have made on various marxist texts on my personal website (Harris, 2003b). These provide a quick overview to guide fuller reading, and I have notes on Adorno, Althusser, Hall, Marx, Mulvey (a feminist and '*Screen* theorist'), and Williamson, with some additional commentaries on Marx's 'theory of value' (see the notes on Elson). Each of these has some further references to follow up.

REFERENCES

Adorno, T. (1991) 'Free Time', in T. Adorno, *The Culture Industry: Selected Essays on Mass Culture*, London: Routledge.

Althusser, L. (1977) 'Ideology and Ideological State Apparatuses (Notes Towards an Investigation)', in L. Althusser '*Lenin and Philosophy' and Other Essays*, London: New Left Books.

Bourdieu, P. (1977) *Outline of a Theory of Practice*, Cambridge: Cambridge University Press.

Clarke, J. and Critcher, C. (1985) *The Devil Makes Work. . . Leisure in Capitalist Britain*, London: Macmillan.

Curran, J., Gurevitch, M. and Woollacott, J. (eds) (1977) *Mass Communication and Society*, London: Edward Arnold in association with the Open University Press.

Harris, D. (1996) *A Society of Signs?*, London: Routledge.

Harris, D. (2003a) *Teaching Yourself Social Theory*, London: Sage.

Harris, D. (2003b) 'Dave Harris (and Colleagues): Essays, Papers and Courses' [online] http://www.arasite.org/

Marx, K. (1977) *Capital*, vol. 1, London: Lawrence and Wishart.

Sayer, D. (1991) *Capitalism and Modernity: An Excursus on Marx and Weber*, London: Routledge.

Turner, B. (1981) *For Weber: Essays on the Sociology of Fate*, London: Routledge and Kegan Paul.

Williamson, D. (1987) 'Language and Sexual Difference', *Screen*, 28 (1): 10–25.

Illegal Leisure

Some activities, including the consumption of some drugs, are actually illegal. The claim here is that these activities can still be understood as leisure activities, suspending judgement on their desirability, rather than as criminal or deviant ones. Leisure studies can offer important insights into these activities even though they are forbidden.

Section Outline: Making leisure activities illegal: policy-making, ambiguity, protest and the loss of legitimacy. Regulating the use of dangerous drugs. Sociological studies of illegal drug-taking. Recent work on the 'normalization' of drug-taking and the implications for social policy.

The case of illegal leisure leads to us asking about the role of the State in making certain leisure activities illegal. This is clearly an area of some controversy, and it would take us too long to investigate it fully here, although McGuigan (1992) has a basic introduction.

Making some activities legal or illegal raises some quite fundamental political questions about how modern states operate. Banning leisure activity is one of the few things that can be guaranteed to get people out on the streets protesting about the way government works, as seen very clearly in the recent large demonstrations about the UK Government's intentions to ban hunting with dogs in England and Wales. It is clear that the protesters saw the issue as a very fundamental one, involving an attack on their 'way of life', threats to the rural economy, or the unfair treatment of particular minorities. Their opponents felt just as strongly, not only about the particular characteristics of hunting as a leisure activity, but also about making social progress, modernizing Britain, enforcing the democratic wishes of the majority of the people of Britain, and so on. The whole issue could still produce a minor constitutional crisis involving the relationship between the two Houses, and the rights of Parliament itself.

The UK Government has criminalized a number of leisure activities from the beginning of the modern democratic era, including other kinds of blood sports, and has intervened to regulate others, as we can see in the entry on rational recreation (in **social class**) . At present, it is illegal to download (or otherwise publish) what a jury might consider to be obscene material, and to possess certain categories of banned drugs, although it seems probable that both kinds of activities are both widespread and popular. We discuss **pornography** in another entry, but we might examine some of the work on the consumption of illegal drugs in this entry as a major case study.

There may well be general justifications for governmental action which could be deployed here. For example, there is the idea of 'social harm', which suggests that the rights of individuals to enjoy leisure activities can be restricted if it causes other people harm. In early political theories such as utilitarianism, it was suggested that we could quantify the amounts of happiness and unhappiness that might be generated by criminalizing some activities, and then choose a policy that generates the most happiness: if banning fox hunting leads to more happiness than unhappiness, the legislation should go ahead. In practice, it is not so easy, since no simple measures of happiness are available.

The State can decide to act on other theoretical or philosophical bases too. It could simply represent the will of the majority as expressed in a vote or referendum on drug use, but, again there are problems here if we allow for the possibility that an ill-informed majority, or one incapable of foreseeing the long-term consequences of an action, might choose the 'wrong' option. Asking the right question in a referendum is also likely to be important, as we know. Then there are problems of what happens if the majority is a narrow or temporary one – should minority groups be forced to follow the will of such a majority, or should we protect minority interests? There are other problems too, such as whether we consider the voters to be making up their own minds, or fear that they may have been unduly influenced by powerful interests, say, those in the media. Nevertheless, the alternative seems equally undesirable – that the government sets itself up as some kind of committee of the wise, banning things that are bad for us (perhaps on the advice of anonymous experts) even though we do not happen to think so ourselves.

When we come to look at actual legislation affecting leisure, the position seems annoyingly inconsistent. In Britain we ban dangerous drugs such as cocaine or ecstasy, but the consumption of alcohol and tobacco is merely licensed. By most measures of social harm, including the costs of treatment and the effects on health, alcohol and tobacco are dangerous drugs as well. Even prescription drugs are known to be dangerous in some circumstances, although the UK Government has long dragged its feet over making consumers aware of possible side-effects. There is some variation between national governments too, where different sorts of drugs are seen as more or less dangerous as in Britain. British Governments have not even been consistent over time: various kinds of opiates were commonly included in medicines in Victorian England, for example, while the status of cannabis is the subject of constant debate. Without consistency, it might be difficult for people to give their consent to laws regulating their leisure activities. It could look as if the government was being rather arbitrary in its choice of what to ban, or even as though it was affected by powerful pressure groups, and not the social good at all (brewers and tobacco manufacturers are quite capable of attempting to influence Parliament, while few speak up for the cannabis user). Given the lack of broad consent, the cost of policing illegal leisure activities is likely to rise, and may be already at the level where it becomes easier to ignore moderate levels of illegal activity rather than insist on prosecuting in every instance (which may be a factor in the recent UK decision to soften the legal category applying to cannabis).

We can now turn to studies of drug-users themselves. It is important to do so, regardless of our personal views, since there seems to be no consistent and agreed set of beliefs about the practice of drug-taking. Even if we believe that drug-taking should be severely regulated by the state, it becomes important to understand why people do it, so that we might control it more effectively. For example, if people are likely to be deterred by an increase in sentences on conviction, or by the development of a new technology to detect drug use, then that should affect the precise actions that are taken by the government.

Illegal Leisure

There is the possibility that the results of actual research could lead to a different sort of policy altogether, directed at educating people about the health risks, rather than stressing the criminal nature of the activity (which is clearly the view of Hammersley et al., 2002). More generally, other social policies might be made more effective. The sort of literature that people receive about illegal drugs as part of schools programmes, for example, often contains information only about the most severe health risks, but do not even mention the aspect of drug use that most appeals to the users – the pleasures. As with other examples, leisure studies can make a genuine contribution here.

There have been several major sociological studies of drug-taking, ranging from Becker (1973) to Hammersley et al. (2002) . What emerges is an awareness of the social dimension of drug use, the ways in which group support is required to understand the pleasures of drug-taking, and the ways in which drug-taking has become part of a normal way of life for some. This immediately changes the focus from the individual towards more social factors. There are also some interesting studies of drug use and its connection with other leisure activities, particularly clubbing, especially Malbon (1999) (see **ecstasy**).

The study with the greatest relevance to the themes we have introduced, however, is the one undertaken by Parker and his associates on a group of young people in the north-west of England (Parker et al., 1998; Parker et al., 2002). To summarize some of the findings, taking recreational drugs is best understood as a matter of the complex calculation of risks and benefits, as with many other consumer activities, including driving or pursuing a dangerous sport. Users estimate the main hazards as damage to their health, or getting caught, and the main benefits as gaining 'time-out' from stress or distress, as leading to leisure and relaxation or to 'escape'. Although this varies by age and generation, most users get started as a result of factors such as the availability of drugs, and their own curiosity about the effects. The presence of peers or friends who can encourage, reassure, and supply know-how is also important. The later study (Parker et al., 2002) says the main route of supply is through friends and contacts too.

There is a perceived social division between recreational drug-users and what might be thought of as hard drug-users: the users themselves identify matters such as whether injection is required. Recreational users refrain from using hard drugs as a result of their personal calculations of risks and pleasures: they have a sophisticated awareness to offer, not blanket hostility towards 'drugs'. Using cannabis seems to be the easiest thing to admit to parents. Those who abstain altogether report some additional social exclusion (some evidence for 'peer pressure').

Parker et al. are aware that adolescents may not be the most effective judges or calculators of risk. They do not perceive the health risks as being particularly large, for example, but then they suffer from a sense of 'adolescent invulnerability'. However, immediate health risks are recognized, and usually described in terms such as 'bad experiences', or 'scary moments', especially when drugs are combined. There is also a methodological problem with studies that use self-reporting, as this one does (and as many studies of deviant activities do): direct observation may be more valid, but it is much harder to arrange. Parker and his team did find some independent signs of dependency, for example, despite denials and disguises. They also recognize a minority of 'quite damaged and vulnerable' young people who 'misuse' drugs.

The move of recreational drug-taking from the margins of social life to the centre is not just a phenomenon related to teenage life, and the majority of users will continue to try illicit drugs beyond their teens. Further, drug use is not associated with social failure or being a loser. 'Excessive individualism' might be associated with drug use, though (among those who can resist peer pressure towards moderation?). Drug use is associated with clubbing, although the use of Ecstasy now extends beyond the club scene. Even abstainers accept drug use as normal. Finally, drug use is not as tightly linked with subcultural formation as once it was, although hard drug users are more likely to belong to subcultures (see **youth subcultures**). Overall, then, there is a new type of recreational drug use, taking its place alongside other widespread leisure activities.

Parker et al. want to trace the emergence of this large group of recreational users to features of 'late modernity' as in Giddens (1991): the traditional social constraints have become 'disembedded', and people have to find new ways, largely personal ones, of managing the 'risk society'. There is an immediate policy implication: attempts to restore controls using traditional remedies, as in launching a 'war on drugs', are misguided, and the State should be seeking to assist the regulation and management of normalization instead. Recreational drug use is so widespread that it cannot now be regulated using the existing legal and policing framework. Traditional policing makes too many assumptions about drug use anyway – that it is invariably associated with crime, that users are addicted, or that young people are largely pressurized into taking drugs. All campaigns based on these assumptions have failed, the team argues.

There are unhelpful consequences of such campaigns as well. There are so many inconsistencies in the regulation of drug use in Britain, for example, in different police force areas, so that enforcement

172

becomes 'a lottery'. The unintended effects of labelling drug-users as criminals are still likely to be serious. Overall, policies of 'informed choice' seemed to offer the best prospects (these are already adopted by some youth agencies and voluntary organizations dealing with drug use). Drug-users should be informed about the effects of drugs, including health and safety aspects, especially those connected with effects on driving performance.

The study also sparked off much debate about the concept and process of 'normalization'. This term has several meanings, all of which relate to the theme of the illegality of the leisure pursuit. One view suggests that despite being illegal, the practice of drug-taking is common enough to appear as a normal part of life. This is developed in the 1998 study and also in the follow-up (Parker et al., 2002). The team estimates that up to 25 per cent of young people may be regular recreational users, and drug use has risen in frequency from 1 or 2 in 10 people in the 1970s to 5 or 6 people in 10 during the 1990s. The phenomenon seems to cross gender and class barriers, although middle-class groups are slightly more likely to be users. The 2002 study confirms the persistence of this kind of pattern, with some slight variation.

However, 'normalization' also refers to a growing social acceptance of drug use. For example, most studies 'Note the presence of a rational, consumerist, decision-making process which distinguishes between drugs, their effects and dangers and identifies a style of recreational drug use which can be accepted or at least tolerated by non-users or cautious drug triers' (Parker et al., 2002: 948). Tolerant non-takers include even politicians and policy-makers who are increasingly coming to accept the views of the 'drugwise', especially about the need to consider cannabis separately from the other drugs. We may be seeing a move from illegality back to legality, possibly, as old solutions are seen not to work, and as greater tolerance grows with the growing numbers of users.

There is one final sense in which 'normalization' might be studied, and this is only hinted at in the Parker studies – how do those engaged in illegal acts explain and justify their law-breaking to themselves and maintain their identity as 'normal' people? Parker has noted an attempt to explain the decision to take drugs in 'rational-consumerist' terms, demonstrating a calculation of risks and benefits. Clubbers seemed to use a different technique by trying to timetable their lives into clubbing and 'normal' episodes, as expressed in the idea of temporary escape: the 2002 study makes much more of clubbers' separateness from routine cannabis users (and see the work on clubbers in the entry on **ecstasy**).

Other possibilities still are provided by some classic work in deviancy on 'techniques of neutralization' (Matza, 1964). Here, juvenile law-breakers were interviewed and asked about their attitudes to the law. Most were not members of a totally hostile subculture that rejected the law outright, but seemed to share many of the values and beliefs of 'normal' people, just as Parker's drug-takers do. However, they explained their law-breaking in ways which tried to minimize or neutralize the immoral aspects of what they had done in order to show they were not really hardened law-breakers. For example, they denied there had been a real crime or any real victims (easily applied to drug-taking), or they appealed to some higher law or morality – perhaps as in making a religious or spiritual justification for cannabis use. Matza argues that these techniques are fairly effective in removing guilt from deviants, and also that we all use them in everyday life as well to explain minor lapses. If the general tenor of Matza's work is right, we are all perfectly capable of engaging in a good deal of illegal leisure, and have been rather fortunate not to have been involved in more!

FURTHER READING

The later work by Parker et al. (2002) might be compared with the more focused study of Ecstasy takers in Glasgow in Hammersley et al. (2002). Parker et al (2002) also have several useful references to follow up from their particular survey work. Matza (1964) is a classic work on delinquency, advocating the concept of 'normalization' long ago and with a more general compass. The references to 'risk society' could be pursued, in Giddens (1991) or in the frequently cited Beck (1992).

174

REFERENCES

Beck, U. (1992) *Risk Society*, London: Sage.
Becker, H. (1973) *Outsiders: Studies in the Sociology of Deviance*, New York: The Free Press of Glencoe.
Giddens, A. (1991) *Modernity and Self-Identity: Self and Society in the Late Modern Age*, Cambridge: Polity Press.
Hammersley, R., Khan, F. and Ditton, J. (2002) *Ecstasy and the Rise of the Chemical Generation*, London: Routledge.
Malbon, B. (1999) *Clubbing: Dancing, Ecstasy and Vitality*, London: Routledge.
Matza, D. (1964) *Delinquency and Drift*, New York: John Wiley and Sons Inc.
McGuigan, J. (1992) *Cultural Populism*, London: Routledge.
Parker, H., Aldridge, J. and Measham, F. (1998) *Illegal Leisure: The Normalization of Adolescent Recreational Drug Use*, London: Routledge.
Parker, H., Williams, L. and Aldridge, J. (2002) 'The Normalization of "Sensible" Recreational Drug Use: Further Evidence from the North West England Longitudinal Study', *Sociology*, 36 (4): 941–64.

Illegal Leisure

Leisure Policy

A policy is more than just a document expressing an intention to act. It requires the marshalling of knowledge and power in order to be implemented, often against the resistance, non-co-operation or sabotage of other groups. Developing and implementing leisure policies involve analysis of a complex political and social context.

Section Outline: *Leisure policies in totalitarian and democratic societies. General themes in British leisure policies. Direct and indirect ways of implementing leisure policies. General analyses of power: gramscian and Foucauldian, with examples. Leisure and the 'Third Way'.*

Given what we know about the diversity of leisure, and the tendency for the boundaries between leisure and other spheres of social life to be flexible, perhaps even collapsing, it is not surprising that leisure policy is going to face some complex problems. Colebatch (2002) points out that any policy development in a pluralistic liberal democracy is going to face considerable difficulties, because although policy may be formulated in the central organs of the state, once it begins to be implemented, all sorts of other parties find they have the power to amend or resist. Any example of a policy initiative will display this characteristic, including some we have discussed in other entries, such as the one to combat obesity with new sporting **disciplinary apparatuses**.

The organizations that regulate leisure, in both a positive and a negative sense, are not even united in one particular government department. For example, policies regulating schools can affect leisure, as in the well-known examples where devolving financial power to schools led to sales of local sports pitches. Facilities provided for educational uses also permit leisure uses: no one wants young people to use their computer literacy skills to download **pornography**, but it is quite possible that they will do so. On another tack, the government clearly does not directly control the commercial providers of leisure, and may wish to encourage them for the economic benefits that they bring – they are hardly in a position to complain if commercial leisure appears to be increasing at the expense of traditional team sports. If intangibles such as **fantasy**, 'flow' and **ecstasy** are integral to (post)modern leisure, perhaps policy should not attempt anything too ambitious, but try to amplify existing positive trends and just campaign or try 're-education' against the others – to 'flow with the flow' as Coalter (1999) puts it.

Leisure covers such a wide variety of activities enjoyed by such a wide variety of people that it becomes extremely difficult to think of a policy that will balance regulation and free choice without some controversy. Some totalitarian societies have developed coherent leisure policies, but even there, there have been rather mixed results. The Nazi policy of co-ordinating leisure activities in order to encourage 'strength through joy' seems to have been relatively well accepted by the population, although even in Nazi Germany rebellious youth cultures developed in opposition to the regime (Peukert, 1987). In fascist Italy, despite considerable state efforts and the provision of leisure resources, the policy never achieved high levels of compliance on the part of the population (De Grazia, in Donald and Hall, 1986).

McGuigan (1992) has identified a number of over-arching themes in recent UK Government leisure policy initiatives, ranging from 'rational recreation', through building national prestige (mostly centred on sport and athletics), to providing access for all (and social inclusion), to achieving sporting excellence (and possibly reviving traditional British team games). A major recent initiative aims to sponsor sport and leisure in policies of social inclusion (PAT 10, 2003). Less directly, the use of health and safety regulations to control leisure activities by refusing to license premises has been used in a number of cases to express government disapproval, from limiting public houses and children's cinemas (Staples, 1997) to effectively criminalizing free festivals and large-scale raves (Redhead, 1993). One specific policy associated with Thatcherism featured a classic indirect attempt to stimulate a private market in the provision of leisure facilities run by the local state – the policy took the form of insisting that each proposal for development be put to compulsory competitive tender, and not automatically given to the local authority suppliers (McGuigan, 1992).

The State has also been prepared to be openly prohibitive, as in attempts to ban obscene displays or the consumption of dangerous drugs (see **illegal leisure** and **pornography**), but there are formidable problems of definition, and serious obstacles in the way of being consistent. It is important for the government to appear to be consistent in their development of policy, of course, because they are supposed to be acting in the interests of society as a whole according to agreed general principles, and not acting in the interests of specific groups only.

Turning to a more positive use of policy, the UK Government has been able to exert an influence by targeting financial resources in specific policy initiatives. Membership of the European Union, and the huge success of the National Lottery have put considerable funds at the disposal of the government, even if this has to be mediated through other bodies (see National Lottery, 2003). Using the discussion of utilitarian principles in the entry on **functionalism** as a guide, we might predict some problems in the implementation of social engineering of this kind. There are doubts whether there are common and agreed goals for leisure, we might question whether the government is able to articulate social needs and separate them from their own, and we might predict a rash of dysfunctions (such as increasing social division between those who receive funds and those who do not) to accompany the proposals.

Turning to a more general level, thinking about policies and their fates also raises the issue of what the State is and how it works. We have already raised suspicions that the State in fact acts in the interests of dominant groups, in the interests of capital for marxists. Having arranged things so that capital expands to colonize the field of leisure, the State also has to manage any discontent or problems of adjustment, and it does this by pursuing hegemony (we discuss this concept in the entry on **gramscianism**, and we focus on specific policy developments such as 'rational recreation' in the entry on **social class**). It is this overall project, we could argue, that explains the specific twists, turns, interventions, and inconsistencies of actual policy – the State is engaged in a kind of political fire-fighting to manage specific crises and their manifestations, or to incorporate popular trends before they turn subversive. In Bennett (1998), however, we find a criticism: such a perspective means that specifics are ignored, that policies are always 'looked through' to find some deeper political struggle at work. We argued this with the criticisms of work stressing the use of leisure and sport as disciplinary apparatuses as well – the actual pleasurable subjective experiences of sport and its pleasures almost have to be ignored.

We might use Bennett to develop an alternative, and perhaps to reinterpret the notion of 'disciplinary apparatus'. Bennett's work is actually devoted to cultural policy, and it draws upon the work of Foucault instead of Gramsci. The connection between the work of these two authors is the subject of much debate, but we can isolate particular emphases associated with Foucault, all of which concern power: power is not concentrated in the hands of the State or the ruling class, but is widely

177

diffused throughout society; power is not only used to forbid or compel, but to enable and actually bring practices into being; power and knowledge are intimately related, in several senses, which includes the idea that the growth of new sciences and other forms of knowledge offers new possibilities for the exercise of power.

What this implies overall is that actual policies are formed in an unpredictable way from a combination of knowledge and the ability to develop a practice. To take an example in Bennett (1998), the development of museums can be explained in terms of a complex combination of the emergence and consolidation of scientific disciplines such as natural history, together with a struggle over the meaning of evolution, working on the raw materials provided by various collections of objects, often donated by powerful individuals in imperial service. No single one of these factors actually caused the development of the London Natural History Museum in the particular ways that it manifested itself, although there are social and political implications in what actually resulted. Very briefly, Bennett argues that the particular forms of display in that museum show the traces of past knowledges and power struggles, over evolution, for example, but more generally contain assumptions about a 'restless self', a particular conception of the human subject.

The interest in the subject or individual that is produced by this kind of activity is also a central theme in Foucault. In general, he argues that the model of social control and the exercise of power change from a rigid hierarchy with an untouchable monarch at the top of the social scale, to one which emphasizes the need for individuals to control themselves, to act responsibly, and to be law-abiding and disciplined. One of the best examples of this argument is contained in his work on the development of the modern prison (Foucault, 1977), which emerges as an institution to model the new self-disciplined subject (before the development of the prison, public punishment or banishment of a most exceptionally cruel kind were the ways to punish criminals socially and emphasize the contrast with the law-abiding). I hope it is now possible to see these Foucauldian notions in the use of the term 'disciplinary apparatus' as well, and we also discuss this idea in the entry on **gazes**.

To speculate on implications for leisure policy, we would need to resist the temptation to see leisure policy as part of a general struggle towards hegemony. However, conventional specific historical analyses would also not do: there is far more at stake than the alternation of particular party political manifestos, and even **figurationalist** analysis would not serve to pick up the general trends as they affect subjectivity.

It would be possible to see leisure policy as an ideal topic to analyse in terms of the coming together of different discourses as Foucault suggests. For one thing, leisure is as good a topic as sexuality (one of Foucault's examples) for focusing a number of different political and social concerns – health, taste, differences between the genders and the generations, issues of national prestige, the proper stance to take towards work and work discipline, and so on. Specific leisure policies could be seen as a combination and an embodiment of particular knowledges, including sociological knowledge of its social functions; scientific knowledge of matters such as the effect of exercise or drugs; commercial and vocational knowledge about how to 'add value'; historical knowledge about any evolutionary trends that might be detectable, and so on. There is the same sort of conjunction of discourses cited in the entry that discusses **bodies** as a similarly suitable topic.

We might begin to understand recent New Labour policy in terms of one of those conjunctions of discourses. We can isolate as an example the commitment to the 'Third Way' as a focus of political, electoral, religious and sociological concerns (see Jary, 2002, for a review). Notions of the Third Way clearly underpin using leisure as a form of social inclusion. There is the political context itself which has to be addressed – the legacy of earlier administrations and the possibility of acquiring funds without raising taxes that we mentioned above, and the declared intention to seek best practice wherever it is found, either in state or commercial sectors.

FURTHER READING

One way forward would involve researching specific policies, such as the UK Government's leisure policies (Department for Culture, Media and Sport, 2003), or to trace the debates about a controversial one like building the Millennium Dome (Guardian Unlimited Special Report on The Millennium Dome, 2003). There are also examples of controversial policies in other sections, such as **illegal leisure**, or **pornography**. The US Government's policy on obesity can also be examined conveniently (Virtual Office of the Surgeon General, 2003). These might be analysed using the framework in Bennett (1998). Jary (2002) is worth pursuing as a general discussion about current UK (and recent US) policy.

REFERENCES

Bennett, T. (1998) *Culture: A Reformer's Science*, London: Sage.
Coalter, F. (1999) 'Sport and Recreation in the United Kingdom: Flow with the Flow or Buck the Trends?', *Managing Leisure*, 4: 24–39.
Colebatch, H. (2002) *Policy*, 2nd edn, Buckingham: Open University Press.

Department for Culture, Media and Sport (2003) [online] http://www.culture.gov.uk/sport/default.htm.

Donald, J. and Hall, S. (1986) *Politics and Ideology*, Milton Keynes: Open University Press.

Foucault, M. (1977) *Discipline and Punish: The Birth of the Prison*, London: Peregrine Books Ltd.

Guardian Unlimited Special Report on The Millennium Dome (2003) [online] http://www.guardian.co.uk/dome/archive/0,3332,223662,00.html

Jary, D. (2002) 'Review Article: The Global Third Way Debate', *The Sociological Review*, 50 (3): 437–49.

McGuigan, J. (1992) *Cultural Populism*, London: Routledge.

National Lottery (2003) [online] www.lotterygoodcauses.org.uk/

PAT 10 (2003) [online] http://www.culture.gov.uk/

Peukert, D. (1987) *Inside Nazi Germany: Conformity, Opposition and Racism in Everyday Life*, London: Batsford.

Redhead, S. (ed.) (1993) *Rave Off: Politics and Deviance in Contemporary Youth Culture*, Aldershot: Avebury Press.

Staples, T. (1997) *All Pals Together: The Story of Children's Cinema*, Edinburgh: Edinburgh University Press.

Virtual Office of the Surgeon General (2003) [online] http://www.surgeongeneral.gov/topics/obesity/

McDonaldization

McDonaldization is a term originally coined by the American sociologist George Ritzer in a series of best-selling books about the spread of the fast food industry and the implications raised for modern society (including other types of leisure). More general theoretical arguments are also involved. Controversy has greeted the work and has led to new emphases.

Section Outline: Weber on rationalization. Ritzer on the characteristics of McDonaldization. Critical evaluations of the McDonaldization thesis. Weber on the 'ideal type'. Developments and applications to other leisure activities – package tours, Disney and the re-enchantment of the (baseball) ballpark.

Ritzer (1993) tells us that he was originally hoping to illustrate a major approach to the development of modern institutions associated with the German sociologist Max Weber, and he provides an account of Weber's sociology in his equally famous social theory book, Ritzer (1996). Ritzer sees the growth of the McDonald's chain as an excellent illustration of the tendencies that Weber described as rationalization, although the later work also suggests that **Disneyfication**, or certain aspects of globalization, including the development of international credit cards and the increasing exchange of 'nothing' (that is, 'weightless' goods like expertise and credit) would also serve as equally good examples. Since much of the discussion of McDonaldization points to the strengths and the weaknesses of Weber's analysis, it is best to begin with a brief account of Weber's theory of rationalization.

Weber had analysed rational human action as falling into four basic types, but he wanted to focus attention on the relationship between two of those types of rationality in particular. One was 'value–rationality', where social life was organized in order to rationally pursue some good life, some ultimate value, as in Christian notions of salvation or virtue. The other type is more familiar, so much so that it has become more or less identified with the concept of rationality itself. Weber called this type 'purposive–rationality', and it takes the form of a much more scientific and calculating pursuit of effectiveness. Here, overall values are important only insofar as they can be translated into specific, ideally measurable, goals. Any matters outside these specifics are left as purely private concerns, no longer to be debated in public life.

The most effective means to achieve these specific goals, with maximum benefit and minimum cost, are then selected, regardless of sentiment, subjective or emotional attachments, or tradition. This second kind of rationality has obviously dominated the modern corporation or state bureaucracy. Weber went on to define his notion of bureaucracy (in the rather special form of an 'ideal type', to which we shall return below) to reflect this overwhelming importance of rationality: work was rationally subdivided, and organized in a hierarchy, there were technical rules and procedures to cover every operation, people were appointed exclusively according to their merits or experience. Modern corporate life would be impossible without the development of this kind of rationality, Weber thought. If an insurance company is to process a large number of clients, for example, it has to be completely rational in the way that it assesses risks and pay outs. It would be no good trying to judge the risk of applying insurance cover to drivers by making personal and subjective judgements about them.

Instead, standard information is required, and forms are filled in. The status and risks attached to the policy are then calculated using a set of objective rules. Decisions whether to provide cover or not are managed by having a hierarchy of offices, with specialist claims assessors and actuaries at the top, and reception staff at the bottom. It is in no-one's interests, least of all the customers', to leave such decisions in the hands of traditional elites, or people who happen to appeal to the shareholders regardless of their merits. It can even be a great relief and refuge to work in a rational organization, instead of one run by prima donnas and bullies permitted to express their 'bad' subjectivity.

It might be obvious immediately that these characteristics can be applied to leisure businesses specifically. The first step is to take a thorough look at a key example, the task of providing recreational foods, in this case, burgers. It is clear that the whole process can be modernized and developed by abandoning the traditional craft methods of producing burgers in small local stores. Something more like a factory is substituted instead – the burger becomes a standard combination of a particular kind of sandwich or bun, a standard portion of meat, and a standard combination of salad and gherkins. Standardization enables exactly the same kind of economic benefits that Henry Ford received after standardizing the production of motor cars; in particular, fine calculations can be made which balance the quantities offered in the meal, the cost of those inputs, the volume of sales, and the price of each item. Such burgers are produced on a kind of factory production line to a standardized formula, and are dispensed in measurable packages. Craftwork disappears, and machines come increasingly to regulate the whole process. Ritzer describes the key qualities overall as:

1 Efficiency (choosing the most efficient means to achieve specified ends as above, giving the assembly-line philosophy of McDonald's, drive-throughs, making the customer work to assemble their own meals and dispose of waste, and so on),

2 Calculability of process and product (the quantification of meals, portion size, times to cook fries).

3 Predictability (standardized meals and Mcworkers all over the world, often trained in-house by the Hamburger University).

4 Control, as in the use of non-human technology (factory farms, microwaves, computerization in cash tills or drinks dispensers – and robot workers).

5 'Irrationality of rationality' (the costs which rationalized organizations

can impose on their environments or customers – what is rational for the company may be damaging or costly for these others, a clear reference to pollution or health issues).

High overall productivity clearly has been a factor in the huge success of McDonald's. Prices are low, and customers get the same value and (in general terms) the same menu wherever they go. However, there is a social price to pay, again well foreseen by Weber. The human and cultural meanings involved in producing **food** are stripped away. Weber used the rather ambiguous term 'disenchantment' to describe this process – cold, abstract, scientific procedure replaces the (often illusory) mystery and charm of the old-fashioned ways of cooking. Ritzer (1999) uses this term to describe the dislike that people feel for coldly rational organizations that seem inhuman, especially in leisure, but goes on to look at processes of 're-enchantment' as well, in a way which rescues him from many critics, as we shall see.

It is clear that Ritzer heartily disapproves of the trend towards McDonaldization, so much so that he urges readers to resist these trends, to press for quality instead of quantity, for diversity rather than uniformity, for human contact rather than the anonymous consumption of products after queuing at the delivery end of a production line. This clearly strikes a chord with many cultural critics as well. Rather as with Disney, many middle-class intellectual academics clearly despise McDonald's and the whole fast food syndrome. Again, we might use Bourdieu to explain why (see **social class**) – the quick anonymous consumption of bland and probably unhealthy food is clearly going to be anathema to those sharing the 'high aesthetic' with its central values of cool, abstracted judgement and denial of immediate gratification (see **food**). This structured distaste for fast food is so common among bourgeois groups that it might be difficult for them to see why anyone would ever want to eat in McDonald's in the first place. Indeed, Parker, in Alfino et al. (1998), suggests this distaste is the real impulse behind Ritzer's analysis rather than the attempted technical application of Weber.

We have already acknowledged the convenience and predictability of the fast meal, but, as usual, deeper cultural manipulation might be at work. Given that rationalization serves to strip food items of any cultural meaning by reducing them to industrial products, there is a need to supply alternative meanings for the consumer. These are going to be ones that lead to further commercial exploitation. McDonald's has worked hard on its image as a family restaurant, for example, and, like Disney, its workers are trained to be hospitable and friendly (although not too friendly, since this might impede efficient processing of large numbers of customers). Children and adolescents like fast food, because it is tasty (salty or sweet), and because McDonald's tries very hard to market their products with a whole range of toys and spin-offs for children. Although Ritzer does not mention it explicitly, we know from other studies of children's diet that they tend to like 'junk' foodstuffs that directly invert adult food values, as in the fascinating study by James (in Waites et al., 1982) of children's desires for cheap, sticky and unwrapped sweets. Fast food offers these pleasures, not least in the way in which it can be eaten with minimal table manners. These clever marketing strategies are particularly sinister, perhaps, because vulnerable people like children are involved, and because there are serious anxieties about the overall effects on health of an excessive diet of burgers. There is a suspicion that ruthless business practices underscore the friendly image: McDonald's has also had a spate of bad publicity about the damage to the environment for which the company allegedly is responsible.

For some critics of Ritzer, however, the familiar accusation is made that this simply under-estimates the capacity of the customers to choose or to resist. To take some quick examples, Rinehart, in Alfino et al. (1998) argues that feminists are perfectly capable of resisting the blandishments of the company, while Turner, in Smart (1999), suggests that customers are much more likely to be playfully consuming rather than be completely dominated by the ideology of rationality. Kellner (in Alfino et al., 1998) suggests that Ritzer simply has missed out the slightly subversive uses to which people can put the McDonald's restaurant, such as when young Taiwanese meet in local Macs to discuss politics. As might be expected, advocates of the 'skilled consumer' thesis see a much more active and measured acceptance of the pleasures of rational consumption, as Miles argues (in Alfino et al., 1998): the predictability of McDonaldization can be welcome in an otherwise risky and changing world of consumerism, and this value is capably calculated even by young consumers. As with all celebrations of the skilled consumer, though, this particular argument can look very uncritical and blandly optimistic. There are some undoubted advantages for rationalized food production though, despite their drawbacks – they can relieve women of the constant responsibility of providing meals for the family, and McDonald's restaurants can provide a kind of temporary refuge for the culturally threatened (like American visitors to the UK, see Caputo, in Alfino et al., 1998).

There is also much more diversity and subjective variability in concrete examples of McDonald's restaurants. To take some of my own experience,

I quickly spotted that you can buy alcohol in French ones, and one McDonald's I visited in the Place de la République in Paris was playing Verdi on the sound system (almost unknown in Britain, I would think). Menus vary as well, between Britain, America and France, and there is, I gather, a whole menu on offer in the Middle East described as 'MacArabia'. The current 'new tastes' menu in the UK is also more diverse, offering salads and pasta, Greek-style burgers, or 'Premiere' burgers in healthy focaccia buns.

These comments often lead on to a methodological argument as well, expressed best perhaps by Kellner (2003). By relying on Weber, Ritzer leaves out a number of theoretical models that would have explained the missing aspects of his analysis. Marxism might have helped provide an assessment of the capitalist background of rationalization, and the impact on the workforce. **Semiotic** analysis could clarify the ways in which meanings are attached to burgers, both by the company and by the customers, as Caputo demonstrates in his analysis of the appealing American 'food, folks and fun' myth displayed in the advertisements (in Alfino et al., 1998: 49). Certainly, in order to understand McDonald's itself as a phenomenon, and not just as an illustration of Weber's work on bureaucracy, we would need to draw upon other theoretical resources, including **postmodern** ones, see Wynyard in Alfino et al (1998). In fact, this is taken up by Ritzer himself in his later work on disenchantment and re-enchantment, when he adds to his account additional insights drawn from marxist and postmodernist theorists to consider consuming more fully (see **adding leisure values**).

However, there is one aspect of Weber's work which might be deployed in the defence of Ritzer's analysis. It is clear that subjective variations do take place in particular McDonald's restaurants, as they must whenever human beings are involved. Some managers will offer different decor or music, as we have seen. Some people will attach particular meanings to visiting McDonald's, as do the (possibly mythical) divorced fathers who take their children for a Big Mac on the weekends they have access. Muscovites apparently queued for hours to be among the first to sample a burger on the opening of the first restaurant in Russia, possibly because they saw eating a Mac as an essential step towards a post-communist future. We know from other studies of corporations that the participants relate to each other in all sorts of subjective ways, not just following the technical rules, but pursuing micropolitical strategies (see Weick, in Westoby, 1988), imposing their own structures of dominance, and even falling in love with each other. As we said above, these are not always 'good' activities, and, increasingly, they may actually be put to commercial purposes after all by apparently humanising or 'enchanting' the workplace.

However, the point is whether these subjective variations are important enough to weaken the central analysis. There will never be a pure type bureaucracy, complete in every detail, as Weber knew only too well. That is why he offered instead an 'ideal type'. This term has been much discussed in social theory, but the word 'ideal' is usually seen as referring to an idea, a central definition, the essence of the organization (the 'type' part refers more to the commonly found features in existing typical examples). If we see Ritzer's work as offering not a simple description of McDonald's but this rather special 'ideal type' of the organization, it becomes possible to rescue it from many of its critics. Despite all the variations we have found, does the central logic of McDonaldization show any signs of weakening or changing? Are the alternative menus themselves produced using the principles of calculability, predictability, and so on? Asking this sort of question might lead to far more support for Ritzer's position, and, indeed, it is a feature of his later work on enchantment. He does use questions like this in reply to his many critics, and he does explicitly mention ideal-type analysis in his reply to critics in Smart (1999). However, he does not refer to this particular interpretation of the ideal type, but sees it instead as a simple template or yardstick!

In conclusion, we might briefly consider some attempts to apply this work to other aspects of leisure. Ritzer himself has always seen the package tour as an excellent example of McDonaldization (even in Ritzer, 1993), and we might compare this with the discussion of **authenticity**. He has also pursued the implications for Disney theme parks and **shopping** malls (Ritzer and Liska, in Rojek and Urry, 1997), and a wide range of other 'cathedrals of consumption' such as cruise ships or museums, and, in the process, tried to incorporate some of the criticisms. Perhaps the best single short piece on this is the analysis of the postmodern ballpark (Ritzer and Stillman, 2001).

Other writers are less certain of the general application of the McDonaldization model, at least in its earlier stages. Bryman, for example, tries out the five characteristics pretty explicitly in his revisit to the Disney theme park (in Smart, 1999), and finds a good fit except for the characteristic of calculability. Disney parks seem to stress the overall quality of the experience rather than attempting to calculate cost-effectiveness in a detailed and local manner. Jary has explored two major applications of McDonaldization – to the university (Parker and Jary, 1995), and to leisure and sports in general (in Smart, 1999). The first example has provoked much amusement and irony among academics trying to debunk the new managerialism in British universities, but Parker and Jary find many exceptions to the overall trend to McDonaldization even in modern universities. In terms of leisure more generally, Jary finds the model too limiting, and he wants to add additional stages or dimensions to the analysis (including the history of leisure in **figurationalist** terms as a precursor to McDonaldization, and to analyses of commodification of sport, of the kind we explore with Nike, in the entry on **adding leisure values**). Ritzer reacted rather sternly to this attempt to both extend and localize his model in his reply (also in Smart, 1999), and claimed he was already working to add some missing elements (in the work on enchantment that became Ritzer, 1999).

FURTHER READING

Apart from following up the collections of criticisms (Alfino et al., 1998 and Smart, 1999) Kellner's (2003) online essay summarizes the critiques and offers new insights. Ritzer and Stillman (2001) on baseball illuminate the power of the new approach to re-enchantment. Those interested in the Weberian background might consult Ritzer's own best-selling textbook on social theory (Ritzer, 1996), or Ray (1999), and compare the sections on the 'ideal type' especially.

REFERENCES

Alfino, M., Caputo, J. and Wynyard, R. (eds) (1998) *McDonaldization Revisited: Critical Essays on Consumer Culture*, Connecticut: Praeger Publishers.

Kellner, D. (2003) 'Theorizing/Resisting McDonaldization: A Multiperspectivist Approach' [online] http://www.uta.edu/huma/illuminations/kell30.htm.

Parker, M. and Jary, D. (1995) 'The McUniversity: Organization, Management and Academic Subjectivity', *Organization*, 2: 1–20.

Ray, L. (1999) *Theorising Classical Sociology*, Milton Keynes: Open University Press.

Ritzer, G. (1993) *The McDonaldization of Society: An Investigation into the Changing Character of Contemporary Social Life*, London: Sage.

Ritzer, G. (1996) *Sociological Theory*, 4th edn, Singapore: McGraw-Hill.

Ritzer, G. (1999) *Enchanting a Disenchanted World: Revolutionizing the Means of Consumption*, Thousand Oaks, CA: Pine Forge Press.

Ritzer, G. and Stillman, T. (2001) 'The Postmodern Ballpark as a Leisure Setting: Enchantment and Simulated De-McDonaldization', *Leisure Sciences*, 23: 99–113.

Rojek, C. and Urry, J. (eds) (1997) *Touring Cultures: Transformations of Travel and Theory*, London: Routledge.

Smart, B. (ed.) (1999) *Resisting McDonaldization*, London: Sage.

Waites, B., Bennett, T. and Martin, G. (eds) (1982) *Popular Culture: Past and Present*, London: Croom Helm in association with the Open University Press.

Westoby, A. (ed.) (1988) *Culture and Power in Educational Organizations*, Milton Keynes: Open University Press.

McDonaldization

key concepts *188*

> *A narrative is a particular sequence of signs (words, images or any other kind) designed to convey meaning – to tell a story, for example. Defining signs as broadly as this enables us to examine the narratives of films and texts, but also of theme parks and exhibitions. Narratives have certain characteristics that enable them to be recognized, connected and predicted, and this is a major source of pleasure for the reader.*

> *Section Outline: Typical narrative structures in myth, folk tales, cinema and Disney theme parks. Realist narratives and dominant values: ideology, marxist and feminist critique. Breaking with conventional narratives in avant-garde film and fiction: destroying the authorial voice. Postmodernism and the collapse of narrative: electronic games and children's television. Harmful effects on child development.*

In the entry on **semiotics**, we argue that individual signs gain in meanings by being organized in sequences, running over time. Some sequences become narratives. We are well used to constructing and reading particular sequences in order to deliver a meaning, and thus pleasure as the meaning unfolds. A classic example of the general structure of a narrative is one that is widely found in a number of folk tales and myths. In the beginning, human beings live together harmoniously in a community of some kind; then something happens to break the equilibrium and introduce a disturbance (a stranger rides into town, a spaceship is discovered, someone dies); that disturbance is finally managed somehow and resolved, so that peace and harmony are restored again in the end. This is, of course, the structure of many novels, movies and television programmes as well. There are several other common mythical structures as well, some of them discovered in Lévi-Strauss' study (see Glucksmann, 1974); human beings are locked in some unending struggle with nature, with the gods, or with strangers, and then some magical creature appears, human, animal, or divine, who is able to reconcile the two sides and achieve some equilibrium again. It is easy see how this common structure might fit, if we think of, say, the mediating role of Mr Spock in *Star Trek*. Other commonly found myths include the story of the oedipal struggle or the (structurally similar) coming-of-age narrative.

Many leisure pursuits can also be seen as structured in this way, as delivering a kind of narrative as they unfold over time and through space. A good example is provided by early analysis of the physical layout of Disneyland in California (Marin, 1977). The argument here is that the visitors' suggested paths around the attraction serve as a kind of walking story. In particular, the paths lead around various exhibits in a particular order, and then always converge on Main Street as the 'happy ending'. It is easy to see this kind of embodied story in the exhibits in Walt Disney World too, where, for example, in the famous Golf Ball exhibit, visitors enter cars and are exposed to a story about communication as the ride unfolds, this time with the giant corporation AT&T as the happy ending (see **Disneyfication**). On a less sinister note, perhaps, some of the more popular rides, say, Nemesis at Alton Towers, involve a little narrative of their own; as you approach the ride, the tension increases, enhanced by clever route planning, then you experience the ride and then are returned to the normal world. The experience of adventure tourism has also been described as taking place in this classic narrative form – we start from a state of equilibrium, then we deliberately seek out experiences that will disrupt this equilibrium and cause us some danger, and then we return from the adventure to normal life. Kjølsrød (2003) has described the ways in which more cultural 'adventures', including collecting objects of various kinds, help sequence and structure, confirm and illustrate personal narratives to do with **identity** (we discuss this work in the entry on **escape**).

We also discuss the tension which sets in as soon as the equilibrium of a football game is disturbed by the opening whistle, and the pleasure that is delivered when this tension is resolved, in the entry on **figurationalism**. The narrative of a football game overall includes many smaller narratives, authored by different players and combinations of them. This again is fairly common in written and filmed versions of narratives, which often tell several stories at once, signalling the leap from one story into another in various ways (for example, through 'flashbacks'), and revealing at the end how the different stories fit together. Barthes (1977) has shown how this complex interlinking and 'nesting' of narratives can deliver pleasure in the Bond movie.

A particular version of such interconnected narratives has been the subject of considerable debate in media theory about how realism is constructed in the cinema. Partly, the effect of realism is produced by simulated **authenticity** sufficient to make the audience believe in reality, which can include providing accurate costumes and sets, and deploying unobtrusive camerawork and editing. However, a particular narrative structure can also induce this sense of realism in a rather specialized way. MacCabe (in Bennett et al., 1982) has suggested that a common way to proceed is to offer a number of plausible stories or accounts of a particular set of events, and then to suggest discreetly that only one of them tells the correct or real version of events. This is clearly found in films such as detective stories.

The general structure is called the 'classic realist narrative', and it refers to realism in the rather special sense of understanding the reality of the situation; one particular account becomes the 'reality', and all the others are seen as imperfect versions of it, or even as lies or fictions. There are also some variants where the reality is that no-one is correct. Viewers are led to the underlying reality by the way in which the story is told or the narrative unfolds – we gradually come to see that one character's perceptions are limited, or that we cannot trust them because we have seen how they behave, or we are able to predict behaviour on the basis of clues that we are given, and so on. MacCabe happened to be writing in order to establish a marxist theory of cinema, and he was to argue that 'the classic realist narrative' was a useful device in conveying **ideological** views of social realities.

This is easier if we think of films that are specifically about politics, such as films made during the Second World War in Britain which allow the characters to offer different analyses of events, including, say, communist or pacifist interpretations; then the characters holding these views are shown to be limited, naïve or ridiculous, and good old British common sense emerges as the master narrative, the one that tells us what really is the case. Sometimes, in the more committed efforts, the master narrative is punched home by having one of the characters make a speech, usually following the conventions of the 'propaganda shot' (the character making a speech is filmed in three-quarter-length close-up, often against an inspiring landscape or sky). The same narrative structure has been detected beneath documentary or current affairs programmes on television as well (Bennett et al., 1982), as various participants offer their limited views of a particular event, and the narrator, who can even be off-camera, sums up at the end or relates the master account. Sometimes, the authoritative accounts are supported by devices such as using 'factual anchors' – statistics, precise times and

Narratives

190

dates, location shots in the places where the events actually took place, and so on.

It is not just those obvious examples of political ideologies that can be reinforced by a classic realist narrative, but more or less any dominant view of a particular society. The classic realist narrative can privilege an account that says that 'human nature' is irredeemably aggressive and competitive, or that women are a permanent threat to social order, or that ethnic minorities present permanent social problems. In each case, alternatives can seem to have been presented fairly and openly, while the privileged view appears innocently as 'reality'. Viewers can even think that they have used their skill and judgement to arrive at these conclusions all by themselves.

Of course, there has been much discussion of this argument and many film critics have denied the centrality of realist narratives in mainstream cinema (see, for example, Williams, 1994). Nevertheless, I have often found them in academic writing or teaching sessions, where a number of limited or flawed positions are advanced, and then a master discourse is introduced to solve the problems of the earlier ones and deliver to the audience some feeling that they have learned and can now make progress. **Gramscian** analysis often offers a perfect example of this kind of pedagogical strategy, in my view.

Some feminist analysis has also pointed out that the classic realist narrative often privileges male values, including those that find pleasure in destruction and adventure (see Beezer, 1995). As is often the case, feminist work has also produced some notable experiments with narratives, precisely to try and break the hold of the narrative in delivering values smuggled in with a feeling of having gained knowledge. Diaries have often been used to good effect instead of structured accounts, for example. We can see this approach used in what we called 'disclosure' approaches in **ethnographic** recording as well (in Burgess, 1984). Feminists interested in making film have also decided to attempt to break with the classic realist narrative. A famous short film (*Amy*) about the life of Amy Johnson, the female flyer, deliberately attempts to break most of the conventions of the documentary, and has the characters try to tell their own stories, again often in diary format, or an audience allowed to comment on their understanding as part of the actual film.

Other experimental film-makers have attempted to deliberately break conventional narrative forms as well, precisely to deny this powerful authorial voice that a narrative can adopt, and to attempt to shock the audience into making its own sense of events. Thus, the French film-maker Jean-Luc Godard has made films that break the story into episodes (such as *Vivre sa Vie*), separated by titles appearing on screen. Another of his pieces (*Pravda*) deliberately set out to reverse the conventions of documentary by making the camera or the editing process visible to the audience, or having the characters speak their own language (Czech) without providing subtitles (see Monaco, 1976). British film-makers like Peter Greenaway have adopted artificial narratives, as in his *Drowning by Numbers*, which uses a structure based on numerical sequences and games (see Greenaway, 1988). There is an excellent example in written fiction of reversed narrative, where time runs backwards (*Time's Arrow* by Martin Amis). The events depicted are those of a Nazi's participation in the death camps of Auschwitz, but when reversed, a dark irony can be depicted – Auschwitz becomes a life camp, drawing smoke and particles from the atmosphere, condensing them through chimneys into bodies, which are carried into gas chambers only to emerge as living people, who are gradually fed so that they grow from their emaciated state into healthy individuals, and who finally leave the camp on trains and return to their destinations in European cities.

It is common to attribute experiments with narrative, or even the abandonment of narrative to **postmodernist** forms of pleasure as well. We can get a quick fix here by pointing out that these experiments have no political or educative intent at all, unlike those described above, but experiment playfully, purely to provide pleasure. In my view, the MGM Theme Park section of Walt Disney World is much more playful than the 'serious' itineraries on offer in the EPCOT Park, for example. Postmodern films offer a series of spectacles instead of an narrative, or a random collection of episodes (my favourite example is Linklater's *Slackers*), or 'slices of life' with no attempt to prioritize one of them as real (perhaps as in *Pepi, Luci, Bom . . .* by Almodovar). A halfway house here would be Tarantino's *Pulp Fiction*, with its interlaced narratives and its experiments with time – the restaurant hold up takes place at the beginning and the end of the film, and one of the stories in the middle depicts the John Travolta character being shot, only to have him turn up at the end.

Perhaps the best example of postmodern media is to be found in children's television, however, such as in the series *Muppet Babies*. Here, the muppet characters have no educational function, unlike their predecessors in *Sesame Street*. *Muppet Babies* can offer the viewer a bewildering variety of episodes and spectacles, sometimes involving film, sometimes animated reconstructions of sequences from film, with many intertextual references to other famous films or television programmes, and with a peculiar tendency for the Babies to both watch television and then take part in it. Just about all the conventions of the classic realist

192

narrative have been abandoned here! Other examples might include electronic games, which also can minimize narrative, and offer instead a simple sequence of fairly repetitive and spectacular scenes – 'shoot-'em-ups' with an endless variety of different characters to take on and defeat. It might be possible to see the slightest traces of narrative structures in both *Muppet Babies* and in games such as *Doom*, but they no longer provide the main structuring principles or the main sources of pleasure.

For the critic Marsha Kinder, the abandonment of prominent narratives raises the possibility of definite social harm for the childhood viewer. Kinder (1991) thinks that the ability to construct and follow a narrative offers an important way of making sense of the world for children, and to abandon them means to risk an inadequate psychological development. She draws support for this view from some well-known child psychology. We might add here work such as that of Lyotard (1984) who suggests that narratives fulfil an important social function, not only in relaying knowledge, but in managing social participation (as listeners join in the narratives, or predict the next turn). Narratives might also be important as devices to articulate meanings, or construct stable identities and biographies.

Kinder's suspicion is that postmodern experiments with narrative will simply produce a lack of understanding of the social world among the young (she also cites the dangers of unstable representations, as in series such as *Transformers*, or those depicting transformations from humans into superheroes). Lacking the ability to develop narratives of their own, children will be particularly vulnerable to those whose profession it is to supply meaningful narratives instead; she has in mind, of course, the advertising industry that is well suited to develop their own narratives about the products they are trying to attach to children's television. We might add another danger here, this time from people such as televangelists who often develop a form of their own classic realist narrative, which McLaren and Smith (in Giroux et al., 1989) call 'prime knowledge' – if you find the world confusing, and you are no longer sure of your ethical or moral principles, it might be tempting to take the advice of someone who has waded through this confusion and has now apparently reached new certainties on the other side.

Kinder's analysis contains no actual empirical research, apart from some anecdotes about the perceived effects on her own son. Of course, it would be useful to know if children are as incapable of imposing narratives on confusing television programmes or electronic games as she thinks. It seems equally likely that children will strive to assign some meaning to the series of spectacles, or impose some narrative sequence of their own on the events. If the electronic game lacks an adventure narrative, it seems quite possible that the player will supply one, drawing upon their own intertextual resources to do so. These personal narratives need to be researched in more depth. One study (de Certeau, 1984) suggests that adults are perfectly capable of constructing their own narratives as they walk around familiar cities, for example, ignoring if not resisting the narratives imposed by **visitor interpretation** devices.

FURTHER READING

Cook has a good section on narrative theory, especially as developed in films. LEO (2003) is an online literacy education site that offers practical guidance on the conventions of narrative. Barthes (1977) is far more theoretical but insightful on the characteristic narratives of Bond novels and films. Barthes (1975) is a close examination of the narrative 'codes' at work in a famous novel by Balzac. Bryman (1995) summarizes work on Disney narratives, including that of Marin (1977).

REFERENCES

Barthes, R. (1975) *S/Z* London: Jonathan Cape.

Barthes, R. (1977) *Image-Music-Text*, London: Collins.

Beezer, A. (1995) 'Women and "Adventure Travel" Tourism', *New Formations*, 21: 119–30.

Bennett, T., Boyd-Bowman, S., Mercer, C. and Woollacott, J. (eds) (1982) *Popular Television and Film*, London: BFI Publishing in association with the Open University Press.

Bryman, A. (1995) *Disney and His Worlds*, London: Routledge.

Burgess, R. (ed.) (1984) *The Research Process in Educational Settings*, London: Falmer Press.

De Certeau, M. (1984) *The Practice of Everyday Life*, Berkeley, CA: University of California Press.

Giroux, H. and Simon, R. and contributors (1989) *Popular Culture, Schooling and Everyday Life*, Massachusetts: Begin and Garvey Publishers Ltd.

Glucksmann, M. (1974) *Structuralist Analysis in Contemporary Thought: A Comparison of the Theories of Claude Lévi-Strauss and Louis Althusser*, London: Routledge and Kegan Paul.

Greenaway, P. (1988) *Fear of Drowning by Numbers/Règles de Jeu*, Paris: Dis Voir.

Kinder, M. (1991) *Playing with Power in Movies and Television: From Muppet Babies to Teenage Mutant Ninja Turtles*, Berkeley, CA: University of California Press.

Kjølsrød, L. (2003) 'Adventure Revisited: On Structure and Metaphor in Specialized Plays', *Sociology*, 37 (3): 459–76.

LEO (2003) [online] http://leo.stcloudstate.edu/acadwrite/narrative.html

Lyotard, J-F. (1984) *The Postmodern Condition: A Report on Knowledge*, Manchester: Manchester University Press.

Marin, L. (1977) 'Disneyland: A Degenerative Utopia', *Glyph*, 1 (1): 50–66.

Monaco, J. (1976) *The New Wave*, Oxford: Oxford University Press.

Williams, C. (1994) 'After the Classic, the Classical and Ideology: The Differences of Realism', *Screen* 35 (3): 275–92.

194

Pleasures

It is fairly easy to tell when we are feeling pleasure subjectively, but more difficult to study and explain it and especially to measure it. A number of theoretical approaches are available to try to do all three and to arrive at general categories of pleasure detectable in leisure activities. Classic work here involves seeing pleasure as rooted in the experience of being able to participate immediately, or of experiencing 'judgement' or 'beauty'.

Section Outline: *Specific pleasures in leisure activities. Generalizing about pleasure: tension balance. The pleasures of bodily participation and the pleasures of intellectual detachment. Academic pleasures. Barthes:* plaisir *and* jouissance. *'Flow' and its characteristics: operationalizing flow; flow and its social dimensions.*

It is clear that leisure activities are pleasurable ones. Indeed, the presence of pleasure may be the defining characteristic of leisure, as figurationalists have argued. A number of specific pleasures have been mentioned throughout this text in the course of discussing the various concepts. When we examine the pleasures offered by electronic games, for example (in **virtual leisure**), we might note that most commentators seem to identify the pleasures of participation and control, on the one hand, and mastery of the program and machine on the other (and perhaps more symbolic pleasures of maintaining your autonomy as an author, or of resisting the capitalist urge to drain you of your money, at least with arcade games, see Fiske, 1989). In the entry on **figurationalism**, we examine work on the pleasure of watching or playing football, which turns on the management of safe and socially respectable tensions generated between our need to be spontaneous and emotional, and the need for social constraint and civilized behaviour. We note that various **illegal leisure** activities offer pleasurable combinations: in the case of illegal drug consumption, these arise from the management of personal excitement and taking risks of various kinds, including risks of ill-health, marginalization, or being caught by the police. We discuss the pleasures of following a **narrative** in commercial film and television, and of letting the narrative deliver particular satisfactions such as a feeling that one understands, or has become knowledgeable enough to 'read' a particular story. In the case of viewing **pornography**, we are on more familiar Freudian ground by adding specifically sexual pleasures of scopophilia and the breaking of sexual taboos.

Is it possible to generalize from these examples and to produce an abstract theory of pleasure which all leisure activities can deliver? We have already seen one that turns on the successful management of tension. It would be quite possible to generalize this figurationalist insight to include all the specific examples mentioned above; it is just that tension is produced and managed in different forms when one plays an electronic game or watches a James Bond film. It is certainly appealing to think of common-sense accounts of the pleasures involved in these terms as well. When a participant in extreme sports talks about the challenge of the activity and the 'rush' in overcoming it, or a clubber mentions the need to balance individual expression and the 'oceanic' delight in being one of the crowd (Malbon, 1999), it is possible to see these activities too as coping with tension and bringing it to a satisfactory resolution. Finally, the notion of tension balance and resolution could also explain the more obvious bodily pleasures of satisfying various needs and appetites, whether for **food**, esteem, relaxation or sex.

We have considered mostly popular bodily pleasures so far. These arise when we identify ourselves with the action, through actual participation, or through **fantasy**. In all these cases, the tension arises precisely because we become, or at least take the part of, participants directly and experience their emotions. What about the more intellectual pleasures, however, which seemed to involve, as Bourdieu (1986) reminds us, the very opposite of this stance – an unemotional detachment, an interest in abstract form and 'higher' qualities which require us to exercise not passionate involvement but judgement? This notion of pleasure can also be detected in much of the academic, critical and philosophical, commentary on leisure activities. We saw, for example, critics of **Disneyfication** or mass tourism raising serious doubts about the effects of emotional participation in the activities on offer. The Disney visitor naïvely identifies as the sentimental and nostalgic fond parent addressed by the Company, and this leaves people vulnerable to the less obvious ideological messages on offer. The same idea haunts the critique of modern consumerism; the identification process in fantasy works so well that the naïve viewer imagines themselves to be David Beckham, playing glamorous football matches, and, uncritically, wearing the same clothes and using the same kind of mobile phone just as the advertisements indicate. 'Mimetic' leisure may indeed have a useful social function of regulating tension in a socially acceptable direction, but the pleasures it delivers make us dangerously vulnerable to ideology and the hard sell.

What do the 'higher' pleasures look like? We might turn to some of the influential work of Roland Barthes for an initial answer (especially Barthes, 1977). Barthes is referring to the pleasures offered by reading novels, and he is at pains to deny that the 'higher' pleasures are simply associated with the tastes of an elite. What is at stake here really is the ability to generate different kinds of pleasure. One of the more obvious pleasures in reading novels or watching films is the ability to come under the control of the narrative and to let the narrative work to deliver its pleasure to us, ideally so that we seem to discover it for ourselves as we proceed. In a famous discussion, Barthes (1977) wants to reserve the term *plaisir* for this sort of pleasure, and to contrast it with another kind – *jouissance*. This term, which has undertones of sexual release, refers to something much more intellectually ecstatic, the pleasures detectable in being able to recognize the effects of the narrative for yourself, and, maybe, to begin to play with the novel or film, to weave your own narratives in and around it. Only some novels and films permit this kind of activity, Barthes argues, and he reserves the term 'text' for those, as opposed to mere 'works' for those that offer only *plaisir*. This whole analysis probably depends not only on a rich and complex text, but a skilled and culturally rich reader as well who can unpack and depict these playful readings. However, a number of commentators have found the ability to treat television programmes as texts to be quite widespread – such as those viewers of television news who, Fiske (1989) reports, can take pleasure in seeing how the programme is actually assembled, and how the smooth surface of the finished product occasionally parts to reveal signs of its own artificiality and contrivance.

As indicated in the entry on Disneyfication, one view is that a lot of academic critique which claims to see 'beneath the surface' delivers this kind of intellectual pleasure to the critic, although this is often concealed beneath expressions of stern duty or liberating intent. However, it is important to stress this as a real pleasure in doing academic work, to explain the appeal of **education as leisure**. It might also help to motivate students who are struggling to come to grips with academic work, and who must ask themselves frequently why anybody bothers to do it. It is quite possible that experience and commitment can lead to both kinds of pleasure in other leisure activities as well. As stocks of **cultural capital** increase, fans can become connoisseurs, theorists and historians of their leisure pursuits.

Yet, to return to the question we began with, is it possible to see even these two kinds of pleasures as sharing some common characteristics, despite all the social and political attachments, as well as philosophical effort to separate them? One approach might be provided by the work on 'flow' produced by Csikszentmihalyi (1975). The descriptions of being in a state of 'flow' refer to a pleasurable 'loss of self', an absence of self-awareness, where one's body and mind simply 'flow' into the activity without any conscious awareness of control. The task itself seems to 'flow' of its own accord, to take on a direction of its own, to become 'autotelic' in Csikszentmihalyi's terms. This state has been described in other literature, referring to religious experiences as well. Csikszentmihalyi refers to Buddhism, but the description also reminds me of Durkheim's work on early forms of religion, where participants develop a state of **ecstasy**, literally leaving behind their normal lives to focus on some purified social relations instead of the vexed and problematic ones of everyday life.

Csikszentmihalyi's classic work mentions leisure activities such as mountain climbing or dancing to rock music. Participants describe a wonderful ability to act calmly without worry or fear, taking a detached objective look at the problems presented by the task. The task itself has to offer the right level of absorption and challenge, in that too challenging a task can prevent flow, just as surely as an undemanding one can. The challenges presented have to be of an intensity and frequency to provide insufficient room for everyday worries, so to speak. Skilled practitioners are able to adjust the challenges offered by different tasks until they achieve a suitable level of 'flow'. After 'flow' has taken place, participants often express the view that they have been restored to health, or granted particular insights into themselves and the way they live. Csikszentmihalyi is well aware that some work tasks can also have this structure, and indeed, one of the more practical outcomes of his work has been to try to design tasks in the workplace that will encourage participants to enter a state of 'flow'. I am interested in the implications this might have for educational tasks such as coursework assignments. However, the main point to consider here is whether notions like 'flow' can also be used to bridge the divide between lower and higher pleasures (as well as between **work and leisure**); did Barthes experience a state of 'flow' when unpacking the complex layers of some of the texts he mentions? Does practising the high aesthetic in analysing photographs as in Bourdieu (1986) deliver 'flow'?

Perhaps much depends on the degree of abstractness and involvement concerned, and on the structure of the task again. To turn to academic work again, some attempts to apply objective academic frameworks of judgement and critique to everyday activities can become monotonous and repetitious, and turn into 'lazy theorizing': the concepts are so familiar and so powerful that it becomes a matter of routine to apply them to just about any example. Much depends on the task as well – more of a challenge is offered if the objects of study are allowed to be more concrete, specific, and object-like, if 'object adequacy' is increased, or processes are allowed to take place in full detail, instead of being reduced to a simple mechanism. More generally, is the high aesthetic actually deployed unconsciously and uncritically, without much thought, and largely to support one's existing social class position and opinions, as Bourdieu tends to imply it is, or can it be used to generate challenge, novelty, and a sufficient level of problems to enable one to become absorbed?

It is with these thoughts that we might be able to add some sociological dimensions to what has become a burgeoning field of research on 'flow'. There are attempts to specify and measure 'flow', on the one hand, and attempts to generalize the notion into a whole way of life as human energies and desires 'flow' past institutional settings and obstacles on the other hand. The ability to experience 'flow' is not just a quality that resides in individuals, however. It requires social support, a network of people that value it and that can help to develop it. For Bourdieu, the ability to experience the 'higher pleasures' (maybe including 'flow') depend on cultural capital and **social class**. More broadly, it might be the case that the sorts of tasks required to generate 'flow' are changing as society changes itself. Rojek (2000) explores an important distinction between 'fast' and 'slow' leisure, for example.

FURTHER READING

Rojek (2000) critically develops the idea of 'flow'. Several recent pieces attempt to apply the idea, such as Bryce and Haworth (2002), and there has been a controversy over 'flow' and gender (Fox and Walker, 2002). Jones et al. (2003) have attempted to operationalize the concept of 'flow' and compare it with other measures of pleasure. Neale's introduction to the work of Barthes (1977) develops the important and much-quoted notions of *plaisir* and *jouissance*. The specific pleasures mentioned in other entries might also be pursued.

Barthes, R. (1977) *Image-Music-Text*, London: Collins.

Bourdieu, P. (1986) *Distinction: A Social Critique of the Judgement of Taste*, London: Routledge.

Bryce, J. and Haworth, J. (2002) 'Wellbeing and Flow in a Sample of Male and Female Office Workers', *Leisure Studies*, 21 (3, 4): 249–64.

Csikszentmihalyi, M. (1975) *Beyond Boredom and Anxiety*, San Francisco: Jossey-Bass.

Fiske, J. (1989) *Reading the Popular*, London: Unwin Hyman.

Fox, K. and Walker, G. (2002) 'Reconsidering the Relationship between Flow and Feminist Ethics: A Response', *Leisure Studies*, 21 (1): 15–26.

Jones, C., Hollenhorst, S. and Perna, F. (2003) 'An Empirical Comparison of the Four-Channel Flow Model and Adventure Experience Paradigm', *Leisure Sciences*, 25: 17–31.

Malbon, B. (1999) *Clubbing: dancing, ecstasy and vitality*, London: Routledge.

Rojek, C. (2000) *Leisure and Culture*, Basingstoke: Macmillan.

Pornography

Pornography can be defined literally as involving writing about the activities of prostitutes. More generally, it is the written or pictorial depiction of explicit sexual activity, following a 'popular aesthetic' (Bourdieu, 1986). It is designed to invite immediate erotic participation and bodily gratification and uses a minimum of artistic conventions. Legal definitions often involve terms referring to possible effects on subsequent behaviour: aggressive sexual activity, a disregard for consent, some sort of moral corruption, a departure from 'normal' tastes, or a general lowering of respect for others.

Section Outline: Pornography and social harm: the problems of research; feminist cases for and against censorship. Pornography as playful, 'carnivalesque', or subversive. Sex therapy, sex documentaries and ambiguity. Gay pornography, its conventions and effects. The libertarian case: de Sade, Annie Sprinkle; critical theory and its critique. The limited forms of pornography: viewer creativity.

Discussing pornography may present particular problems, especially when considering some of the more exotic genres. Even calling the consumption of pornography a 'leisure activity' might imply some acceptance of the practice. My argument is simply that consuming pornography seems to be a major pastime, and so it should tell us something about leisure in modern societies: it is necessary to suspend moral judgement at first, as with other activities.

There is a clear link with discussions of **illegal leisure** here, since, in the UK at least, publishing pornography is a criminal offence, which has been extended to cover downloading, storing, and reproducing pornographic images from the Internet. We have yet another case to analyse of the role of the State in leisure activities. Why does the State claim the right to punish people for pursuing this kind of leisure activity? The usual answer, as with drugs, is that some social harm is caused, especially to vulnerable people in particular – to children, who might lose their sexual innocence, or acquire misleading ideas about sex, and to women, who are exploited by the pornography industry and become the object of a controlling **gaze**. At its most developed, the 'social harm' argument suggests that there may be a direct linkage between the consumption of pornography and the committing of various sexual crimes, especially rape.

There is considerable ambiguity surrounding the 'social harm' argument. For one thing, it is very difficult to agree on a definition of pornography, especially when we consider the large grey area between illegal pornography and acceptable erotica. Trying to make lists of prohibited behaviours in this area, whether in the form of codes for films or broadcasts or parliamentary legislation, is likely to end in public ridicule or contempt. The Hays Code for the US motion picture industry, for example, insisted that 'Miscegenation (sex relationships between the white and black races) is forbidden' (see Arts Reformation.Com, 2003) The BBC once tried to ban smutty subjects in comedy programmes. The British Government recently attracted some ribald press comment for trying to ban outdoor sex, even when accomplished in one's own garden, and it has now dropped the proposals (see Travis, 2003). The values of the people drawing up these codes come under immediate and scurrilous question: what repressed views of sex must they have?

Various attempts to legislate by defining categories of pornography led to ambiguity and the failure of juries to convict, and were replaced, in the UK, by a provision that material can be deemed to be pornographic if a jury agrees that it is likely to 'deprave and corrupt' people who consume it (which seems no easier to determine). Again, juries could be really unpredictable in these matters, and, as a result, it seems that the police are now unlikely to prosecute unless the material concerned is likely to attract widespread public condemnation – child pornography is the obvious example.

The same sort of problem is going to affect researching the social harm of pornography. We explore the general difficulties in more detail in the entries on **effects analysis** and **virtual leisure**, but they are similar here. We would have to take care to reach an agreed definition of pornographic content, perhaps by having users rate the material themselves, or try to achieve some expert consensus. We could not really be content with researching a sample of users based on people who had been convicted of sexual offences since these might not be typical of normal users. We would face the difficulty of trying to isolate the consumption of pornography as a factor in engaging in harmful activities. It is reasonable to think that all sorts of experiences and social factors affect criminal behaviour, and these would have to be taken into account as well. In particular, we would need to know whether consuming pornography alone causes criminal behaviour, or whether, for example, people with a predisposition towards violent sexual activity would be drawn to both consume pornography and to commit sexual crimes. I do not claim to have investigated this topic very far, but to my knowledge, there seems to be little research on the topic which meets these basic requirements; clearly, some seems to be urgently needed.

One possible way forward is provided by the work of Shaw (1999) who interviewed a sample of women about their tastes for and feelings about pornography. The results overall indicated considerable fear and reservation about pornography, which was seen as almost entirely a male leisure commodity. Likely adverse effects included risks of degrading women or raising male expectations about women's bodies. The women also seem to have been 'silenced' and capable of only muted reactions to male uses, partly because they did not want to be seen as prudish or intolerant of the freedom of others.

Certainly, feminists such as Dworkin (see Andrea Dworkin Web Site, 2003) have been convinced of the likelihood of tangible harm by the research they have read. For her, pornography displays the ultimate form of objectifying women, reducing them to a sex object to be used for sexual gratification, and also to be looked at for the same reason. The kind of pornography that she describes reduces human beings not only to bodies, but to parts of bodies, and sexual relations become reduced to mechanical acts. Conversely, ordinary objects become sexualized as they are used for sexual purposes. In this way, social life itself gets 'pornographed'. Not surprisingly, violence, including sexual violence against women is normalized.

Pornography

However, not all feminists agree with this viewpoint. The contributors to a collection of feminist writing against censorship (Church Gibson and Gibson, 1993) offer some interesting arguments. Segal, for example, reviews the research on offer and notes some serious measurement problems like the ones cited above (including the difficulties of isolating the effects of explicit sexual violence in pornography particularly). She notes the ambivalent effects of depicting violent sexuality (men do not really like it either and display a typical pattern of 'anxiety and depression, of revulsion rather than arousal', Church Gibson and Gibson, 1993: 14). She finds no conclusive evidence of a general connection with real sexual violence, and points to the dangers of encouraging censorship in alliance with intolerant political groups, like those who support (anti-feminist) 'family values'. She also introduces one of the main difficulties in that the meaning of the images is so open to interpretation. Echoing a point made by Plummer about sexuality in general (which we discuss in the entry on **fantasy**), she points out that any image can be 'pornographized', that even nuts and bolts are called female and male in a general and pervasive sexualizing of objects, but also that the most violent sado-masochistic images can be used to stimulate fantasies in 'caring and consensual encounters' (ibid.: 15).

This theme is developed in an essay on fetishisms by McClintock in the same volume (Church Gibson and Gibson, 1993). McClintock notes the taste for male humiliation in activities such as sado-masochism (S/M), which inverts all the usual objections to the female body being subject to a contemptuous and exploiting male gaze. Other matters of identity are also challenged: 'It publicly exposes the possibility that manhood is not *naturally* synonymous with mastery, nor femininity with passivity . . . eroticism is sundered from the rule of procreation' [original emphasis] (ibid.: 222). She also notes the politically subversive potential of S/M in the liking for uniforms, ritual and the mechanism of punishment. Similarities are found both in the activity itself and in the legal processes that ensue if participants are prosecuted:

> The sex trial and the flagellation scene mirror each other in a common liturgy . . . the Judge, like the Dominatrix is theatrically costumed . . . Both Judge and Dominatrix are paid money to exercise the right to punish, while fetish elements are common to both . . . voyeurism being an indispensable element in both scenes . . . S/M thus emerges as a private parody of the public trial. (Church Gibson and Gibson, 1993: 221)

For those who spot these similarities, the subversive thought occurs that in real trials, 'Under his purple robes the judge has an erection' (ibid.:

221). Other costumed fantasies subvert other forms of authority such as schools, prisons, police stations or families. The whole symbolic significance of S/M needs to be understood, says McClintock. For example, it is not so much about the infliction of pain or power as experiencing the 'signs of power: images, words, costumes, uniforms, scripts' (ibid.: 225). The whole point is to dramatize and manage risk (there are echoes here of the **figurationalist** notion of mimetic leisure, of course), and this can involve trust and respect for each participant, even love, although McClintock recognizes that sometimes 'real anger or hate' can also be found (ibid.: 227).

It is quite possible that some of the pleasures involved in more conventional pornography also lie in the playful inversions of bourgeois discourses about sexuality, which are notoriously disguised in 'artistic' paintings, 'romantic' or 'erotic' writing, or hidden under the pretext of being educational, anthropological, scientific or therapeutic. Such inversion is a theme identified in the British 'soft' pornographic magazine *Fiesta*. Attwood (2002) examines the 'carnivalesque' appeal of the writing, and traces the connections between the world of 'real sex' in the magazine (a curious mixture of instant access and male humiliation) and the broader British tradition of vulgar bawdy humour, often intended to mock bourgeois refinement.

In a relatively rare analysis of gay pornography, Dyer (2002) notes some of the basic conventions at work – we have moved far from the low production values of 'blue movies'. For example, he notices the common deployment of conventional techniques of realism (we discuss realist **narrative** in another entry). Dyer's chosen examples have a documentary look, for example, with the usual deployment of a privileged camera (showing us things that mere spectators would not be able to see), and all the conventions of real-life settings, naturalistic sound, and 'point-of-view' shots. With those shots, the camera assumes the characteristic viewing position of one of the characters in the action and thus permits viewers to feel they are that character, really in the action.

Pornography does have conventions of its own, and these are also found in gay variants, for example, frenzied action and other signs of 'abandon' represent passion. In Dyer's examples, the actors are extremely convincing in showing the signs of gay abandon, including the maintenance of erections and what look like authentic ejaculations. Dyer goes on to make some insightful comments about how the stardom specifically of gay porn stars is maintained, and he summarizes some popular gay porn plots – an attractive man appears who is 'innocent . . .

[but] willingly but almost passively gets into sexual encounters' (2002: 195), for example.

Porn exceeds realist conventions in certain ways too, using unusual camera angles, slow-motion, split screens and conspicuous editing to add pleasures for the viewer. These can include devices that make the viewer well aware that they are watching a video – Dyer's favourite gay porn star addresses the camera directly (which adds a different meaning to the similar scenes in Annie Sprinkle's videos – see below); explores lot of optical analogies with mirrors and cameras; looks at porn films while on camera himself; and generally shows pleasure in being involved in making a pornographic video (ibid.: 199). Dyer says this matches a lot of aspects of gay culture such as a delight in parody, pastiche, and artifice. There is an intellectualised pleasure to watching gay porn for Dyer. He likes to enjoy these textual elements as well, and to see how the video is actually being assembled (see **pleasures**). This gives an erotic charge to his viewing as well, raising the definite possibility that gay porn permits both intellectual appreciation and full involvement: Dyer is watching sex as display, presentation and excess, and there are clear links here with the idea of sex as performance (see **identity**). Dyer clearly sees gay pornography not as contagious and leading to imitation so much as transgressive, in that it 'affirms the delights of that most common, most unadmitted, at once most vanilla and most politically incorrect of all sexual activities, masturbation' (ibid.: 202).

The libertarian case for ending censorship might be examined more generally. The argument goes that the free and healthy exploration of sexuality has always been limited in the interests of social control and oppression (a theme which can be found in the works of Marx, Freud or Foucault), and that the consumption of pornography encourages a more open discussion and the lowering of inhibitions. To some extent, this is echoed by some sexual therapists dealing with particularly inhibited couples, as in the once-controversial work of Dr Martin Cole who ran a notorious sex therapy clinic at the University of Aston and publicized his work with well-attended lectures in university lecture halls (see Cole and Dryden, 1988).

The work of Annie Sprinkle (AnnieSprinkle.org, 2003) is often discussed in this context too, and two admiring essays in the Church Gibson and Gibson collection describe her work. Straayer, for example, describes Sprinkle as offering a postmodern combination of 'pornography, feminism, art, spirituality, sex education, advertising, political activism, performance art, body play and the self-help health, prostitutes' rights and

205

safe sex movements' (Church Gibson and Gibson, 1993: 156). She deconstructs commercial sexiness in commentary on her own pin-up pictures, offers a parodic 'educational' commentary direct to the viewer while performing in her own pornographic movies, displays an always-positive sexuality in her activity with burns victims, amputees, transsexuals and persons of restricted growth, encourages the audience to examine her cervix, and has done much to explore the mysteries of female ejaculation. This reflective, flexible and positive sexuality is much admired, although I have always had doubts about whether it emerged actually from or merely survived work in the sex industry. Liberationists can easily find themselves in the dangerous company of professional pornographers, of course (see Russell, 2003).

One of the first pornographers to make the libertarian case, for example, was the Marquis de Sade. The stories ostensibly deal with young women who discover that they have been seriously repressed by the Church and other authorities, and that the pornographic expression of their sexuality brings with it both political and personal liberation. For critics such as Horkheimer and Adorno (1979), however, they can be no finer example of a false kind of liberation, one that escapes constraint only to produce a new barbarism produced by a 'bourgeois individual freed from tutelage' (ibid.: 86). Sade's notion of social relationships, for example, is shown in his description of an orgy; it permits a form of work, the totally efficient sexual exploitation of every possibility. Sade may have liberated himself from feudal constraints but not from capitalist ones. The same kind of anxiety was echoed in Marcuse's (1968) fears that the sexual revolution of the 1960s also only released a harmful kind of exploitative subjectivity and a kind of commercialized promiscuity, rather than leading to any increase in genuinely liberating eroticism in social life.

There is, of course, a strong suspicion that, overall, the whole debate reflects the tastes of powerful groups who have been successful in influencing policy. We need only think of the 'high aesthetic' in the work of Bourdieu (1986) to realize how much pornography is going to disgust bourgeois opinion. It offers the 'lowest' of pleasures, such as immediate gratification and involvement, and a literalness about sexuality that avoids all mediation and intellectual activity (hence the use of the term 'obscene', which literally means that which should not be seen). Attempts to analyse the conventions of written pornography such as the classic by Marcus (1977) point to the serious limits of its narrative form. It cannot really rely on surprise to deliver pleasure, since there is none about the outcome of sexual activity. The narrative has to deliver the same story, in effect, at more or less the same pace, leading to the serious problem of repetition and thus boredom. As the Marquis de Sade's musings showed long ago, one obvious way to avoid this is to introduce as many sexual variations as possible, involving homosexual or bisexual couplings, sex with objects, group sex, costume sex, rituals involving sex, and the like. Even these are fairly limited in the end.

Against this view, though, is the sort of reading offered by Dyer (2002), which we have discussed above, which points to the creative use of media conventions. McClintock's argument (above) also suggests that consumers can perform creative readings despite any lack of inspiration in the actual product. Perhaps recent pornography can be seen as genuinely creative, once bourgeois prejudices are overcome?

It is clear that the term 'pornography' covers a very wide range of material, much of which seems to be consensual, commercially produced, and no more exploitative than other commercial activities. Pornographic content seems to be appearing in a variety of guises or literary forms as well, as in the notorious 'sex documentaries' which have become a staple of late night viewing on British TV. It is also now far more widely available, and can be effectively obtained by downloading material at home, with minimal risks of being detected or being socially embarrassed by contacts with professional pornographers. In these circumstances, it is clear that the State has great difficulty in enforcing particular views of what counts as illegal material, although the dangers of encouraging even one case of violent sexual behaviour might outweigh these difficulties, of course. We might borrow a term from the discussion of illegal drugs, and suggest that the consumption of pornography as well has become 'normalized'.

FURTHER READING

The pros and cons of censorship can be pursued via Dworkin (Andrea Dworkin Web Site, 2003), Russell (2003) or Church Gibson and Gibson (1993). Ross (in During, 1993) has a thoughtful essay on the popularity of pornography. Shaw (1999) offers some useful methodological guidance on studying possible effects. The Starr Report (CNN.com, 2003) offers an interesting case study to explore the boundaries between pornography and the explicit reporting of sexual activity.

REFERENCES

Andrea Dworkin Web Site (2003) [online] http://www.nostatusquo.com/ACLU/dworkin/

AnnieSprinkle.org (2003) [online] http://www.anniesprinkle.org/

ArtsReformation.Com (2003) http://www.artsreformation.com/a001/hays-code.html

Attwood, F. (2002) 'A Very British Carnival: Women, Sex and Transgression in *Fiesta Magazine*', *European Journal of Cultural Studies*, 5 (1): 91–105.

Bourdieu, P. (1986) *Distinction: A Social Critique of the Judgement of Taste*, London: Routledge.

Church Gibson, P. and Gibson, R. (eds) (1993) *Dirty Looks: Women, Pornography, Power*, London: BFI Publishing.

CNN.com (2003) 'The Starr Report', [online] http://www.cnn.com/starr.report/

Cole, M. and Dryden, W. (1988) *Sex Therapy in Britain (Psychotherapy in Britain)*, Milton Keynes: Open University Press.

During, S. (ed.) (1993) *The Cultural Studies Reader*, London and New York: Routledge.

Dyer, R. (2002) *The Culture of Queers*, London and New York: Routledge.

Horkheimer, M. and Adorno, T. (1979) *Dialectic of Enlightenment*, London: Verso.

Marcus, S. (1977) *Other Victorians: A Study of Sexuality and Pornography in Mid-Nineteenth Century England*, New York: New American Library.

Marcuse, H. (1968) *One-Dimensional Man*, London: Sphere.

Russell, D. (2003) 'Nadine Strossen: The Pornography Industry's Wet Dream' [online] http://www.echonyc.com/~onissues/russell.htm

Shaw, S. (1999) 'Men's Leisure and Women's Lives: The Impact of Pornography on Women', *Leisure Studies*, 18: 197–212.

Travis, A. (2003) 'Government Backs Down on Sex Laws', *The Guardian*, 16 April.

key concepts

Postmodernism

208

Postmodernism refers to a cultural development after modernism, featuring playful experimental combination of previously separate styles and elements. Particular combinations are taken as especially characteristic. Postmodernization usually refers to social processes such as the decline of modernist social groups (such as social classes and nation–states) and the subsequent development of differentiation and cultural autonomy. Theoreticians debate whether and how the two are connected.

> **Section Outline:** *Postmodernism and the disillusion with modernism ('scepticism towards metanarratives'). Collapsing boundaries in film and television. Postmodern leisure: hyperreality, 'death tours', virtual leisure, 'casual leisure'. Postmodernization as differentiation and dedifferentiation: commodification, rationalization, post-Fordism. Possibilities to resist and reverse these trends and the implications for leisure.*

This entry might best be read in conjunction with the entry on **posts**; in that discussion we suggest that a critical distance has apparently been opened up with something that went before. This meaning is retained with the term postmodernism, although it is important to begin right away by saying that the term is ambiguous, and that the academic writers usually associated with postmodernism (Lyotard and Baudrillard) have both dissociated themselves from the uncritical celebration of cultural changes that the term often implies.

However, we can get into the debate by thinking about what it is in modernism that has been left behind after radical criticism. The usual guide here is Lyotard (1984), who has used the phrase 'scepticism towards metanarratives' to summarize the kind of criticism that has been made of modernism. To be brief, one characteristic of modernist social science in particular was that it offered 'foundational' concepts (see **posts**), but also claimed that it could lead human beings towards emancipation, towards a new freedom. Both claims have been challenged, but it is probably that lack of faith in emancipation that has proved decisive in the scepticism that Lyotard refers to. Many people who used to believe in progress have been disillusioned; marxism as a science that would lead towards a new freedom for everyone looks doubtful; freudianism, as a way of freeing ourselves from repression and infantilism so that we could be mentally healthy and happy, seems suspect. For academics, disillusionment is clearly associated with an equal suspicion about the scientific status of these approaches.

We can see a similar disillusionment associated with many of the promises once made by natural science. The promise of limitless cheap energy as a result of being able to develop nuclear power, based on advances in nuclear physics in the 1940s, has turned sour. Post-war enthusiasm also extended to a belief in town planning as a rational scientific way to design towns and cities, to end forever the old slum conditions, and inaugurate a new era of community. That did not really work either, whether we look at mass housing developments in Glasgow,

209

or Milton Keynes. Finally, post-war economics also promised a way to solve economic crisis, to control inflation, to end mass unemployment, and to introduce international financial stability – again, no one really believes in those possibilities these days.

The cultural aspects of postmodernism also stem from a rejection of the ways in which things were done in modernism. We can see this clearly in examining the media. It was common, for example, to develop a system of generic film-making, so that both the industry and the audiences could immediately understand that they were viewing a Western or a melodrama. Television operated with a series of categories of its own, such as drama, documentary or children's television. A set of conventions had emerged to govern the ways in which stories were told, and characters represented, both in fictional film and in documentary television. Postmodernism inaugurated an era of new experimentation in all of these areas. We see a 'collapse of internal boundaries', for example, as film genres are abandoned or mixed, and as one film cheerfully quotes from another. What sort of a film is Tarantino's *From Dusk Till Dawn*, for example? (For those who do not know the film, it begins as a story about a set of robberies, but, when the robbers meet up to divide their spoils, they realize that the other people in the club with them are monsters, and the film becomes a vampire movie.) Michael Jackson's *Thriller* (the best-selling rock video of all time) is riddled with references to and borrowings from American youth movies and vampire movies, and is directed by the same person who made *An American Werewolf in London*. Entertainment and education become collapsed into 'edutainment'. Children's television is made with an acute eye on the adult audience, who enjoy watching it ironically. It is difficult to tell the difference between a 'straight' detective programme and a parody, or a pornographic television programme and a documentary on the sex industry. Instead of single options for viewers, postmodern media offer multiple options (they are 'polysemic', to use a common term). Other features of postmodern media can include experiments with **narrative** or authorship, or the mixing of national styles (as in anime, for example, which often combines Japanese and American elements of animation).

This collapsing of boundaries is not only found in media, but also in cooking (as in the emergence of the chicken tikka pizza), or in the odd combinations found in niche tourism (sport tourism, sex tourism, educational tourism, cognitive tourism). We can also notice the collapse of internal boundaries in discussing the new flexible **identities** that now seem to be available, as in 'queer theory'. The old social constraints have ceased to control our behaviour, tastes, leisure pursuits, and the categories we used to classify them. Formerly, it was an artistic elite who used to experiment with clothing, painting, politics or religion, but now we all have the cultural resources to do so. The only difference, possibly, is that artistic experiment maintained modernist ideas of 'seriousness' and emancipation arising from new insight or knowledge, whereas in postmodernism, experiment is for the purposes of **pleasure** or fun. It is also fair to say that experiment has a commercial value. The sphere of commerce used to be rigidly separated from the sphere of art, but this is another internal boundary that has collapsed, so that we see surrealist or expressionist advertisements, Dadaist influences on popular music, or Russian futurism used in a pop video. Is there a serious critical point being made about American society in *Blue Velvet* (Denzin (1991) finds it a politically conservative film), or in *Brother, Where Art Thou?*, with its rendition of a Ku Klux Klan rally as a Busby Berkeley musical scene?

Rojek (1993) lists the characteristics of postmodernism much as we have done here, while adding to the list time–space compression and velocity, both examples of the erosion of particular boundaries. Rojek focuses on leisure examples to test postmodernist analysis. He discusses theme parks, heritage sites and literary landscapes, for example, all of which can offer a cheerful combination of fictional and real characters, blurring the boundaries between 'fact' and 'fiction' (and the separation of historical periods) and heading towards **hyperreality**. Literary landscapes in particular can become real enough to inform political struggles to preserve them. His discussion of popular but odd leisure activities such as visiting death sites, including cemeteries, and 'black spots' offers further evidence of 'dedifferentiation', the collapse of boundaries between categories once separated (such as cemetery and tourist site). At the same time, he reminds us that traditional societies also offered these pleasures, and notes that traditional leisure activities have not been entirely replaced.

In a later review of the literature, Rojek (1995) emphasizes the democratizing potential of postmodern tendencies towards collapsing boundaries – between high and low culture, for example, which provides access to the cultural raw materials for leisure on an unprecedented basis. It is worth pointing out that this particular boundary might well have collapsed in a special way, permitting much more traffic one way (middle-class interest in popular culture) than in the other, a point reinforced by a British survey (Roberts and Parsell, 1994), and a recent study of participation in sport in the USA (Wilson, 2002); one needs more **cultural capital** to cross into high culture than vice versa. Rojek also notes the collapse of two more important boundaries – between **authentic** and inauthentic forms, and between **work and leisure**. In a later review (Rojek, 2000), we are pointed towards home-based virtual leisure as the likely future postmodernist activity.

As an alternative, we might consider the work of Stebbins (1997) on 'casual leisure' as a more characteristic and non-electronic postmodern leisure pursuit. Casual leisure complements Stebbins' (1982) work on 'serious leisure' (the pursuit of a hobby or pastime with work-like commitment). Moorhouse (in Rojek, 1989) also has a discussion of labour as leisure. Casual leisure involves browsing and sampling a variety of leisure pursuits without particular commitment; its pleasures include immediate gratification, easy access and participation because of low skill levels required, and 'serendipity' (the bonus as a new and unexpected pleasure is unveiled).

It is this lack of commitment and 'depth', of political intent and seriousness, the ever-present possibility of irony and mockery that has disappointed marxist and feminist critics in particular, as might be imagined. For them, all the experiments in postmodernist culture leave the essential bases of oppression (especially patriarchy) untouched; in his witty commentary on performance in *Mulholland Drive*, Lynch exposes his female stars to the same old male **gaze**, one might argue. Advocates of postmodernism also tend to ignore the commercial and political agenda of experiment, seeming to think playfulness as above constraint. We find this kind of criticism directed against postmodern children's television (see **narrative**), and the reassuring accounts of the **heritage** industry or the Disney site offered by postmodernists. In these cases especially, commercial interests in novelty are too closely allied to postmodernist joy in experiment, the critics suggest.

Whatever the intentions of producers, it is still also possible for cultural consumers such as subcultures, 'tribes', 'taste publics', audiences, followers and practitioners (such as football supporters), new social movements, and even social classes or sections of them to reconnect meanings back to narratives and add depth to them. Giddens (1991) also notes the new role for gurus and popular experts offering advice on lifestyles, health, sex, plastic surgery and much else. This may indicate a new form of consumer empowerment and the extension of opportunities for genuine choice.

Baudrillard (Baudrillard and Lotringer, 1987) remains resolutely sceptical of the political possibilities, however, arguing that what political movements of any kind offer is the mere simulacrum of politics, that talking about power is all that remains. As even totalitarian societies learned, it is impossible to marshall sufficient authority to purse any serious political process. A possible retort is to suggest that this political fatalism, and the rather gleeful pleasure at the failure of 'serious' projects is characteristic of a particular class fraction, the 'new petite bourgeoisie' as Bourdieu (1986) calls them. This fraction stakes its claim to social privilege on the possession of particular kinds of cultural capital, including knowledge of recent trends and events and an academic ability to criticize. Its main rivals are both the traditional working class 'beneath' and the old aristocratic class 'above'. Not surprisingly, its distancing activities focus on relentless critique of both tradition and elite culture, and it invests in transitory and fleeting cultural fashions and styles – in postmodernism.

Partly in order to stave off the view that it is a mere style associated with a particular group, and possibly because of a lingering desire to assume the role of public intellectuals, postmodernists invoked a notion of real and irreversible social change that has been sufficient to inaugurate a new era, leaving modern society behind. However, the social theory here is much less well developed, and usually implies more than it explains. This is why some critics separate out postmodernism as a description of cultural trends, and postmodernization as a social process: this also restores the issue to the proper control of traditional experts such as sociologists and economists, of course. Leaving aside academic micropolitics for a while, though, questions do arise about the origins of these cultural developments; how exactly is it that boundaries which had been important in culture for decades suddenly managed to collapse, how have cultural projects designed to touch upon the deepest of human issues become fragmented and 'depthless', lost their seriousness, and become mere materials for playful intertextual comment or pastiche?

A comprehensive review of the different theoretical possibilities is provided in Crook et al. (1992). In essence, Crook et al. define a series of social processes as 'differentiation', 'hyperdifferentiation' and 'de-differentiation'. What happens is that in modernism culture becomes subjected to various processes of differentiation: culture itself separates out as a specialist area in social life, and then divides into more specific specialisms, such as literature, music, painting and so on. Hyper-differentiation refers to the much accelerated processes of differ-entiation that have occurred in cultural areas more recently: this has been so acute that cultural traditions have themselves become entirely fragmented, subdivided, specialized to an advanced extent. The paradox is that this process allows a subsequent phase of dedifferentiation, since fragments are much more easily assembled into new collections and cultural practices than were the traditional cultural specialisms. Crook et al. use the example of the ways in which fragments of music are used in advertisements. This fragmentation and recombination explain most of the features that we have listed above as postmodern. It is important to realize that the process of transition is by no means as simple as I have rendered it here, and there have been various attempts to reverse it, to reunite cultural specialisms into overall projects, for example (one is the avant-garde project to make art connect back to everyday life).

Crook et al. identify a number of sociological processes at work which drive differentiation and hyperdifferentiation. It is clear that the marxist process of commodification plays a major role here. Commercial processes have long extended into cultural areas as well, and produced a huge amount of novelty and specialization in the production of cultural goods. At the same time, commodification reduces those goods to a common factor, that they are commodities and that they have in common an exchange value, to use the technical term. This produces a radical indifference (dedifferentiation) to any quality other than exchange value, the ability to be bought and sold in markets. The work of Jameson (1991) is usually cited as the most common example of an application of this model to postmodern culture specifically, as we saw in the citing of his name in the debates about **heritage**. For Jameson, the ability to transfer cultural objects into commodities is what lies behind the seemingly separate and distinct qualities of postmodern culture – the cheerful thefts of cultural elements that belonged to definite cultural traditions, stripping away any depths in the process, and their reappearance in loose collections or pastiches. Other marxists have slightly different takes on the argument, for example, critical theorists argue that culture has become fully transformed into a culture industry, with all the novelty and cultural invention provided by the remarkable flexibility and creativity of capitalism and its production processes.

For **gramscians**, a rather elliptical argument based, inevitably, on some analysis offered by Gramsci, suggests that it was changes in production that underpin the cultural changes found in postmodernism. The shift is seen as the Fordist accumulation process encountered difficulties and evolved into post-Fordism, involving small-scale flexible forms of production, with minimal stocks, and with effective links to the changing demands of the consumer. This understanding of economic changes and their social consequences (new opportunities to enter production for excluded groups, new divisions in the workforce between multi-skilled core and under-skilled periphery), together with the increasingly linguistic turn described in post-marxism, informed the 'New Times' project (Hall and Jacques, 1989) that was the culmination of the analytic work (see Harris, 1992, for a critique).

However, Crook et al. insist that commodification alone is not enough to explain the changes. Processes such as rationalization, associated with Weber, and with Ritzer, whom we have discussed in the entry on **McDonaldization**, also lead to important developments. Rationalization also encourages cultural specialism and differentiation, and there is a role here for cultural experts and specialists in their own right, regardless of any ties they may or may not have with the culture industry. In Giddens's view, (1991), such expertise is not confined to the professionals, but increasingly informs everyday life as we become more and more reflexive about our conduct. Such differentiation can still lead to dedifferentiation, as specialisms become more and more esoteric, and open to fewer and fewer specialists. It is clear that Ritzer's later discussion of (re-)enchantment can be used to illustrate this argument. In order to compensate for the excessive rationalization of the game of baseball and its stadia, for example, various 'enchanting' elements are added, such as additional entertainments. As a result, the game of baseball seems to be in danger of losing its specificity and different-ness, and the experience of attending a match seems to blend with that of attending a theme park (Ritzer and Stillman, 2001).

Finally, Crook et al. do not think that the local forms of solidarity listed above (lifestyle, taste publics, and so on) will resist the dedifferentiating trends, which extend far beyond culture to affect work and politics as well. For this reason, although we are not there yet, postmodernism seems the most likely future, and we can expect more cultural fragmentation and recombination, and thus more new forms of leisure.

FURTHER READING

The classic pieces by Rojek (1993, 1995, 2000) and the much-quoted work of Stebbins (1982, 1997) are worth following up. I have 'reading guides' to key works by Lyotard (1984) and Baudrillard (1983) on my web-site (Harris, 2003), specifically accessible via www.arasite.org/sagelist.html. Crook et al. (1992) is detailed and useful. There are several main online sources for postmodernist work, including PopCultures.Com (2003), The Theory.org.uk Directory (2003), Cultural Studies Central (2003). Taylor (2003) is an excellent online archive of Baudrillard's more accessible work.

Baudrillard, J. (1983) *Simulations*, London: Semiotext(e).

Baudrillard, J. and Lotringer, S. (1987) *Forget Foucault and Forget Baudrillard*, New York: Semiotext(e).

Bourdieu, P. (1986) *Distinction: A Social Critique of the Judgement of Taste*, London: Routledge.

Crook, S., Pakulski, J. and Waters, M. (1992) *Postmodernization: Change in Advanced Society*, London: Sage.

Cultural Studies Central (2003) [online] http://www.culturalstudies.net/

Denzin, N. (1991) *Images of Postmodern Society: Social Theory and Contemporary Cinema*, London: Sage.

Giddens, A. (1991) *Modernity and Self-Identity: Self and Society in the Late Modern Age*, Cambridge: Polity Press.

Hall, S. and Jacques, M. (eds) (1989) *New Times: The Changing Face of Politics in the 1990s*, London: Lawrence and Wishart, in association with *Marxism Today*.

Harris, D. (1992) *From Class Struggle to the Politics of Pleasure: The Effects of Gramscianism on Cultural Studies*, London: Routledge.

Harris, D. (2003) 'Dave Harris (and Colleagues): Essays, Papers and Courses' [online] http://www.arasite.org/

Jameson, F. (1991) *Postmodernism, or, the Cultural Logic of Late Capitalism*, London: Verso.

Lyotard, J-F. (1984) *The Postmodern Condition: A Report on Knowledge*, Manchester: Manchester University Press.

PopCultures.Com (2003) [online] http://www.popcultures.com/

Ritzer, G. and Stillman, T. (2001) 'The Postmodern Ballpark as a Leisure Setting: Enchantment and Simulated De-McDonaldization', *Leisure Sciences*, 23: 99–113.

Roberts, K., and Parsell, G. (1994) 'Youth Cultures in Britain: The Middle Class Take-Over', *Leisure Studies*, 13: 33–48.

Rojek, C. (ed.) (1989) *Leisure for Leisure*, London: Macmillan.

Rojek, C. (1993) *Ways of Escape*, London: Macmillan.

Rojek, C. (1995) *Decentring Leisure: Rethinking Leisure Theory*, London: Sage.

Rojek, C. (2000) *Leisure and Culture*, Basingstoke: Macmillan.

Stebbins, R. (1982) 'Serious Leisure: A Conceptual Statement', *Pacific Sociological Review*, 25: 251–72.

Stebbins, R. (1997) 'Casual Leisure: A Conceptual Statement', *Leisure Studies*, 16: 17–25.

Taylor, A. (2003) 'Baudrillard on the Web' [online] http://www.uta.edu/english/apt/collab/baudweb.html

The Theory.org.uk Directory (2003) [online] http://www.theory.org.uk/directory.htm

Wilson, T (2002) 'The Paradox of Social Class and Sports Involvement: The Roles of Cultural and Economic Capital', *International Review for the Sociology of Sport*, 37 (1): 5–16.

key concepts

216

> The term 'post' means 'after' in Latin, so we can see that some idea of sequence or change over time is indicated by attaching the term to a concept or an approach that was dominant before. Post-marxism is something that comes after marxism, post-Fordism after Fordism, and so on. But there is another implication too, that the new positions come after because they have identified serious problems with the earlier ones, problems which mean that the old positions cannot be held with the same kind of confidence as before.

> **Section Outline:** *General and theoretical problems: floating signifiers and dogmatic foundational concepts. Post-structural anthropology, deconstruction, post-marxism, post-feminism, post-tourism. Celebrating difference.*

This is a rather peculiar section in a way, because I want to discuss a number of concepts each of which are indicated by having the prefix 'post' attached to them. I want to discuss in particular some 'posts' that occur quite frequently in the discussion of leisure, and some that relate to the various 'isms' that we have encountered in other sections. Perhaps the best-known 'post' gets its own section – **postmodernism** (in which I have included a brief aside on the concept post-Fordism as well).

The particular kind of criticisms implied by insisting that something is 'post' an earlier position usually turn on identifying fundamental theoretical flaws. These are of the same general type, and are seen as so devastating that they leave the older positions as wreckage with no hope of renewal or repair. They are also so fundamental that it becomes difficult to see any easy answer to the criticisms raised; any proposed replacement scientific or systematic approach of the old kind will encounter the same problems. In this final sense, then, the prefix 'post' indicates that nothing similar can emerge.

What are these general criticisms that appear to be so devastating? In order to simplify, I am taking a risk here, and suggesting that despite the

217

various positions involved, there are some common criticisms. Specific advocates of 'post' positions will vary greatly in terms of the philosophical resources they use. American critics such as Rorty (1989) draw upon a tradition we also discuss in the entry on **semiotics** – American pragmatism – while French critics such as Barthes, Foucault or Derrida will develop out of the other tradition mentioned in that entry – French semiotics. The connection with semiotics provides an early clue, in that 'post' critiques have something to do with the ways in which language is supposed to work to construct meaning.

We can begin to see how this works by considering French semiotics or 'structuralism' as it is sometimes called. Our very brief treatment indicates that meaning is conveyed by signs arranged into particular sequences, such as **narratives** or codes, which work by comparing and contrasting the meaning of one sign with another set of signs over time. The other dimension involved is a 'paradigmatic' one, where individual signs gain their meaning by being placed in general classes or categories – the sign 'Freud' makes sense because we place it in general collections such as 'German theorists', or 'psychoanalysts'. But there is a problem, since both of these processes are literally endless – signs can always be compared and contrasted with other signs, and individual signs can be placed in an infinite number of classes – in the case of Freud, classes such as 'dead people', 'Viennese', 'inhabitants of London', and so on, forever. There is no way to fix the meaning of signs, except by introducing a set of constructive processes outside the system altogether. Individuals may think they fix the meaning of signs, when they use them in writing, or in making films, but the use of signs is always inherently unstable, and a host of 'ghosts' await (to use Derrida's term, see Kamuf, 1991), ready to be invoked. Now what I have described here, very briefly and simply, is only a problem for those who thought that structuralist semiotics would deliver a definite science of signs, one that would explain how meanings are constructed 'objectively', and with the precision of science. When this claim came to be doubted, by thinking about the ways in which signs and signifiers 'slide', we enter the terrain of post-structuralism. We need to understand how meanings are actually (temporarily) fixed in practice, using various literary devices, and how alternative meanings are deferred – we need to do deconstruction (see Kamuf, 1991).

Let us consider another example with the structuralist anthropology of Lévi-Strauss. Being able to understand the underlying structure of kinship systems forms part of a crucial argument that Lévi-Strauss makes for the scientific status of his kind of anthropology (Lévi-Strauss, 1977). Using just a few terms based on human relationships, and adding the dimension of warm or cool emotional feelings, Lévi-Strauss claims to have been able to reconstruct logically a huge variety of actual kinship systems, which appeared extremely diverse on the surface. We did not raise this problem in the entry on semiotics, but there is an assumption in that argument that turns on the claims to universality of the basic structure which underlies the specific variations. What sort of structure is this exactly? Is it a clever theoretical construction based on Lévi-Strauss's own search for logical order, or does it have some independent and objective status, really out there in the world? Lévi-Strauss seems to be rather vague and ambiguous in describing what sort of underlying structure this is, and how exactly it explains human behaviour, although he favours the latter possibility. The British anthropologist Edmund Leach has some excellent critical points to make here (Leach, 1969), and suggests that Lévi-Strauss is forced to work with some notion of a general human mind or 'esprit', which is, of course, an extremely debatable and clearly unscientific term. A recognition of this problem, and a suspicion that it is really particular dominant groups or individuals who are actually responsible for imposing particular patterns in human life leads to a 'post-structuralist' anthropology.

I hope it is clear that just about any general system can be doubted in this way, by focusing on the important issue of the scientific status that is being claimed for it. One version of this focused doubt turns on the consistency and coherence of the main 'foundational' concepts involved. We can illustrate this by examining marxism, which we have discussed in entries such as the one on **social class**. For Marx, and for much sociology at the time, what appears on the surface is produced by some structure working underneath. In Marx's case, this structure is described by the use of terms such as 'class struggle', the 'extraction of surplus value', and the 'capitalist mode of production', with its different 'levels', one of which features **ideology**. When we discuss ideology, we see that one common claim made by marxists is that this set of concepts provides them with a science in order to understand social life, and this is important in staving off the criticism that marxism is yet another ideology. However, when we examine the nature and use of these foundational concepts, we find that they are not used coherently or systematically at all, at least according to critics such as the British post-structuralists Hindess and Hirst (see Crook, 1991, for a detailed summary of the work undertaken by these two theorists, and I have also summarized their work far more briefly in Harris, 2003). Anyone reading this entry will simply have to accept my word for now that Marx's use of concepts simply fails to meet their test of science (Hindess and Hirst, 1977). The same goes for Althusser, who had enjoyed a reputation for offering the most 'scientific' version of modern marxism (Hirst, 1979). At crucial points, Marx and Althusser resort to rhetoric and persuasion instead of logic. They use ambiguous metaphors, they extend the meaning of concepts in ways that are not fully consistent, and they are not above dogmatism, simply insisting that something just must be class struggle or whatever. I have used a version of this sort of criticism to identify, to my own satisfaction at least, the same kind of incoherence and dogmatism in **gramscian** analyses of popular culture and politics (Harris, 1992). The bad news for all sociologists was that all the founding parents, not just marxists, seemed to have serious flaws of this kind at the heart of their arguments. Nor did the critique go unnoticed in feminism, with considerable debates taking place about whether the concepts 'woman', or 'patriarchy' really did mean something objective, some essential quality which ran beneath the surface of specific gender identities or social systems (see, for example, Bailey in Ramazanoglu, 1993).

No specific system of scientific analysis seemed possible, hence no immediate candidate arose to replace marxism or feminism. One position calling itself 'post-marxism' drew upon those notions of endlessly sliding signifiers discussed in post-structuralism, and insisted that concepts such as 'social class' referred to a linguistic act, an act of **articulation**. People had to come to recognize themselves as members of the social class, and make a linguistic utterance to that effect, so to connect the term with current politics and current concerns, to fix a meaning at a specific time and place. There was no other way to fix the meaning of the term, and it was a delusion to believe that it had some objective meaning independently of those articulations. We pursue a rather similar process with the concept of gender, when we discuss the idea that gender **identities** are a matter of 'performance', that there are no fixed or essential genders, which we need to socially construct them. In this sense, 'queer theory' with its notion of almost infinite possibilities and fluid identities represents one 'post-feminist' position.

It is worth noting that both post-marxism and post-feminism have their critics. It is difficult to resist the philosophical and logical critiques offered of marxism and feminism, but not impossible. For example, Geras (1988) has identified some inconsistencies in the use of the key term 'articulation', as our discussion in that entry indicates. There are certainly some assumptions involved as well about the kind of science that the older positions have been or should be aiming at. For example, Hindess and Hirst seemed to have in mind a fully logical, rigorous and coherent deployment of concepts, but it is not obvious why this version should be preferred. In general, critiques offered by the 'posts' can look extremely abstract, philosophical, or, as we shall argue below, intellectualised. There is a crucial political dimension to the adoption of both marxism and feminism too, of course. People often believe that the analysis offered is good enough for practical political purposes, while admitting that it may not be perfect, and, by comparison, believe rival positions that prop up pro-capitalist or oppressive regimes are far more incoherent and dogmatic. Finally, some critics, including Fraser, see the adoption of post-marxism in particular as a rationalization peculiar to academics, 'only a temporary waystation on the exodus from Marxism now being traveled by the French intelligentsia' (Fraser, 1989: 82).

It is with the notion of fluidity and emergence that we come closest, perhaps, to what might be called the positive implications of the 'post' positions. These turn on the argument that there are no essences or underlying mechanisms that determine social life. Free-floating and fluid possibilities are still socially and politically fixed into seemingly natural options and categories, but this must always be unstable. If post-structuralism has a political position, it is probably along the now familiar lines of wanting to support 'difference', to permit flexible identities, not to attempt to prioritize some as essential, natural, or objective. It is a position that has its problems, ably demonstrated in an excellent critique by Fraser (1989) of a particular version of the politics of difference associated with Derrida's followers. In a nutshell, celebrating endless difference almost inevitably rules out conventional politics of any kind, and leaves the field wide open to those who are prepared to postpone difference and assemble a coalition to act. It is certainly a rather intellectual commitment, depending, as so often is the case, on the willingness of others, even opponents, to take a sophisticated view of difference as well; it is often just as likely, of course, that force will be used to impose a dominant view.

To round off our survey, it is worth discussing post-tourism. Again, broader leisure interests can stand instead of 'tourism' in this phrase. Urry (1990) suggests that conventional tourism is a thing of the past, given the social and theoretical changes associated with postmodernism (and this theme is also developed in Rojek, 1995). Instead, a knowing 'post-tourism' emerges, one that does not seek **authenticity** but accepts or even relishes inauthenticity, one that adopts a playful relativism and ironic detachment rather than a serious attempt to encounter otherness, one that deconstructs and subverts the tourist gaze and all the ideological baggage that goes with it by expressing doubts about its sincerity. There is the same sense that this trend is irreversible and that a sceptical public will never again take seriously the crude simulations and fake anthropology of the tourist industry. The future offers even more examples of post-tourism in the shape of virtual tourism (see **virtual leisure**) – why travel at all when you can manage encounters with otherness at home? Although this is a term describing experience rather than theoretical commitment, post-tourism has theoretical implications in suggesting that if tourism as a separate and special practice has disappeared, perhaps there is no longer a need for a separate academic discipline called tourism studies. Arguments in favour of tight boundaries around this specialism, with the usual mixture of special pleading, dogmatism, incoherence and so on, could also be deconstructed with ease.

FURTHER READING

Very good introductions to the debates about post-structuralism are found in Culler (1976), Crook (1991) and Sarup (1993). Hindess and Hirst (1977) offer an excellent post-structuralist critique of much modern sociology. Fraser (1989) has some telling feminist criticisms of post-structuralism. PopCultures.Com (2003) has an excellent section which includes the theorists mentioned here and others (specifically on http://www.popcultures.com/theorist.htm).

REFERENCES

Crook, S. (1991) *Modernist Radicalism and its Aftermath: Foundationalism and Anti-Foundationalism in Radical Social Theory*, London: Routledge.

Culler, J. (1976) *Structuralist Poetics*, London: Routledge and Kegan Paul.

Fraser, N. (1989) *Unruly Practices: Power Discourse and Agenda in Contemporary Social Theory*, Cambridge: Polity Press.

Geras, N. (1988) 'Ex-Marxism Without Substance', *New Left Review*, 169: 34–62.

Harris, D. (1992) *From Class Struggle to the Politics of Pleasure: The Effects of Gramscianism on Cultural Studies*, London: Routledge.

Harris, D. (2003) *Teaching Yourself Social Theory*, London: Sage.

Hindess, B. and Hirst, P. (1977) *Mode of Production and Social Formation*, London: Routledge and Kegan Paul.

Hirst, P. (1979) *On Law and Ideology*, London: Macmillan.

Kamuf, P. (ed.) (1991) *A Derrida Reader: Between the Blinds*, London: Harvester Wheatsheaf.

Leach, E. (1969) *Genesis as Myth and Other Essays*, London: Jonathan Cape Ltd.

Lévi-Strauss, C. (1977) *Structural Anthropology*, 1, London: Peregrine Books.

PopCultures.Com (2003) [online] http://www.popcultures.com/

Ramazanoglu, C. (ed.) (1993) *Up Against Foucault: Explorations of Some Tensions between Foucault and Feminism*, London: Routledge.

Rojek, C. (1995) *Decentring Leisure: Rethinking Leisure Theory*, London: Sage.

Rorty, R. (1989) *Contingency, Irony and Solidarity*, Cambridge: Cambridge University Press.

Sarup, M. (1993) *An Introductory Guide to Post-Structuralism and Post-Modernism*, Hemel Hempstead: Harvester Wheatsheaf.

Urry, J. (1990) *The Tourist Gaze: Leisure and Travel in Contemporary Societies*, London: Sage.

'Race' and Leisure

The term 'race' is associated with the view that there are biological differences between people with differently coloured skins or other bodily differences; no-one needs to be reminded of the political dangers of such a view. The usual alternative, which is to refer to 'ethnic minorities' is also controversial, however, since, as Sivanandan (1990) points out, the term can imply that people of colour (to use another term) are hopelessly culturally backward or comically 'ethnic', and that discrimination is just a matter of cultural misunderstanding. Leisure activities show a characteristic combination of opportunities and discriminatory practices for people of colour.

Section Outline: Forms and locations of racism. Black and Asian people in popular culture, especially film. 'Jim Crow'. 'Race' as a structuring factor in youth subcultures. Black and Asian people, music and sport: 'natural athleticism' and racism among spectators. Sport as a sidetrack.

223

It is very difficult to avoid controversy when discussing this issue, which begins with the very terminology used as we can see above. It is clear to Sivanandan and his associates at the UK Institute of Race Relations (who produce the journal *Race and Class*) that the politics of skin colour is also closely associated with other forms of discrimination, especially class discrimination.

This has also been the position of marxist analysts who see 'racial' politics as a surface appearance of **class** politics, principally aimed at dividing the working class. This makes sense especially in Britain, it could be argued, since the more recent immigration of those of Afro-Caribbean descent was associated with the recruitment of labour for working-class occupations. However, immigration from other countries, especially Asian ones, presents a more mixed and complex picture, with people being recruited to skilled occupations such as those in the health service as well. The picture in other countries is also significantly different: African-Americans are descended largely from slaves, while Australian Aboriginal people, or native Americans or Africans, are not immigrants at all, but have been colonized by white immigrants. Overall, there has been considerable debate in social theory to attempt to show how the politics of skin colour is connected to, but not exactly the same as, other kinds of politics involving discrimination. For an overview of different approaches to 'race' and leisure, specifically sport, see Jarvie and Reid (1997).

Racism is found in the form of open personal attacks on people or in forms of discrimination in schools or employment. There is some debate about whether it is as permanently well grounded as divisions based on class (essential to the maintenance of capitalism for marxists), or **gender** (coded irretrievably into culture and identity formation according to some feminists). It may be so prominent because of the recent colonial period. Skin colour and other physical characteristics are certainly found as a cultural resource in the **semiotics** of everyday life, offering convenient binary classifications. There is also a set of racialized background repertoires or scripts often used especially to explain and complain about unequal resources, self and others, the past and social change, or normality and deviance. There is no space to explore this racialisation of everyday discourse here, but there are some useful studies by Cashmore (1987) or van Dijk (1987) – the latter offers some examples of how to analyse media discourse in particular. Although we do not discuss the topic in the entry on **effects analysis**, it would be quite possible to consider the impact of mass media on promoting racial stereotypes or racialized scripts, of course, and one famous example is found in the study of racialized press coverage of street crime in the UK (Hall et al., 1978). Hall (in Alvarado and Thompson, 1990) has also explored the effects of the 'white **gaze**'. A critical review of a more recent study of televised commentary concerning black soccer players (McCarthy et al., 2003) is included in the entry on **gramscianism**.

We would expect leisure patterns more generally to exhibit these political forms of inclusion and exclusion, just as with class or gender. It might help to begin with a simplified scheme which charts such patterns in film and television, based on the one in Hall (in Alvarado and Thompson, 1990), or the one by Julien and Mercer (1988). According to such schemas, people of colour began life in mainstream white society by

'Race' and Leisure

being largely ignored and excluded altogether. Hardly any such people were seen in film or television programmes, for example, and black and Asian sportsmen were rare. The first stage in recognizing a black presence was accompanied by stereotyping – people of colour were seen as savages, comics, idiots, child-like, as in the 'Jim Crow' tradition in the USA (Davis, 2003). Slowly, the stereotypes were reduced, and more complex black and Asian characters were allowed to appear, initially as extremely unusually well talented and highly qualified people, for example, or by slightly more sympathetic depictions of people of colour as 'cool'. The final stage, which we may or may not have reached, is one where ordinary people of colour are finally allowed to appear, where their characters are developed regardless of their skin colour, or where skin colour is not used as a particular signifier (see **narratives**). It is clear that each of these stages involve a kind of discrimination, in the form of maintaining that people of colour are different from white ones, and initially, of course, clearly inferior. It is very difficult to avoid this kind of discrimination, since even more positive depictions run the risk of being patronising, or indifferent to skin colour and thus politically naïve. It is always possible for the audience to apply stereotyped readings to the characters as well, regardless of the intentions of the makers of the film or programme.

Similar stages may be detectable in the development of other leisure activities as well. Rather as with gays (see **gender**), black and Asian identities may have had an influence even where they were officially denied a presence. Hebdige argues as much in his account of the development of youth subcultures and musical taste publics in Britain (for example, Hebdige, 1979). Whereas gramscian analysis focused on the development of such subcultures as a result of a 'double articulation', a reaction to the determinants of both age and social class, Hebdige pointed out that there were also complex reactions by white youth to black identities and cultural styles as well. Indeed, in his contribution to the initial collection on youth subcultures (Hall and Jefferson, 1976), Hebdige suggested that the cultural position of the UK 'mod' could best be understood in terms of the model of the 'white negro' in the USA. To give an example of his later work, both white and black (Afro-Caribbean) youth developed similar tastes in styles of music and dress such as 'two-tone', or 'white reggae', but tastes diverged and opposed each other with the development of distinctive black musical and cultural styles, based on notions of black separatism such as Rastafarianism. Black and white youth cultures interact with all the complexity one would expect of cultural productions, showing 'inversions, miscegenation, "deep structural adaptations which symbolically accommodate or expunge the black presence" (Hebdige, 1979: 45), mythologisation and displacement' (Harris, 1992: 92).

Apparently it seemed rather difficult for even gramscians to accept that 'race' was an important and analytically separate strand of discrimination (or example of hegemony), and it required a 'special' collection of writings on black popular culture (CCCS, 1982) to restore the balance. The same unconscious process whereby dominant white perceptions are taken as universally applicable is found in many other fields in leisure studies as well: another media example is provided by bell hooks (1999), who argues that the power of the cinematic male gaze never particularly applied to the viewing experiences of American black women. We have here an argument that 'racial' minorities retain a continuing level of experience derived from their social origins and reinforced by the continued experience of discrimination, and that this provides a set of cultural resources to resist dominant culture. As usual, though, studies of 'normal' people of colour are rare, and so we do not know how widespread this cultural resistance might be.

In Britain today, there is a very visible black cultural presence in leisure pursuits such as the music industry and sport. It is, however, far less certain that these developments represent a growing tolerance of the presence of people of colour more generally. Such occupational specialisms can be easily explained in racist terms, for example, using the old stereotypes that people of colour are closer to nature, have a natural rhythm, or natural athleticism. The origins of a black presence in music can be considered instead as explicable in social and cultural terms: music offered an area of 'free time' which was particularly suitable as an arena in which to develop artistic labour, skill and creativity in contrast to the usual sort of work on offer for people of colour (so Frith, 1983, suggests). It is also possible to argue that although these areas represent genuine opportunities for leisure pursuits and even occupations, they are also compromised in various ways. For example, the creativity and energy of black music run the risk of being re-incorporated into the commercial music industry, usually in a blander and more popular form. Chambers (1985) is one of several analysts who have identified a cyclic process here – independent music, expressing the cultural and leisure interests of particular minorities, reaches the attention of mainstream music and business, gets incorporated in order to revitalize the old tired formulas of popular music, and then calls forth a reaction in the form of new independent music which resists and inverts mainstream trends.

Black and Asian sportsmen may also have experienced discrimination and the effects of mainstream white power of a slightly different kind.

They are still chronically likely to receive racial abuse when they perform, as a study of British black football players indicates (Holland, 1997). Holland takes care to show that the 'burden of abuse' was massively exaggerated for black players on opposing teams, but even black home players also received about eight times more abuse than their white colleagues from home fans. This helps him to seriously question the usual rationalization for abuse that it is just 'part of the game', directed at all players, some of whom happen to be black. It is another example of the risks that participants in leisure can run – far from being a unifying force, the emotions released by spectatorship can also reproduce social division. Holland reports that several black players fear for the safety of their families as well as for themselves. Although his case seems to be established for football, there seems to be less evidence of this kind of abuse in other fields, although Holland does mention isolated cases of black entertainers receiving racist abuse. I know of no study suggesting that black musicians receive racist abuse for a poor performance.

There may be a deeper mechanism at work which has channelled people of colour into sport in the first place. There are of course black star athletes who have made a great success of playing sport, often rather a narrow range of sports in fact, but there is also a large group who have been subjected to a process that Carrington (in Barton and Walker, 1983) refers to as involving a 'sidetrack'. This takes place because of the common mechanism that sees sporting success as an alternative to, and a compensation for, academic or business success. To channel people of colour while at school into a sporting career risks discouraging them from pursuing a more conventional route to financial and social success. The schoolteachers that Carrington examined in his case study saw sport as a chance to get their Afro-Caribbean pupils genuinely involved, and the pupils themselves were not entirely unwilling to choose sport, although they were 'realistic' about their prospects. Nevertheless it is not difficult to trace the residual racism in such sidetracking, building on the view that people of colour are somehow natural sportsman, possessing better physiques and minds attuned best to motor activities, and not natural academics or entrepreneurs. This process goes along with the existence of serious discrimination against people of colour in the education system and occupational system; the integration and social mobility of people of colour are permitted as long as they conform to the dominant views of themselves. Something similar may be what is in effect offered to women (see Coalter, 1999), to gays, and perhaps even to those of working-class origin as well.

227

Back et al. (1999) discusses racism and football culture, and Carrington and McDonald (2001) offer some recent work on 'race' and sport in Britain. St Louis (2003) has a useful discussion of the racist assumptions involved in current discussions of 'natural athletes'. Harrison et al. (2002) review the literature on Afro-Americans and their development of US sporting identities. Van Dijk (1987) is a massive piece of work which is well worth browsing for ideas about researching racist discourse more generally.

REFERENCES

Alvarado, M. and Thompson, J. (eds) (1990) *The Media Reader*, London: BFI Publications.

Back, L., Crabbe, T. and Solomos, J (1999) 'Beyond the Racist/Hooligan Couplet: Race, Social Theory and Football Culture', *British Journal of Sociology*, 50 (3): 419–42.

Barton, L. and Walker, S. (1983) *Race, Class and Education*, London: Croom Helm.

Carrington, B. and McDonald, I. (2001) *'Race', Sport and British Society*, London: Routledge.

Cashmore, E. (1987) *The Logic of Racism*, London: Allen and Unwin.

CCCS (1982) *The Empire Strikes Back: Race and Racism in 70s Britain*, London: Hutchinson.

Chambers, I. (1985) *Urban Rhythms: Popular Music and Popular Culture*, London: Macmillan.

Coalter, F. (1999) 'Sport and Recreation in the United Kingdom: Flow with the Flow or Buck the Trends?', *Managing Leisure*, 4: 24–39.

Davis, R. (2003) 'Creating Jim Crow: In-Depth Essay' [online] http://www.jimcrowhistory.org/history/creating2.htm

Frith, S. (1983) *Sound Effects: Youth, Leisure and the Politics of Rock and Roll*, London: Constable and Company Ltd.

Hall, S., Critcher, C., Jefferson, T., Clarke, J. and Roberts, B. (1978) *Policing the Crisis: Mugging, the State, and Law and Order*, London: Macmillan.

Hall, S. and Jefferson, T. (eds) (1976) *Resistance Through Rituals*, London: Hutchinson.

Harris, D. (1992) *From Class Struggle to the Politics of Pleasure: The Effects of Gramscianism on Cultural Studies*, London: Routledge.

Harrison, L., Harrison, K. and Moore, L. (2002) 'Afro-American Racial Identity and Sport', *Sport, Education and Society*, 7 (2): 121–33.

Hebdige, D. (1979) *Subcultures: The Meaning of Style*, London: Methuen and Co.

Holland, B. (1997) 'Surviving Leisure-Time Racism: The Burden of Racial Harassment on Britain's Black Footballers', *Leisure Studies*, 16 (4): 261–77.

hooks, b. (1999) 'The Oppositional Gaze: Black Female Spectators', in S. Thornham (ed.) *Feminist Film Theory: A Reader*, Edinburgh: Edinburgh University Press.

Jarvie, G. and Reid, I. (1997) 'Race Relations, the Sociology of Sport and the New Politics of Race and Racism', *Leisure Studies*, 16 (4): 211–20.

Julien, I. and Mercer, K. (1988) 'Introduction: De Margin and De Centre', *Screen*, 29 (4): 2–11.

McCarthy, D., Jones, R. and Potrac, P. (2003) 'Constructing Images and Interpreting Realities', *International Review for the Sociology of Sport*, 38 (2): 217–38.

Sivanandan, A. (1990) *Communities of Resistance: Writings on Black Struggles for Socialism*, London: Verso.

Key concepts

228

St Louis, B. (2003) 'Sport, Genetics and the "Natural Athlete": the Resurgence of Racial Science', *Body and Society*, 9 (2): 75–95.

Van Dijk, T. (1987) *Communicating Racism: Ethnic Prejudice in Thought and Talk*, London: Sage.

Semiotics

This term refers to particular attempts to develop systematic theories of communication that examine the ways in which signs (anything that signifies) inter-relate. One controversy turns on the role of human consciousness in this activity. Semiotic approaches have led to attempts to analyse systematically the development of meaning in leisure texts (such as films or tourist brochures) and activities.

Section Outline: *Examples of semiotic analysis: the James Bond novels and movies. Main concepts in (French) semiotic analysis: examples in fashion writing, films and photographs. Tourist brochures. (American) semiotics and the analysis of common shared understandings of shopping malls or theme parks. Construct theory as a practical research application.*

I am going to begin with some examples of modern semiotic analysis (also known as semiology or structuralism) before turning to some of the underlying theories. We can see the power of the approach immediately by considering familiar examples such as the Bond movies. Bond movies have been extremely popular for four decades, and it would be very interesting to know exactly what there is about the Bond movie that has produced this success.

Some people point to a 'formula' which can be found in Bond movies. To be more precise, there might be common themes or elements, and perhaps some typical plot lines as well. If we were going to be really systematic, we might begin by seeing all the films and then try to note down the elements of the Bond formula. This would be far more systematic a method than the usual discussions about our favourite parts of Bond movies, favourite Bond girls, favourite actors or scenes.

The first systematic analysis of this kind was attempted on the Bond novels, not the films (Eco, 1979). Having examined all the Bond novels, Eco suggested that they seem to work by deploying various elements arranged as pairs of terms, or binaries, which enabled the characters to be compared and contrasted with each other. These elements included contrasts between Bond, M, the villain, and the woman; contrasting qualities such as loyalty and disloyalty, duty versus sacrifice, love versus death; and comparisons between Britain and other 'races', or the free world versus the Soviet Union. The complete list supplied all the main options that were used to carry meaning in a Bond novel. To list a few examples, the character of Bond was contrasted with the character of M to signal to the reader that Bond was a modern, rather disrespectful and challenging secret agent, while M represented the traditional values of patriotism, service, and a preference for the old ways. Bond was contrasted with the villain in almost every way – he was physically perfect, able to improvise, civilized, obeying a higher code of loyalty and morality. All the other comparisons and contrasts were used in a similar way, sometimes in clusters, so that the villain stood for the values of different 'races' and nations, and represented death instead of love.

Eco then went on to list some of the dynamics of the Bond plot. This time he identified nine major 'moves' in the overall game that was played between the characters – M moves and gives a task to Bond, the villain moves and appears to Bond, Bond offers a first check to the villain, the villain captures Bond or the woman, and so on. Having outlined the basic structure of binary elements and plot lines, Eco proceeds to suggest that there are a number of levels which one can use in analysing Bond novels. We have already seen that the plot can be considered as a game, and we can analyse characters and the values they represent, but Eco also draws attention to various literary techniques deployed by the author of the Bond novels (Ian Fleming), and the underlying ideologies (which again are classically simplified into political systems offering the binary options of good and evil, right and wrong). What gives the Bond novel its popularity is that readers recognize this structure, and can admire the way it is actually developed. The structure is flexible enough to permit a number of variations, and it is here that contemporary relevance can be introduced by the author – as international tension rose between the 'free world' and the Soviet Union, this tension could be worked out in the novel; if social change seemed to be taking place, that could be depicted, perhaps in the relationship between the men and women in the novel, and so on. We

key concepts

230

should say immediately that Eco thinks that the Bond novel is particularly clear in its use of this underlying structure.

Other analysts have found different sorts of themes or 'codes' in the Bond film in particular (Bennett, in Open University, 1982). The films developed a momentum of their own, and again it is important to emphasize the unusual production circumstances of Bond films, in that they were, with two exceptions, produced by Eon Productions. Initially, codes and forms of signification particularly relevant to the cinema had to be introduced, such as using the famous gadgets to stand for Bond's ingenuity, which is otherwise quite difficult to illustrate. As the production team became established and successful, links could be developed, so that the later films could introduce modernized themes, and comment upon the earlier films (Bennett and Woollacott, 1987). Bennett and Woollacott actually developed their later analysis from a combination of marxist, feminist and structuralist analysis, not semiotics alone, which could indicate a problem with the classic techniques.

Classic semiotic or structuralist analysis proceeded in the systematic way we have outlined. The example here is the work of Lévi-Strauss. Lévi-Straus attempted to understand and systematize existing amounts of anthropological data, including some that he had gathered himself. We examine some of the work he has done on the use of **food** and its preparation as a form of communication in another entry: just to explain briefly here, we can see the binary oppositions between types of food, especially raw and cooked food, as standing for or signifying important social matters such as the relationship between nature (raw) and culture (cooked). The clearest example of his work, though, refers to his attempt to explain the huge variety of kinship structures found in different societies across the world, which is not particularly a leisure example, but which is instructive. Again to be very brief, Lévi-Strauss (1977) proposes that all these displayed different variants of a simple underlying structure and set of values. The structure consists of the basic social relations between relatives in the same family, relatives and strangers from other families united in marriage, and parents and their offspring. These relations can either be 'cool' or 'warm' in emotional terms. The reading guide to Lévi-Strauss on my website (Harris, 2003) spells out the implications in more detail, but I hope it is already possible to see that, for example, some kinship structures (like ours) save the warmest relationships for marriage, but others save them for relationships between brothers and sisters, so much so that children tend to be raised by their maternal uncles and not by their fathers. Correspondingly, this warm relationship between adult siblings tends to be balanced by a cooler one between parents and offspring. Lévi-Strauss had found a simple underlying system of communication, using relationships and emotions as its terms, to explain what had seemed an impossibly complex system of forms of kinship that seemed to have no rational explanation at all. Such is the power of structuralist analysis.

More contemporary examples can be provided. Barthes, according to Culler (1976), set out to provide some logical structure to explain the otherwise inexplicable shifts in fashion writing. Having collected a large set of such writings, Barthes set out to show that certain binary terms were at work in them as well, turning on contrasts between and clusters among textures and colours. There was also an attempt to use the turning of the seasons to orchestrate shifts from one combination to another, as in writing about 'autumn fabrics', for example. As seasons changed, so did garments. Fashionable garments in one period turned into their opposites in the next: heavy warm fabrics gave way to light diaphanous ones, pastel colours to strong colours, single colours to tartan and tweed, and so on. Things like moods or aspects of personality can also be worked into this writing, so that a need for novelty or change can be used to introduce a new combination of the basic qualities, and if, say, sophistication is 'in' one month, its opposite, say, innocence, freshness or naturalness, can be introduced next as a natural sequence.

Not all the writings of Barthes follow this systematic approach. His work on modern 'mythologies' (Barthes, 1973) indicates other ways of making meaning, using a basic vocabulary of meaningful objects. The famous example of the analysis of a photograph of a black soldier saluting his nation's flag clearly operates at two levels. It has a literal meaning (denotation) as an illustration of what is taking place, but it also has another kind of meaning (connotation) in representing the idea of the nation, its democratic attempt to include everyone, even black soldiers, and so on. There are detectable elements of marxism in this account too, with its interest in how **ideologies** work. (The essays in this collection are just worth reading for the insights they deliver, however, without worrying too much about the implications for method.)

At this stage it is important to note that beyond this basic agreement so far, there are in fact several theories of semiotics: Eco has developed one, Barthes works with several variants, and Charles Peirce has quite a different approach (see Lechte, 1994). However, it has become common in general commentaries to focus on a particular variant, partly through the influence of the seminal Open University course on Popular Culture (Open University, 1982). This variant has certainly provided the starting point for the more recent writers we have cited. The implications are developed at the most abstract level by considering not only words, but objects, pictures and actions – all alike can be considered as acting as signs; they signify something, or in more formal terms, they are related to a signifier, a concept. Sometimes this is easy to see as when a photograph of a cat clearly signifies the concept 'cat-ness' (rather than any particular cat), or when the location of the Shire Horse Centre in Devon is indicated by a road sign which bears the outline of a horse. These are iconic signs.

For Saussurian semiotics, iconic signs are not actually the most common way to signify, however. Many signs do not have an obvious relation to their signifier at all. The actual words in English 'cat' or 'Shire Horse' do not contain any immediate clues as to what they might signify, and indeed, those concepts are described by quite different sounding words in other languages. The meaning of those signs can only be understood from seeing how they work in sequences of words. If I were trying to teach someone English, I might say 'cat' and point to a real cat or to a photograph of one, but I have other options as well. I might utter a sentence about a cat and its qualities. I might contrast cats to dogs. I might employ more poetic devices such as metaphor to illustrate 'cat-ness', perhaps by saying that a true cat is an iron spike in a velvet glove. Abstracting from these very simple examples, we can see that specific signs get their sense by the relationships developed with other signs. Their meaning might unfold in sequences, narratives, stories, or rituals (the syntagmatic or diachronic dimension, to use the jargon), or it might be revealed in a sudden sideways leap into metaphor (the paradigmatic or synchronic dimension) (see Culler, 1976).

Rather than elaborate more theory at the abstract level, we might stop and consider the implications for analysis of, say, films and how they managed to communicate with us. We might want to pay particular attention to the sequences of images and speech offered by a film, as it delivers additional meanings. We have already hinted at how the character of Bond emerges as we see him compared and contrasted with the other characters such as M, the girls, the villain, and so on. We might also want to pay particular attention to the metaphors in the film, often the visual images that we see while the action is taking place. The game of golf in *Goldfinger* is a metaphor for the overall conflict between Bond and the villain, for example, showing their attitudes to playing and winning (and thus to honour, morality and expediency). We explore some more of these devices in the entry on **narrative**. Some other work by Roland Barthes (1975) points to the way that the weather is commonly seen as a metaphor for the mood of the characters, for example; as a relationship breaks down, we see stormy weather, and so on. These narratives and metaphors themselves can be patterned, just as they are in the Bond movie, offering only a few basic options or 'codes'. Barthes notes five common ones.

Semiotic analyses of tourist brochures have developed (see Dann, 1996, for an excellent summary profusely illustrated with examples, of the range of ways in which 'sociolinguistic' analysis, including the sort of semiotics described here, have been applied). Dann has also produced several shorter and more specific analyses himself, including the one in Selwyn (1996). This piece adopts a 'dilettante approach, utilizing insights from a variety of frameworks which were found to be interesting' (Selwyn, 1996: 62-3), and begins with Dann coding the brochures he has sampled according to whether they feature photographs of tourists only, locals only, or no people at all. The analysis goes on compare the presence or absence of tourists with codes based on settings 'Beaches, transport, hotels and their surroundings, tourist sights, local scenes, entertainment, sport. . . and animals' (ibid.: 64). The codes are eventually used to describe different scenarios as 'different kinds of paradise . . . Paradise contrived . . . Paradise confined . . . Paradise controlled . . . Paradise confused' (ibid.: 67). Impressive as this analysis might be, a classic semiotician might find it lacking in rigour. It is easy to spot binaries or construct themes of this kind, on the basis of only a brief acquaintance with photographs, but the choice of themes can look rather partial. Rigorous semiotic analysis would do something rather different. As in the examples from Eco on the Bond novel, Barthes on fashion writings, or Lévi-Strauss on kinship systems and myths, there is much more involved. A proper semiotic analysis would try to identify the features common to a whole set of phenomena, and then demonstrate how all the specific variants displayed by those phenomena could be explained in terms of the basic structure.

The principles of Saussurian semiotic or structural analysis have been criticized precisely on the grounds that there may be no underlying structure to explain specific variants in sets of writings or photographs. Post-structuralist analysis starts from the principle that we should radically doubt the existence of such an underlying universal structure or foundation. There are certainly privileged or dominant structures which attempt to limit and steer meaning, but these cannot claim some privileged philosophical status. Instead, we need to ask political questions about where these underlying structures come from, whose interests they represent, and what efforts are made to maintain them as universal. We discuss some of the implications in the entry on **posts**.

Finally, it is possible to encounter another kind of semiotic analysis, this time associated not with French theory but with American, and especially the work of C.S. Peirce. I think the most useful way to approach Peirce is not through the formal work on signs and their functions (which is how Lechte, 1994, does it), but rather by considering him as interested in a 'logic of enquiry', as in Habermas (1972). Briefly, Peirce is interested in how people acquire knowledge, develop it progressively (in the interests of practical intervention primarily, according to Habermas), and how they come to develop a working consensus about the world with others (an essential step if knowledge is to progress). These interests are developed in a philosophical approach usually known as American pragmatism, and this approach has led to a good deal of sociological work, including one strand that led to **ethnography** (see Joas, in Giddens and Turner, 1987). Peirce thought the same basic procedures underpinned both the specialist efforts of scientists and logicians and the 'everyday' procedures used by non-specialists to try to understand, say, a Disney park or shopping mall (as in Gottdiener's, 1995, applications), or a tourist sight (as in MacCannell, 1989).

Thus, we all use a form of deduction and induction respectively to try to pin down a knowledge of specific cases and to establish general beliefs or 'laws' which can attract consensus. There is an important third process too, known as abduction, which offers a chance to generate new speculation or hypotheses about the world – if I know there is a general view that cities are large and anonymous, and if I have heard that shopping malls can also be large and anonymous, this leads me to wonder to what extent cities and shopping malls are alike. If there are important differences between them, I may be forced to rethink, and perhaps to supply an additional term that explains the connections between malls and cities (such as suggesting that malls are a postmodern subset of all cities). Of course, these options are never entirely personal or individual but are exercised within whole frameworks of cultural resources – this is where the different types of signs available and how they work becomes important (some function specifically to guide the formation of new knowledge, for example).

Finally, on a methodological note, there is a procedure to guide research on this practical matters which looks rather like this kind of American semiotics, although it takes a more psychological line and tends to ignore the wider social context of communication. It is usually called 'construct theory' (see Enquire Within, 2003) and it takes the form of asking people to make explicit the constructs they use to compare and contrast objects and experiences. You might begin by asking Disney visitors to compare and contrast the parks to others they have visited, for example, and note the terms they use: Disney parks might be 'American' rather 'British', 'clean' rather than 'sordid', 'family-centred' rather than 'youth-centred' or whatever. Note that the constructs involved are usually thought of as binary again. Having got a list of constructs like this, it becomes possible to see if they are shared. Their structure can also be examined – are some more important than others?; do people change their minds after visiting?; and how widespread is the change? (for example, do people reverse their judgements using the same constructs, or are they forced to develop whole new constructs?). Are there higher-order constructs that qualify the lower ones? For example, was the Disney site cleaner than cities in the old days (an historical construct 'now' versus 'then' which limits or qualifies the original)? There is a brief account of how this approach might be used to study the meanings of tourist photographs in Botterill (1989).

FURTHER READING

Dann (1996) is a well-stocked resource, not specifically on Saussurian semiotics though. The actual examples in Barthes (1973, 1975), Culler (1976), Eco (1979) or Lévi-Strauss (1977) are worth examining, and you might want to explore these first (depending on your preferred learning style). The definitive online source for semiotics is Chandler (2003), and see the book (Chandler, 2001).

REFERENCES

Barthes, R. (1973) *Mythologies*, London: Paladin.
Barthes, R. (1975) *S/Z*, London: Jonathan Cape.
Bennett, T. and Wollacott, J. (1987) *Bond and Beyond: The Political Career of a Popular Hero*, London: Macmillan Education.
Botterill, T. (1989) 'Humanistic Tourism? Personal Constructions of a Tourist: Sam Visits Japan', *Leisure Studies*, 8: 281–93.
Chandler, D. (2001) *Semiotics: The Basics*, London: Routledge.
Chandler, D. (2003) 'Semiotics for Beginners' [online] http://www.aber.ac.uk/media/ Documents/S4B/semiotic.html
Culler, J. (1976) *Structuralist Poetics*, London: Routledge and Kegan Paul.
Dann, G. (1996) *The Language of Tourism: A Sociolinguistic Perspective*, Wallingford: CAB International.
Eco, U. (1979) *The Role of the Reader: Explorations in the Semiotics of Texts*, London: Hutchinson.
Enquire Within (2003) [online] http://www.enquirewithin.co.nz/HINTS/skills2.htm
Giddens, A. and Turner, J. (eds) (1987) *Social Theory Today*, Cambridge: Polity Press.
Gottdiener, M. (1995) *Postmodern Semiotics: Material Culture and the Forms of Postmodern Life*, Cambridge, MA: Blackwell.
Habermas, J. (1972) *Knowledge and Human Interests*, London: Heinemann Educational Books Ltd.
Harris, D. (2003) 'Dave Harris (and Colleagues): Essays, Papers and Courses' [online] http://www.arasite.org/

236

Lechte, J. (1994) *Fifty Key Contemporary Thinkers; From Structuralism to Postmodernity*, London: Routledge.

Lévi-Strauss, C. (1977) *Structural Anthropology*, vol. 1, London: Peregrine Books.

MacCannell, D. (1989) *The Tourist: A New Theory of the Leisure Class*, revised edn, New York: Schocken Books.

MacCannell, D. (1992) *Empty Meeting Grounds: The Tourist Papers*, London: Routledge.

Open University (1982) *Popular Culture (U203)*, Milton Keynes: Open University Press.

Selwyn, T. (ed.) (1996) *The Tourist Image: Myths and Myth-Making in Tourism*, New York: John Wiley and Sons.

Shopping

Not all shopping is a leisure activity, but much of it can be seen as offering the characteristic pleasures. Shopping as leisure is facilitated in certain circumstances and perhaps certain locations. There are powerful economic reasons for encouraging this kind of shopping.

Section Outline: *Shopping centres and city redevelopment: post-Fordism and postmodernization. Design and theming in retail culture. Shopping malls as idealized cities. Consumerism, resistance and reinterpretation. Window shopping, symbolic politics, the uses of the mall: an ethnographic study.*

Interest in shopping as a leisure activity has emerged as a result of the growth of affluence, the economic dominance of the retail industry, and the discovery of women's leisure in leisure studies. Very often, discussion of it also takes on an additional 'policy' dimension, since as the activity changes, so do the sites, buildings and locations associated with shopping – from inner-city markets to shopping malls, for example. There are also strong links with the themes raised in discussions of consumerism, such as whether shoppers are the victims of consumer capitalism seduced by the dubious pleasures of the centres and malls into realizing the capital of the manufacturers and retailers, or whether shopping is a genuinely meaning-oriented activity, with pleasures of its own.

It is possible to focus the history of shopping development by examining one large city in the UK – Newcastle upon Tyne (Tyne and Wear Metropolitan County as it was known in the 1980s) – drawing on the account by Davies in Dawson and Dennis-Lord (1985). I do not know if this is a typical history, if indeed there is such a thing, but it will help us grasp some points. Newcastle upon Tyne and environs (the 'metropolitan county') is a city in the industrial North-East of England that used to specialize in heavy traditional industries such as coal mining and heavy manufacture including shipbuilding. These have declined dramatically in the UK in the past 25 years, leading to social effects like the decline of organized manual labour, new middle-class affluence, the growth of service industries and suburbanization. For some people, these trends are typical of economic changes in the UK, and support the case for 'post-Fordism' or 'New Times' (see **gramscianism**, and **postmodernism**). Tyne and Wear responded in several ways including undergoing a substantial redevelopment combining a new light railway transport system, new sports and athletics stadia, and a huge retail shopping centre – the Gateshead Metrocentre.

City planners in Tyne and Wear had attempted to develop retail outlets before, Davies tells us – first, local precincts, based on existing street patterns, then specially enclosed centres and finally interconnected malls with 'attractor stores'. This had been partially successful in promoting city growth as intended. Later phases included suburban developments, some funded privately, some by local government, built around the new (then) 'superstores' as anchors and attractors. New local administrative bodies (like metropolitan counties) helped consolidate and plan these developments for the whole region, which eliminated overlap and competition and also helped overcome some local residents' discontent at the constant upheavals (and at a famous scandal involving corrupt links between a prominent architect and developer, and a powerful politician). The large interconnected developments mentioned above were the final result. We can see here a growing realization of the value of shopping as an activity in its own right, capable of generating economic growth or reversing economic and population decline, offering an outlet for the new working groups entering the labour market (especially women) as traditional labour declines, and playing a major part in whole redevelopment plans based on transport, sport and leisure.

Featherstone (1991) uses the Gateshead Metrocentre as an example of postmodernization, which in this case involves the redevelopment and gentrification of inner cities. Themed and simulated environments, financed by local and global capital, act as attractors to service industries and the people who work in them, services grow up to cater for these new gentry, and the whole area rises in value – 'cultural capital' serves to generate finance and mercantile capital (see Zukin, 1990). The petite bourgeoisie benefit most – artists, intellectuals, professionals, 'yuppies' – who settle in these areas, often with gated estates and extended security devices to protect them.

For marxists, this would indicate that the old class struggle as before is still driving these events, but there are problems; the events also indicate a growing independence and flexibility of culture in our societies, offering new pleasures which are not confined only to dominant groups. Indeed, it would not make economic sense to aim to benefit just the petite bourgeoisie. Shopping is an activity that offers genuine pleasures to a wide range of people, and, indeed, must do so for economic success. At the very least, the activity must be 'open' enough to permit a wide range of people to find pleasure in it (to borrow a point made by Fiske (1987) about commercial television and its need to become populist).

As with other areas (like **heritage** or **Disneyfication**) we must turn to the issue of **pleasure** to explain the developments. Shopping has turned from being predominantly a functional activity into predominantly a pleasurable one, associated with culture and lifestyle and with the general 'aestheticization' and playfulness of life (these matters are often discussed under the broader heading of 'consumerism'). This theme has been much discussed, and there are considerable policy implications, as Gorter et al. (2003) argue in their article on the development of out-of-town shopping centres in Holland. Briefly, all will be well if those shopping centres specialize in offering the customers particular types of shopping, such as either 'fun' or 'run' shopping, to use their terms (shopping for pleasure, or shopping dedicated to the modern habit of buying large quantities cheaply). Specialization will enable a diversity of shops to survive, including those in traditional city centres – otherwise, out-of-town shopping will produce deserted inner cities.

In order to attract shoppers, especially 'fun' shoppers, pleasures have to be 'added', to the business of buying goods. As in other sections, we can consider this from the point of view of the producers and the consumers. Producers add meanings and values by designing 'themed' shopping environments, for example. Gardner and Shepherd (1989) chart the rise of the design business in retail, which grew, they claim, by 300 per cent in the 15 years before their book. Designers are no longer advisers to manufacturers and retailers, but are becoming the dominant force in retail, able to control manufacturers and persuade retailers to undertake frequent expensive transformations of their premises. This designer-generated restlessness and future orientation, and the need to cater for the needs of a fickle public (and to create these needs too) have been major factors in the move towards small-batch, networked production of consumer goods that post-Fordist theorists have discussed

A number of techniques and developments are charted by Gardner and Shepherd. The development of the distinctive generational look of 'youth', for example, began in the 1960s, and still provides a certain restlessness as each generation wants to look different from their predecessors. Thus, exotic souk-like retail interiors of trendy shops like Biba in the 1960s gives way to the uncluttered simple look of Conran and Habitat, and then to the unspecified 'concept' of Next. Segmentation also appears as the category of 'youth' itself splits into fragments (some based on **social class**). Later, 'niche' stores take this to extremes, selling only specialized 'impulse buy' items like ties (in Tie Rack), or knickers (in Knicker Box). The triumph of the design industry comes with the conversion of the big established chain stores to seeing 'design' as a key factor. These stores had always had brand names and their own designs, say Gardner and Shepherd, but in the 1980s they began to go in for substantial redesign of their premises, at least in the London showpieces – Debenhams in Oxford Street was redesigned as a galleria, others offered themed departments. Stores turned in to 'consumer pleasure domes' in a style described as 'retail theatre' (Gardner and Shepherd, 1989: 87).

The next step was to design the themed shopping mall. These have also sprouted in recent years. We can specify the key ingredients – major attractor stores, facilities for adequate transport to out-of-town sites (on cheaper land), and additional pleasures via some design and theming. Themes are often based on popular elements in leisure pursuits, such as heritage and nostalgia (what Gottdiener (1995) calls 'Ye Olde Kitsch'); holidays (Lehtonen and Mäenpää in Falk and Campbell, 1997, point out the similarities with tourism); cosmopolitan cities; hi-tech futurist; nature; exotic locations. Malls are embodiments of safe locations, pedestrianized, specially designed modern shopping environments often with air conditioning and security systems – **hyperreal** cities.

Turning to the perspective of the shoppers, we need to question whether they are simply passive victims of the designers' guile, lulled into a pleasurable mood so as to convince them to buy goods they do not really need. There are subjective pleasures on offer too, it seems. Thus, Fiske's (1989) piece on shopping takes the familiar line that shoppers are able to resist the official intentions of the designers and impose their own, often contrary meanings. The young and homeless can invade the mall, for example, and engage in a kind of cultural politics via symbolic contests with the security guards and affronted respectable shoppers. Alternatively, people can walk around and window shop or try clothes on, but not actually buy anything, taking some of the pleasures but not paying the price.

Morris's account (in During, 1993) is a different one, based on trying to explain less politicized pleasures – malls as places to visit (although the piece is written in a spirit of showing that women shoppers are not fools). Borrowing an idea from de Certeau's (1984) piece on how every walker can impose their own meanings and narratives on the cityscape as they walk, Morris argues that malls can occupy a place in local **narratives** of family reunions, or revisits to home towns, for example.

Gottdiener (1995) offers perhaps the best single account that tries to relate the economic functions of the mall to the pleasures on offer to the consumers and visitors. Shopping malls arise as part of the movement of 'deconcentration' of cities – city centres lose their functions which are dispersed into nearby (or even global) smaller locations instead. Yet shopping malls also offer an image of city centre life which has been lost, the centre as a safe public space, one devoted to play and pleasure. This simulated city space contrasts strongly with real cities outside, which are unsafe and not playful any longer (meanings work by deploying these contrasts, according to the framework Gottdiener is using, based on the **semiotics** of Peirce). The very design of (American) malls emphasizes this contrast, with their blank external walls and their inward-looking orientation. Meanings are also complemented by images provided by mass media encountered well before entry to the mall, providing visitors with a stock of intertextual meanings they can recognize once they enter (and there is a certain convergence between malls too, as designers try out already successful themes in new ones).

This intertextuality allows a certain experience of individuality, rather than a tightly closed and controlled identity for the visitor (although, as all the commentators note, there are security guards able to police or expel anyone with particularly undesirable identities). We have the basis for the main ingredients of safe pleasure here – nostalgia (including visions of restored cities in the future) and recognition. Indeed, Gottdiener argues that the mall allows us to become, for a while, the 'ideal self' of modern capitalism – the playful consumer and community member with a public life again, but this time, one structured around insistent economic imperatives. As this ideal self becomes less and less capable of being realized in the 'real world', so simulated 'themed' environments which permit it to appear become more attractive – 'the virtual self of the "amusement society", created and reproduced by the media and advertising . . . exists alone and unfulfilled until it enters the mall' (Gottdeiner, 1995: 97).

Lehtonen and Mäenpää (in Falk and Campbell, 1997) follow what looks like a very similar analysis in their account of the biggest mall in Scandinavia – the East Centre Mall near Helsinki. This mall apparently offers a sanitized version of Helsinki city centre, takes on undertones of popular Baltic cruises, and gives a chance to recreate playful sociability in its main thoroughfares. However, their work then proceeds along the classic lines of a study in **ethnography**. The visitors observed and interviewed by Lehtonen and Mäenpää seem to be able to reproduce many of the independent pleasures of city tourism, including *flâneurie* (see **hyperreality**), managing a mixture of engagement and detachment, gaining the pleasures of being able to observe things without the annoying mediations of shop assistants, and to manage shopping and sightseeing with periodic withdrawals to eat or be entertained by street performers. The mall helps punctuate people's lives, as a kind of half-way house between work and home, or day and evening. There are other pleasures too, those of managing familiarity and strangeness, just as in tourism, and, above all, of 'playful trial and anticipatory longing' (Falk and Campbell, 1997: 164).

The whole tone of the account is more active, based on the ability of visitors to **fantasise** for themselves. Shoppers may look like the docile virtual citizens of Gottdiener's account, but Lehtonen and Mäenpää suggest this may be a mask donned by skilful players. Fantasy may perhaps escape even the controls of advanced capitalism: 'In the playful street sociability, in the freedom and looseness of its anonymity and in the touristic disengagement from everyday life, can be detected '[a] . . . trance-like aspiration reaching out from the demanding self and towards other people' (ibid.: 164).

FURTHER READING

Falk and Campbell (1997) have a good collection of pieces. Ritzer (1999) has appeared in the entry on **McDonaldization**, but he includes some work on shopping malls as 'cathedrals of consumption' as part of his general thesis. Online shopping malls seem to offer still more possibilities for the development of a 'postmodern self' – see Directory Search (2003) for a database. Newitz et al. (2003) offer some online essays on shopping, and demonstrate an analytic approach (involving critical participation) associated with the Bad Subjects Project. Slater (1997) offers a useful introduction to the wider issues of consumerism.

242

Dawson, J. and Dennis-Lord J. (eds) (1985) *Shopping Centre Development: Policies and Prospects*, London and Sydney: Croom Helm.

De Certeau, M. (1984) *The Practice of Everyday Life*, Berkeley, CA: University of California Press.

Directory Search (2003) [online] http://www.directory-search.org/?c=3-1

During, S. (ed.) (1993) *The Cultural Studies Reader*, London and New York: Routledge.

Falk, P. and Campbell, C. (eds) (1997) *The Shopping Experience*, London: Sage.

Featherstone, M. (1991) *Consumer Culture and Postmodernism*, London: Sage.

Fiske, J. (1987) *Television Culture*, London and New York: Routledge.

Fiske, J. (1989) *Reading the Popular*, London: Unwin Hyman.

Gardner, C. and Shepherd, J. (eds) (1989) *Consuming Passion: The Rise of Retail Culture*, London: Unwin Hyman.

Gorter, C., Nijkamp, P. and Klamer, P. (2003) 'The Attraction Force of Out-Of-Town Shopping Malls: A Case-Study on Run-Fun Shopping in the Netherlands', *Tijdschrift voor Economische en Sociale Geographie*, 94 (2): 219–29.

Gottdiener, M. (1995) *Postmodern Semiotics: Material Culture and the Forms of Postmodern Life*, Cambridge, MA: Blackwell.

Newitz, A., Rubio, S. and Caffrey, A. (2003) 'Bad Tourists at the Mall' [online] http://eserver.org/bs/08/Newitz-Rubio-Caffrey.html

Ritzer, G. (1999) *Enchanting a Disenchanted World: Revolutionizing the Means of Consumption*, Thousand Oaks, CA: Pine Forge Press.

Slater, D. (1997) *Consumer Culture and Modernity*, Cambridge: Polity Press.

Zukin, S. (1990) 'Socio-Spatial Prototypes of a New Organization of Consumption: The Role of Real Cultural Capital', *Sociology*, 24 (1): 37–56.

Social Class

243

Social class is one of the forms of social division that have been at the heart of debates about equality, access, and social policy for some years. We discuss other main forms of social division, such as gender *and* 'race' *in other entries, and it is advisable to look at those too in order to get a fuller picture of social divisions and how they might interact. Social class divisions are classically rooted in occupation or differences in* cultural capital *or economic power. Leisure activities can both diminish and reproduce class divisions.*

Section Outline: *Social class and occupation: empirical patterns in leisure choices, measurement problems. Class and culture. Bourdieu and the shaping of 'taste' in leisure: general class 'aesthetics' and specific fractions, leisure and class distinction. Marxist views: Clarke and Critcher and the patterns of settlement and crisis in class relations, rational recreation. Social inclusion and exclusion.*

It is entirely possible to discuss these social divisions without taking any sort of immediate political position on them – to research class divisions is not necessarily to approve or disapprove. The other main problem that students often have is that they come from slightly unusual social class locations themselves, and, indeed are going through university courses which can have the effects of placing them in occupations that belong to a different social class. Sometimes they think that sociologists are offering some kind of 'bleeding-heart liberal' line on social class (or the other social divisions) and they resent being preached at. My task here is to try to get beneath these immediate perceptions and get on to the academic issues as such – how has social class been defined, and how has the concept been used to explain differences in leisure pursuits?

Social class is a controversial and much discussed concept, and some of the best arguments about it and its effects are found in other applied social science areas, especially in debates about the effects of the education system in breaking down social class barriers (for recent contributions, for example, see Saunders, 1995, for UK data, and Bowles and Gintis, 2002, for US data). The arguments often feature a good deal of empirical ('factual') data, and much debate and discussion goes on about how the terms are defined. The demonstration of empirical patterns of leisure use, and the attempt to show how these are related to social class memberships are an important area. Current British Government data on leisure pursuits are irritatingly patchy, but it is still possible, for example, to show that choice of holiday destinations do seem to be connected to occupation, and that social class seems to be connected to patterns of consumption for items like alcohol and tobacco. Even here, the figures are not entirely decisive, and indicate only limited patterns and broad trends. What is more, it is clear that other factors blur the picture – age and gender are also very important in patterning leisure choices.

Nevertheless, there is some support for the view that individual choice is not as individual as it appears, that, somehow, broad patterns of leisure choice are connected to social class memberships. In this tradition social class is defined largely in terms of occupation. This is a convenient measure, used in a lot of official UK and US research; occupation clearly affects income, wealth and purchasing power, and work conditions, including the number of holidays you are entitled to, and the amount of sheer physical effort demanded. It is reasonably easy to see how these factors might seriously limit or expand the leisure opportunities available. It is also the case, though, that occupational definitions of class are never entirely satisfactory. Where would the unemployed, or the student population be placed, for example? Notoriously, the kind of work at home that women particularly do, which is unpaid but still crucial, is also not taken into account. Indeed, the practice of taking the 'main occupation' of a family as an indicator of the social class of its members classically over-represents male occupations and has been the subject of much controversy. The same practice can also under-estimate the amount of social mobility which people undergo – the movement from one occupation to another, especially a movement 'up' the social scale. Finally, an average picture might conceal significant recent changes in the occupational system – after all, we might be combining data provided by people who started their work careers 50 years ago with those who are just in their first jobs. There are several other technical objections, well discussed in pieces like Saunders (1995).

It is easy to see how differences in income and time away from work might affect leisure choices, but social class has broader effects too. Work in the sociology of education, for example, has investigated a whole range of cultural factors associated with occupation, ranging from parental interest in school to expectations for offspring. Whole perceptions about social life, what we can expect out of it, and what we want for our children seem to be involved in social class membership. These broader factors are also prominent in the work on gender and 'race' in leisure. Perhaps what is needed is a broader investigation of cultural perceptions of leisure and the way in which they might affect people's leisure choices.

Bourdieu (1986) has completed a substantial survey-based study of general cultural tastes in France (in the 1970s), including interests in particular leisure pursuits, such as attending the cinema, eating, and doing sport. There seem to be quite different perceptions based on the membership of social groups. To summarise, Bourdieu discovered the existence of two major forms of general preferences or tastes – 'aesthetics'. Where the 'popular aesthetic' valued emotional contact, a sense of involvement, an opportunity for immediate participation, and a consequent similarity with everyday life, the 'high aesthetic' valued quite different qualities, the opposite qualities in fact. The more distanced, formal, abstract and intellectualised the cultural experience, the more it was preferred and valued in this 'high aesthetic'. These different aesthetics were associated with broader social divisions: they represented differences in 'social class'.

Bourdieu has a rather different notion of social class here and the way it affects the conduct of everyday life. It is not based on occupation alone, unlike the usual British material. As he points out, occupations themselves can also indicate gender or 'racial' composition as well – those occupations lowest in status are quite often also the ones taken up by women or people from ethnic minorities. Occupations alone are insufficient, but they do indicate some deeper structure at work. In Bourdieu (1986), we are told that cultural practice depends on a combination of two things, a 'habitus' and the ownership of various kinds of capital. To explain these terms briefly, 'habitus' refers to a set of 'dispositions' or informal categories used to describe the social world; in the case of leisure and culture, these classificatory systems appear as the different 'aesthetics' we described above. This stems from an old sociological argument that we get our ideas about the world from the social surroundings we live in when we are brought up. It is not just the ideas of our parents we inherit, but their actual practices as well – the way the family meal is organized gives us an idea of what the 'proper' differences are between men and women, for example, how they should eat and who should serve whom.

The two broad aesthetics give us two 'objective classes', abstract classes in theory, so to speak. The actual concrete picture is more complicated and depends on the type of capital we possess and how we use it. Bourdieu means by 'capital' more than just economic wealth – there is 'educational capital', 'social capital' and 'cultural capital' as well. All of these are resources which can be used to pursue leisure interests. We discuss this more in the entry on **cultural capital**. In class terms, different combinations of such capital provide further splits in the 'objective classes'. The middle classes, for example, are divided according to whether the main form of capital possessed is economic, social or educational – the former grouping represent the 'aristocratic' or traditional middle class, while the latter fall into the category of 'new middle class' or 'petite bourgeoisie'.

We are a long way already from the rather simple picture of classes as occupations, and just differences of income and time as explaining cultural differences. Tastes do not line up neatly with just income, but with something more complex, a combination of habitus and capital.

Sometimes this provides a fairly simple picture – the preferences of the working-class respondents to Bourdieu's survey for heavy 'filling' diets is easy to explain, since this is all that working-class families can afford to eat. But there is more to it. Such diets go along with a cultural preference for strong manly bodies, for simple things with no pretensions, for quantity rather than quality, for family life that values males as 'breadwinners' and allows males and females to show the 'proper' ways of eating and relating to each other. Some of these working-class tastes persist even when income rises, Bourdieu found, as in the case of some of the foremen he surveyed. As we would expect, the picture among the more fragmented middle-class groups is more complicated: those groups occupy different positions within the overall 'social space' or 'field' opened up by the various combinations. Thus one fraction has high stocks of cultural capital but low stocks of economic capital, they feature high status for women but offer them little spare time, they show a conservative attitude to culture in general, but a less conservative one towards food. Overall, the combination accounts for their taste for 'raw or grilled, healthy, natural-sweet' foodstuffs like fish and fruit, yogurt, fruit juice, jam and frozen foods. Different combinations of the same factors (such as low cultural capital but high economic capital, more spare time and high status for women) in another fraction produce a predominant taste for 'rich, strong-fatty-salty [foods], wine, spirits, aperitifs and patisserie'(Bourdieu, 1986: 186). The whole picture, an entire map of occupations, their typical tastes in the arts and politics as well as in food, and their relation to this underlying structuring combination of culture and economics, is represented in a quite beautiful diagram in Bourdieu (ibid.: 128–9). Sport is used as another example (in Bourdieu, 1993), and we discuss that in the entry on **bodies**.

Bourdieu has been accused of wanting to explain everything by using these sociological factors (a flaw which is sometimes called 'sociologism'). One aspect which is worth noting is that this relentlessly sociological approach does at least claim to be an improvement on even more simplistic approaches, such as those which claim to identify some underlying human essence behind all the diverse leisure practices, as expressed in notions like 'man' as 'homo ludens' (see Kew in Mangan and Small, 1986).

No one habitus can possibly be self-sufficient in accounting for new cases, of course, and so some active reinforcement of distinctions must occur as new leisure pursuits arise. Bourdieu knows that the commercialization of leisure puts more opportunities in the way of consumers, and presumably they must experiment a bit before they find the latest offerings 'to their taste' or not. Do particular electronic games offer the sort of 'weightlessness' and intellectualized challenge suitable for petite bourgeois groups, or the kind of immediate emotional involvement and vulgar enjoyment favoured by the traditional working class? People also enjoy social mobility as they take on new occupations, and they have to modify their tastes in order to achieve some harmony or reconciliation between the old tastes and the new. They may even choose to manage their tastes as a matter of 'pure choice', as do some fractions of the petite bourgeoisie again – my favourite examples are those who value abstractness and 'weightlessness' (sometimes quite literally as in their fondness for ballet) as a kind of metaphor for their position (they wish to be 'socially weightless' as Bourdieu puts it).

A more active definition of social class is also found in this work. The fact that the high aesthetic is the precise opposite of the popular one is no accident. The high aesthetic is cultivated deliberately to separate a social group out and raise it above the common level, to claim a superior social status. Kew (in Mangan and Small, 1986) argues that this is a useful emphasis too in questioning the simplistic views that say that sport and leisure unite people in a common interest. This argument is often found in government thinking, as in the 'Sport for All' policies of the 1980s, and the interest in sport for 'social inclusion' in the current period. For all the writers summarized here, to participate in leisure and sport is also to be exposed to discrimination and closure based on social class (and gender and 'race').

We know from British examples of the early modern period that maintaining social distance was an important function of 'culture' or 'cultivation' among the upper classes in Britain as well. More vulgar classes might have begun to acquire equal incomes and wealth, but the true aristocracy had 'culture'; they demonstrated this by being 'literary' or 'artistic' for example, both involving activities which require considerable leisure time and a stock of cultural capital. This sort of argument is also found in study of the 'leisure class', a group which marked itself off from others by its conspicuous pursuit of leisure activities. Leisure does not just reflect social class membership, but is used to indicate and support it because people use their leisure pursuits to make a statement about the social classes to which they belong. Rojek's work (2001) on celebrity explores this further, although his conclusion is that modern celebrities are too diverse and too transitory to form a social class as such.

There is yet another way in which social class has come to be used to understand leisure patterns, and this one turns on a marxist notion of social class. This particular notion is also much broader than the focus on occupations, and refers to the whole economic structure of modern society, or capitalism as marxists prefer to call it. Here, the ownership of economic capital is at the heart of all the other factors which appear to affect leisure. The argument is that capitalism features the systematic exploitation of labour at the heart of its amazing ability to deliver economic growth. This exploitation need not be blatant and unpleasant any more, but it has not disappeared. Given that exploitation lies at the heart of the system, it becomes possible to divide people into two fundamental social classes (exploiters and exploited), which take the particular form in capitalism of capitalists (those who own capital including factories, stocks and shares, and land as well as money in the bank), and proletariat (those who own only the labour power that gets exploited by capitalists). In fact, Marx himself recognizes that there might be other social classes in any actual social formation, including the remnants of earlier forms of production, such as peasants. Yet the two classes I have described remain fundamental, in several senses. This is one reason why class division of this kind can never be reformed away in capitalism, according to marxists, unlike the other forms of social division (based on gender or 'race') which we discuss (although they have their own arguments to claim that they are fundamental as well).

In the fairly recent past, the conflict between these two social classes was open and transparent, involving strong capitalist pressure to control the mass of the exploited people through means which included parliamentary legislation, religious justification, slavery, and colonialism, although even then there were periods of relative social peace. There is still a need to preserve this fundamentally exploitative relation, but modern societies have a battery of social control techniques to supplement the use of naked force. These techniques include various kinds of **ideology** – sets of beliefs or practices which have the effect of making capitalist societies look fair, natural, or inevitable. The development of organized leisure can be understood precisely in this way, as a series of social control techniques to regulate opposition to capitalism and also to help make it seem universal and natural. The link between the emphasis on competition in sport, and competition as a central feature of capitalist production and innovation is an obvious target for suspicion.

One of the best arguments to examine here is provided by the work of Clarke and Critcher (1985). Their historical accounts of the growth of leisure chart a background series of 'settlements' and 'crises' in the struggles between the social classes. The period of 'rational recreation' is perhaps the most famous example. Clearly, from the point of view of a dominant capitalist class, there is considerable danger in allowing working-class males to congregate together in groups, or 'mobs', and engage in drunkenness and rowdy behaviour. Hence the need to prevent or discourage 'traditional football', or the more rowdy activities associated with drunkenness, and to license gatherings of various kinds whether in the streets or in 'sites of disorder' such as fairs, carnivals or football matches. Sometimes such activities were prohibited by law, or at other times substituted by more acceptable, usually more commercialized, alternatives – professional football, cinemas instead of music halls, home-based entertainment, anything that would get working-class males 'off the streets and under control'.

Signs of social class domination in this sense affect modern leisure pursuits as well, and Clarke and Critcher do much to uncover the deep structures of the modern leisure industry. What appears to be individual choice reflects the flexible commercialization of leisure. People think they are choosing to watch a particular television programme, or to drink a particular brand of ale, but they are merely fulfilling their role as customers. Indeed, the role of the individual in leisure shows an increasing disempowerment, from participant to customer to consumer.

The work of other marxist writers such as Adorno on the paradoxes of leisure as 'free time' (see **work–leisure relationships**) is also important. Marxist analysis is a powerful perspective which can offer a very plausible account of a wide range of phenomena. However, its very power makes it difficult to argue with or refute, much as we saw with Bourdieu. The demand for actual evidence of the existence of class domination is not easy to reconcile with a view that says empirical evidence only describes the surface features of leisure, where what is needed is an analysis of the deeper mechanisms beneath the surface. Empirical data may show a considerable diversity of social class groupings and social mobility, but the root structure of capitalism, the exploitative relation that lies at its heart has not changed for marxists, even though the personnel involved might now be different. This 'surface/depth' metaphor is found in other analyses too, as we shall see, and is an important one to consider. Major criticisms of it are also found in the entries on **figurationalism** and **posts**.

FURTHER READING

I have reading guides to some of the key Marxist texts (including Marx and Clarke and Critcher) on my website (Harris, 2003). The debate between Saunders and his critics, and the latest study by Bowles and Gintis are also available in note form there. Bourdieu's (1986) classic text is worth reading for several of the debates cited in other sections. Rather disappointing empirical online data about leisure, usually rendered in terms of 'social grade' or 'income slices', is available for Britain from National Statistics (2003).

REFERENCES

Bourdieu, P. (1986) *Distinction: A Social Critique of the Judgement of Taste*, London: Routledge.

Bourdieu, P. (1993) *Sociology in Question*, London: Sage.

Bowles, S. and Gintis, H. (2002) '*Schooling In Capitalist America* Revisited', *Sociology of Education*, 75 (2): 1–18.

Clarke, J. and Critcher, C. (1985) *The Devil Makes Work. . . Leisure in Capitalist Britain*, London: Macmillan.

Harris, D. (2003) 'Dave Harris (and Colleagues): Essays, Papers and Courses' [online] http://www.arasite.org/

Mangan, J. and Small, R. (eds) (1986) *Sport, Culture and Society: International, Sociological and Historical Perspectives: Proceedings of the VII Commonwealth and International Conference on Sport, PE, Dance, Recreation and Health*, London: Spon Ltd.

National Statistics (2003) [online] http://www.statistics.gov.uk/statbase/Product.asp?vlnk=5748&More=N

Rojek, C. (2001) *Celebrity*, London: Reaktion Books.

Saunders, P. (1995) 'Might Britain Be a Meritocracy?', *Sociology*, 29 (1): 23–41.

Virtual Leisure

251

Any leisure activity using access to the Net or Web is included in the definition of virtual leisure here. There are also forms which are only practically possible via the Net or Web – instantaneous chat, virtual reality, immediate access to leisure materials (including some illegal ones), online communities. The last example links with the use of 'virtual' social realities in social theory.

Section Outline: The Web and the Net as embodying postmodernist leisure: the collapse of internal boundaries and hyperreality. Identity, gender, cyborgs and the Net. Constraints in flexible electronic identities. Virtual possibilities and online (leisure) communities.

Although the early stages of the Internet may have been dominated by military and then educational users, developments such as the World Wide Web mark a shift towards much more decentred and non-hierarchical uses, including uses for leisure. It is not necessary to demonstrate the popularity of browsing the Web, or actually chart its phenomenal growth in the last few years, nor to point out that access is still limited to affluent users, and probably to English speakers. As usual, we shall be trying in this entry to explain the pleasures on offer to those who browse it, and to explore its uses for leisure.

Browsing the Web has been discussed using approaches associated with **postmodernism**, and, indeed, has been seen as a characteristic postmodern development (see Rojek, 1995). In the relevant entry, we suggest that one defining characteristic involves the collapse of boundaries between formerly separate activities and roles. Many enthusiasts have suggested that this is precisely what is offered by electronic communication, through e-mail, bulletin boards, conferences and lists (including multi-user sites such as MUDs or MOOs), web-browsing, and, these days, web logs and person-to-person transfer protocols. It is easy see how boundaries might have collapsed, especially the ones that had separated people by distance, age, nationality (as long as they speak the same language), status or role. E-mail in particular has the astonishing ability to be both immediate and yet subject to control, far more immediate than postal contacts, and far less intrusive than telephone calls. Electronic participation in discussion groups permits far more control over what you choose to reveal to others about yourself: participants can remain anonymous, or can choose to adopt artificial personae ('avatars').

It is still possible to contact celebrities, and even celebrity academics, in ways which would not have been possible in the past (in my view, that is because, luckily, American etiquette, not British, dominates the Net). In academic life, barriers can be broken down between writers, readers and publishers, with the establishment of participatory websites, such as my own (Harris, 2003), which simply ignores the organizational boundaries between academic specialists, and those between lecturers and students. Web browsing offers a delightful chance to transcend cultural boundaries, as one chooses a site on French philosophy, offering the collector a chance finally to access Lacan's Paris seminars (Lacan, 2003), and then turns to Ebay offering a chance to buy British motorcycle memorabilia by way of cultural relief. This abundance promises to end monopolies, and even reverse commodification by offering free resources, whether we are talking about academic courses or pornography.

The freedom and pleasures of Web browsing and electronic

communication have been celebrated by a number of writers, especially those interested in the formation of identities. Feminists such as Turkle (1995) or Haraway (2003) have offered exhilarating outlines of the possibilities offered to transcend the normal constraints on **identity**. Further implications arise for the ability to transcend the limits of **bodies**, to adopt a novel disembodied identity (see Braidotti, 2003). At the same time, of course, female bodies have never been more on display with the astonishing growth of pornographic sites. The issue of possible adverse effects on users and the women themselves is discussed in the entry on **pornography**, but Web-based pornography has specific dimensions. For one thing, it becomes almost impossible for any state to regulate access, at least until the rumoured surveillance technology (such as the 'clipper chip') becomes available. For another, Web-based pornography raises anew some interesting moral problems – as Miah (2000) asks, for example, is engaging in interactive cybersex the same as adultery?

There is no need for women to remain trapped in a conventional gender identity when they communicate electronically. Their bodies are no longer up front and on display, always ready to be used to make judgements. Their imaginations can run free in cyberspace, and they can experiment and play. Even the old cultural boundaries between human beings, animals and machines can be dissolved, as we all experience becoming 'cyborgs':

> The cyborg is a kind of disassembled and reassembled postmodern other and personal self. This is the self feminists must code. . . . Cyborg imagery can suggest a way out of the maze of dualisms in which we have explained our bodies . . . to ourselves. (Haraway, 2003: 163)

Communication networks are now the basis of social relations for Haraway, involving a move away from the 'comfortable old hierarchical dominations'. Women must still struggle to realize the possibilities, however, to develop a 'powerful infidel heteroglossia' (ibid.: 181) based on their multiple identities. The futuristic and utopian possibilities foretold in creative genres such as 'cyberpunk' can be realized and concretized in the privacy of our own homes. It is not only women who would benefit of course, but anyone trapped by their physical identities, including males, the aged, people from ethnic minorities (Haraway has a whole entry on 'women of colour'), the disabled, and so on. To illustrate specific possibilities, 'photoblogs' offer the ability for women to enjoy the pleasures of *flâneurie* (discussed in the entry on **hyperreality**), which they were unable to do in real cities.

253

Of course, there are problems and reservations as well. Early criticism of the more playful statements worked with the view that there was something unique and paramount about actual face-to-face interaction, and that essential human qualities would be lost by electronic communication. Of course, in some ways, this was the whole point, since face-to-face interaction also permits stereotyping, labelling and linguistic dominance, and it would sometimes be a relief to dispense with these. This argument can also be seen as largely redundant, now that electronic communication is so widespread, at least in the affluent West; just as Baudrillard (1983) suggests, there is no point in lamenting the eclipse of the real because hyperreality has triumphed, so we might argue that it has been a very long time indeed since face-to-face interaction carried most of the communication between us. This argument is sometimes associated with the view that electronic communication lacks emotional content. Again, this could be a relief, of course, but I also believe myself that is simply untrue – the combination of anonymity and intimacy offered by email often permits complete strangers to indulge in considerable displays of emotion, including interpersonal warmth. To argue this from the other direction, I am aware of university-sponsored electronic communications that take great care to remind people of their obligations not to exceed the instrumental functions required, not to flirt, not to abuse or intimidate, not to 'flame'.

Another set of reservations turn on the realization that electronic communication offers its own form of constraint. It is true that 'body language' and clues provided by verbal tone or accent may be absent, but this does not imply the removal of all the other conventions, such as those of vocabulary, fluency, grammar, syntax, the ability to use 'standard' English or local argot, and the everyday knowledge they can display. Differences in age, nationality, ethnic origin, and social class, at least in terms of the amounts of **cultural capital** revealed, are equally difficult to suppress in electronic as well as face-to-face conversation.

Gender can also reveal itself quite easily in the actual structure and content of the e-talk that goes on, according to Herring (2003a). Herring's own research collected contributions to academic discussion groups (ten years ago), and found significant differences between men and women in terms of the amount (men made far more contributions, while women seemed to be intimidated or excluded more often); topic (more information-related topics for men and personal-related topics for women); and manner of the communication ('rhetorical and linguistic strategies' employed included apologies and humour for women, and assertiveness and sarcasm for men). Herring concludes that the formal

---

Virtual Leisure

possibilities of unrestrained communication are limited by the conventions and 'genderlects' (gendered dialects) brought over from everyday social life.

Perhaps all is well as long as conversation is confined to either instrumental discussion (a seminar), or to uncommitted light chat, but the more topics are covered, the greater the risk of exposing one's real identity. It may even be the case that participants are now fully aware of the prospect that the person that they are chatting to is not what they seem. It would be interesting to see if special kinds of 'sincerity checks', or, to use more formal terms, the raising of validity claims will develop in electronic forms of communication as much as they do in face-to-face interactions. It seems just as likely that electronic chatters will monitor responses for consistency, compare actual with predicted responses, question motives, set tests and use all the other devices with which we are accustomed to check each other out. Perhaps readers of this entry would like to try for themselves entering a chat room with a completely different identity, and recording how easy it is to maintain it.

These reservations and problems suggest that electronic communication is really not that different from conventional communications, either face-to-face, or as mediated through more familiar technology such as telephones and letters. The field has been dominated from the beginning by exaggerated claims, and announcements of imminent breakthroughs, usually based on some dubious and naïve evolutionary view of social formations and what makes them change (see, for example, Pask and Curran, 1982, for an early cyborg theory). This is also the view of Miah (2000), who suggests that the claims made for the creative breakthroughs of virtual reality especially are much exaggerated, as much as the constant promises of new technology (such as 'teledildonics'). If 'virtual reality' involves a claim that experience can now be mediated through electronic media, then all human communication is virtual reality, unless we are prepared to accept that human beings once communicated through a more privileged medium, such as sense data. We challenge the privilege accorded to sense data in the entry on **fantasy**, and argue that it is as mediated as any other kind of knowledge of the world.

A final meaning of 'virtual' might allude to the almost infinite possibilities of contact with others offered by cyberspace, any example of which can be readily actualized. I think there is something in this view, since the speed of access alone is quite different. As an academic, acquiring access to journal articles would take weeks or months before electronic publication, and I am free to browse scores of sites in one evening (broadband technology really has made a difference here). At the same time, some social theorists have argued that conventional human societies themselves are only a mere actualization of a much larger set of 'virtual' possibilities (Bhaskar, 1989, and Giddens, via the discussion of 'structuration', in Giddens, 1982, for example, are perhaps the best-known advocates of this view). Nevertheless, we can advance an argument used before to suggest that leisure activities offer much more room for experiment than conventional societies. For example, online communities, the best-known of which perhaps is LambdaMOO (MOO Homepage, 2003), have pioneered new thoughts about living in communities. Bromberg (in Shields, 1996) describes her participation and the pleasures it provided, in terms of identity play, erotic appeal, and mastery over the environment. Recent events have shown that participation in LambdaMOO involves some conventional risks too, including the 'first on-line rape' (Miah, 2000).

It might be more interesting to inquire about the conventions that lead specific browsing or communicating individuals into particular channels and possibilities, which help them to manage the enormous abundance and saturation of information on the Web. Again, this problem is clear in an academic context – of all the websites on a particular topic, how on earth can the actual browser decide which ones offer useful or valid knowledge? (On this particular topic, Internet Detective, 2003, offers some useful advice.) More generally, the Web offers us a concrete example of the abstract problems of relativism, again raised best by discussions of postmodernism. To put this in the terms I tried to develop in Harris (1996), we know that there are considerable trends towards cultural relativism represented by the huge number of options available on the Web, but no-one can live in a condition of full relativism, so what forces stabilize this position for actual actors?

FURTHER READING

There are many useful articles online on gender, identity and the Web – Herring (2003b) and SocioSite (2003), for example. Shields (1996) is a bit dated but still useful for raising the issues. Haraway's 'Manifesto' (Haraway, 2003) is a classic. You can still discover the dynamics of LambdaMOO (MOO Homepage, 2003 – FAQs especially). Thornton (2003) reviews some useful recent material on democracy and the Internet.

REFERENCES

Baudrillard, J. (1983) *Simulations*, London: Semiotext(e).

Bhaskar, R. (1989) *Reclaiming Reality*, London: Verso.

Braidotti, R. (2003) [1996] 'Cyberfeminism with a Difference', *New Formations* 29: 9–25, and [online] http://www.let.uu.nl/womens_studies/

Giddens, A. (1982) *Profiles and Critiques in Social Theory*, London: Macmillan.

Haraway, D. ([1991]2003) 'A Cyborg Manifesto: Science, Technology, and Socialist-Feminism in the Late Twentieth Century' [online] http://www.stanford.edu/dept/HPS/Haraway/CyborgManifesto.html

Harris, D. (1996) *A Society of Signs?*, London: Routledge.

Harris, D. (2003) 'Dave Harris (and Colleagues): Essays, Papers and Courses' [online] http://www.arasite.org/

Herring, S. ([1993]2003a) 'Gender and Democracy in Computer-Mediated Communication' [online] http://ella.slis.indiana.edu/~herring/ejc.txt

Herring, S. (2003b) [online] http://www.slis.indiana.edu/faculty/herring/

Internet Detective (2003) [online] http://www.sosig.ac.uk/desire/internet-detective.html

Lacan, J. (2003) 'The Seminars of Jacques Lacan' [online] http://www.lacan.com/seminars1a.htm

Miah, A. (2000) 'Virtually Nothing: Re-Evaluating the Significance of Cyberspace', *Leisure Studies*, 19 (3): 211–24.

MOO Homepage (2003) [online] http://www.moo.mud.org/

Pask, G. and Curran, S. (1982) *Micro Man: Living and Growing with Computers*, London: Century Books.

Rojek, C. (1995) *Decentring Leisure: Rethinking Leisure Theory*, London: Sage.

Shields, R. (ed.) (1996) *Cultures of Internet: Virtual Spaces, Real Histories, Living Bodies*, London: Sage.

SocioSite (2003) [online] http://www2.fmg.uva.nl/sociosite/

Thornton, A. (2003) 'Does Internet Create Democracy?' [online] http://www.zip.com.au/~athornto//

Turkle, S. (1995) *Life on the Screen: Identity in the Age of the Internet*, New York: Simon and Schuster.

257

— Visitor Interpretation —

There is a common view that managers of tourist and heritage sites or museums should make their sites more popular and attractive – hence the rise of visitor interpretation. Materials are displayed, routes are designed and sites reconstructed in order to assist the visitor in understanding the experience and gaining additional pleasures. The techniques are controversial and may involve the sacrifice of authenticity or historical accuracy.

> **Section Outline: Adding value** for commercial and professional reasons. **Postmodernism.** Techniques and links with the media and with education. Management checklists and procedures. Visitor involvement and visitor re-interpretation.

Visitor interpretation has become a growth area in leisure and tourism in recent years, especially in **heritage** sites and museums. In one of those ironic collapses of distinctions attributed to **postmodernism**, there has been interest from both academic researchers and site managers. Academic analyses of the **ideology** of heritage sites or of the tourist **gaze** can be used to expose the values in leisure and tourism, and might enable visitors to engage in some sort of critical analysis or ironic resistance. Yet the same analyses can be used quite differently, by practitioners interested in constructing those controlling narratives in the first place.

In practitioner terms, 'values' can be 'added' to existing sites, to broaden their appeal and attractiveness, to deliver to visitors a sense of involvement and to satisfy a range of visitor interests in a single visit. Thus, if a customer survey shows that visitors to a heritage site are interested variously in history, in educating their children to current British Government standards, in spectacular views, or in architecture, it is a sensible step to try and 'add' those interests in some way. This might be achieved by adding display materials both outside the site and, perhaps, in special displays inside. These materials would offer a popular history of the site, materials for school history projects, selected places for viewing the site and its environs, panels on architectural details, interactive materials to engage children in exploration, and so on.

This sort of thing is not new, but there is recent interest in the techniques for adding such values in a popular (perhaps a populist) way, partly to meet the professional demands for 'liveliness' in presentation, and the development of commercial potential. The older conventions of display and presentation have been perceived to be out of date. It is inevitable that the new presentational techniques should draw heavily on the mass media including using ethnographic studies of the audience, and narrative techniques of the display material (organized under categories like 'thematics', 'poetics' and 'rhetoric') (Silverstone, in Uzzell, 1989). Themes and techniques might also be borrowed from popular culture, and even from modern educational practice.

Thus, we find materials developing strong and conventional narratives and representations to organize the visitors' perceptions, perhaps at the expense of historical accuracy as historians perceive it. Visitor materials tell pleasurable stories about the site, they popularize those stories using techniques such as personification (people tell their 'own' stories), or by using popular stereotypes (of cheery English peasants or rugged frontiersmen), and they guide the visitor around the site from one element in the **narrative** to the next – we might begin with the early settlements, move to a display on a day in the life of an inhabitant or of a visiting dignitary, then on to the next popular period (the English Civil War, say), then on to more recent times such as the Second World War, and so on. Inconvenient elements can be minimized as well; thus, the great British hero Sir Francis Drake is acknowledged to have been in the slave trade, in one local heritage site (Buckland Abbey – see below), but in a fairly obscure piece of display material. The entry on **heritage** discusses the problems in depicting (or even omitting) unfortunate historical facts such as mass disease or squalor to casual visitors who are on holiday.

The display materials might use visual elements (perhaps even video tape or CD) and audio (as in the cassette commentary) to use the site to develop an even more real (perhaps a **hyperreal**) experience for the visitor. The style overall can look very much like that of a propaganda movie extolling the selected virtues of national history in order to involve the people in the struggle against the foe, but as the borrowings from media continue, we might expect to find more subtle 'persuasive' forms emerging, possibly involving the use of 'realist narrative', or moving on to subtleties like those displayed in Nike advertisements (see **adding leisure values**). (For a useful discussion of propagandist and persuasive techniques, see Jowett and O'Donnell, 1999).

As any educator knows, some controlled audience involvement is essential, and this can be attempted by starting with existing visitors' knowledge (perhaps of some of the myths surrounding the site – Robin Hood for Sherwood Forest and Nottingham, to cite a well-known example, discussed in Rojek, 1993). A form of 'discovery' as participation might be offered as visitors are invited to find items for themselves (as in 'treasure hunts') or to complete quizzes. Different media might be selected to pursue particular functions – cassette or CD audio commentaries enable visitors to exercise more control of pace or of topic than video displays, and audio commentary is often seen as more 'atmospheric'. Interactive electronic displays test knowledge or enable the pursuit of 'individualized' enquiries. Learning, for children, needs to be 'active', to use the key word, and is disguised as entertainment, just as in schools broadcasting (*Sesame Street*, say, or in the long-running British TV show *Blue Peter*). Learning materials provided at British sites might also be designed deliberately to conform to the stages of the National Curriculum.

There are implications for visitor management, of course. Distractions from the careful narratives and possibly contradictory experiences should be carefully managed in an overall 'visitor plan', which might begin with designing the drive to the site and the car parks, and include those occasions when visitors step back into real life (when they visit the toilets or shop). Facilities are landscaped, and staff have to be trained to avoid poor impressions and to greet visitors with politeness and that essential smile. Disney sites are often seen as world leaders here, of course, especially the Florida site with its huge expanse of land under the control of the Disney Company, its tightly designed routes through the parks and its control of visitor vistas, and its legendary staff training programmes (see **Disneyfication**).

The British examples can seem rather obsessive and uncritical, however. Laws (1998) provides an exhaustive checklist for managers to help them monitor their site closely. Some of the contributors to Uzzell (1989) seem quite authoritarian too. Rick suggests covert observation, designed to weed out any staff who display uncooperative non-verbal behaviours such as 'shuffling feet' (in Uzzell, 1989: 126); Shettel argues that visitors should be surveyed and tested; Stoep suggests taking time-lapse photographs to estimate visitor damage to the site. Parkin (in Uzzell, 1989) suggests extensive landscaping of the areas surrounding a heritage site, even if it is in the middle of a town – which really is approaching the practice of turning whole places of residence into theme parks for visitors.

Although there has been a great deal of work on the design of visitor materials, there has been little research so far on what the visitors actually make of them. In media studies, there is a great deal of interest in the 'active viewer', who can positively reinterpret the narratives and representations offered in a television programme (see Ang, 1996). One source for much of this reinterpretive power lies in the huge number of other texts that each viewer has consumed, so that the 'preferred meaning' of a film has to battle with lots of alternative and equally plausible ones delivered with equal skill in other texts. It is quite possible to see this happening with tourist and leisure sites too, as Urry's (1990) work on the ironic tourist suggests. Ironic and sceptical tourists might be one outcome, but apathetic and jaded tourists is another, as the touring and visiting public get weary of encountering endlessly skilful communication aimed at 'adding value' to their visits, and sink into the 'black hole' of non-communication predicted by Baudrillard (see

260

hyperreality). My website (Harris, 2003) contains some work on the intended interpretational strategies designed to popularize a local heritage site (Buckland Abbey). The material is dated, but it is still possible to see the dangers of overdoing the strategic communication, as heavy-handed messages are drawn for the state of Britain today and the need to develop individualism and welcome social change.

FURTHER READING

There are some useful case studies and examples in Uzzell (1989) (both volumes, but especially volume 2). Shackley (1998) describes the issues in the broader context of visitor management. Harris (2003) has the example of the local heritage attraction with some detailed examples of the materials used. Some of the suggested reading for the other sections might be useful too – from the entries on **narratives** or **pleasures**, for example.

REFERENCES

Ang, I. (1996) *Living Room Wars: Rethinking Media Audiences for a Postmodern World*, London: Routledge.
Harris, D. (2003) 'Dave Harris (and Colleagues): Essays, Papers and Courses' [online] http://www.arasite.org/
Jowett, G. and O'Donnell, V. (1999) *Propaganda and Persuasion*, 3rd edn, London: Sage.
Laws, E. (1998) 'Conceptualizing Visitor Satisfaction Management in Heritage Settings: An Exploratory Blueprinting Analysis of Leeds Castle, Kent', *Tourism Management*, 19 (6): 545–54.
Rojek, C. (1993) *Ways of Escape*, London: Macmillan.
Shackley, M. (ed.) (1998) *Visitor Management: Case Studies from World Heritage Sites*, Oxford: Butterworth-Heinemann.
Urry, J. (1990) *The Tourist Gaze: Leisure and Travel in Contemporary Societies*, London: Sage.
Uzzell, D. (ed.) (1989) *Heritage Interpretations: The Natural and Built Environment* (vols 1 and 2), London: Belhaven Press.

261

Work–Leisure Relationships

Leisure is often defined as the opposite of work in several senses, but this is too simple and ignores the connections between the two sorts of activity. Several other definitions of leisure are tried out in other entries of this book by contrast, e.g. in the entry on figurationalism.

Section Outline: Assumptions about work and about 'free time'. Parker on the relations between occupations and leisure. Work-like leisure: commercialization and rationality in leisure. Work as leisure in **postmodernism**: 'serious leisure', the role of **fantasy**, escape, irony, 'flow' and the work environment.

The relations between work and leisure have been central to discussions in leisure studies from the beginning. This is quite often the first topic which undergraduates begin to discuss, because it reveals an instructional difference between academic analyses of leisure and 'common sense'. When asked to define 'leisure', most people invoke a contrast with work, so that leisure is something that goes on in 'free time', away from the need to attend the factory or office. Leisure is something that follows personal interest and choice, unlike the experience of being under the control of bosses or timetables. Leisure is a matter of self-expression and pleasure, whereas work involves compulsion, conformity, and the deferment of pleasure.

I think it is possible to see even from this early list, however, that there are substantial assumptions involved. It seems as if it is work that is the important partner, and leisure something trivial or too personal to worry about. Conversely, seeing leisure as the repository of all the 'nice' values relies on possibly outdated conceptions of work as alienating, and can only lead to dissatisfaction in leisure, since it is being asked to bear the whole burden of aspirations towards freedom and pleasure. There are more technical problems as well.

We can begin by examining some of the assumptions made about work. Is work an activity dominated by compulsion, control, discipline, and lack of freedom? The answer might well turn on deciding what sort of work we are talking about. The kind of manual labour that involves daily attendance in a large anonymous factory, servicing noisy and relentless machines attached to a conveyor belt might fit this description, but other kinds of work clearly offer more freedom and autonomy. Middle-class occupations, such as university academic, might seem to qualify here, but so do a range of manual occupations, which are often much sought-after because they do offer some freedom, such as driving jobs or self-employed sub-contracting in some skilled trade. Even factory work has its moments of autonomy and freedom, as a number of studies show (a famous one is Haraszti, 1977). The point is also made clearly in Parker's classic work (1983). Some demanding manual tasks, such as deep-sea fishing or coal-mining tend to produce an 'oppositional' leisure pattern, where the values of work are reversed, and irresponsible pleasure-seeking tends to dominate. On the other hand, for middle-class office work, leisure 'extends' the values of work, and complements them, so that work requiring a great deal of self-direction and autonomy tends to lead to leisure that does the same, as in the well-known tendency for business executives to play golf. Parker also notices a 'neutral' pattern, where work does not exert sufficient impact on people's lives to affect their leisure at all.

Parker's work is also well known for pointing out that 'free time' is not the same as leisure. Time away from work is actually devoted to a number of tasks, including sleeping, eating, routine activities with families, and meeting the basic physiological requirements. In order to isolate leisure as such, we need a more positive definition, Parker argues. Incidentally, he is also well aware that one of the things that women do in their 'free time' is to work at the maintenance of the household, to engage in 'unpaid domestic labour' as feminists were to call it. We have mentioned the importance of this activity before, in the entry discussing **gender** differences. It is the requirement to engage in unpaid domestic leisure that marks women's experience of leisure, so that they tend to think of 'leisure' as that rather small amount of time which is left after both paid and unpaid work.

It is true, however that men also engage in a certain amount of unpaid domestic labour in their 'free time' too, as Moorhouse (in Rojek, 1989) argues. This includes what might be called nowadays 'serious leisure' (Stebbins, 1982), which involves the pursuit of a hobby, or the exercise of a skill (Moorhouse's example of voluntarily restoring old railway engines would be a good example). Moorhouse even suggests that housework and child rearing can reveal some leisure qualities as well. The question really is whether there is a significant difference to the individual and to the experience arising from being paid for some activities and not others.

Some of the other entries in this book suggest that leisure has become penetrated by the norms and ideals of work. This is seen clearly in commercial leisure, where major companies do their best to '**add leisure values**' to their products or to organize the rational production of leisure goods (as in **McDonaldization**, for example). It has long been realized that one person's leisure is another person's work, and it is clear that a great deal of work lies behind the provision of '**authentic**' encounters for tourists, or the management of **escape** experiences. Leisure activity itself has become penetrated by work-like relations, according to some commentators, so that people attempting to cultivate their bodies as a form of self-expression by working out in a gymnasium will encounter a **disciplinary apparatus**, a work-like regime with specific tasks and objectives, and a constant supervisory presence. Even sexual activity has become work-like according to the notorious Hite report (Hite, 1981), and young American males in particular develop considerable anxiety about their performance statistics and the need to satisfy their partners. The pornography industry also shows precisely how sex can become work. Adorno (1991) expresses the same reservations about the whole concept of 'free time', suspecting that it really is a chance to rehearse the values needed for work, and the same suspicion lingers in the use of terms such as 'recreation', especially 'rational recreation', which involved an attempt to develop leisure activities that kept the workforce healthy and fit (and, incidentally, minimized absenteeism at the start of the week or after bank holidays).

If leisure has been penetrated by work, some analysts argue that the reverse has also occurred. Perhaps Rojek is the most consistent advocate of the view that the work–leisure relation has been broken by the development of late modernity or **postmodernism**; to use the terms we outlined in that entry, the boundary between work and leisure has collapsed. Postmodernism has offered a tremendous variety of leisure materials and options and made them available and accessible to anyone with a television set or PC. As a result, it becomes possible to add leisure values for ourselves, to engage in leisure-based **fantasies**, for example, even while we are at work. These moments may be fleeting, but some of the best leisure moments always have been, and the pleasure and satisfaction are just as real. Apart from the more obvious kinds of fantasy,

Work–Leisure Relationships

postmodernism also offers the possibility of a whole range of pleasures associated with irony. Irony in this case involves finding a subversive, often self-mocking meaning in routine activities. It is a way of coming to terms with, yet undermining, something which one is obliged to do. People can lecture ironically, for example, going through the motions of solemnly exercising a pedagogic function, while quietly sending up their performance, certainly for their own amusement, and sometimes for the amusement of the students as well. One obtains a kind of detached observational stance, which can be pleasurable in itself, and ironic performance is also a way of expressing 'role distance', where an old hand indicates that the job is so well known that it can be performed effortlessly, leaving time and space for additional comment.

According to Hebdige (1988) mods were exponents of 'ironic neatness', a tactic that might be recognized by anyone who has been made to wear a school uniform, involving the mildest exaggeration of dress codes, the jacket that is just too neatly pressed, the shoes obsessively clean. For those in manual labour, a form of applied irony can also be detected, in the mocking exaggerated acceptance of the orders of the foreman or the mission statements of the company, often accompanied with the pursuit of personal goals in the guise of working entirely for the company – de Certeau (1984) has some examples of workers producing their own goods while pretending to be producing the company's, for example. Of course, it would not do to exaggerate these possibilities, since they have to constantly patrol a thin line between leisure and real work, and may involve doing what the bosses required of them all along. The ability to avoid an obtrusive presence of work is highly limited, and, just as with escapes, the reality that surrounds temporary absences remains, waiting to claim us again.

The same kind of argument applies to the risky engagement with commerce that so many leisure activities involve. We buy goods and enjoy them in what might be seen as a private moment, where we put goods to our own immediate leisure uses, but it is difficult to avoid leisure values added by advertising and promotion, and we have to guard against 'seduction strategies', where we are allowed to enjoy ourselves, but also left deliberately dissatisfied, so that we will return to purchase more goods. It is this kind of argument that leads Rojek to pessimistic conclusions overall, for example, in Rojek (1993, 1995) – leisure, especially leisure involving fantasy, offers a utopia that we all know is unrealizable.

We have examined some particular forms of escape that do seem to offer a genuine transforming experience, as in the entry on **ecstasy**. Here, collective activity seems to be required together with a special space and some expert guidance in order to generate enough momentum to leave behind the everyday world. We looked at some examples such as clubbing. One implication of this work is that the state of ecstasy is actually rather difficult to attain. Sometimes, it requires chemical assistance, but even this is not completely reliable. For most clubbers, the mundane everyday world seems remarkably persistent, and affects a great deal of what they actually do, including the close monitoring of other people and themselves, and engaging in a time-consuming and rather anxiety-provoking business of social distantiation. Once again, such activity looks rather work-like; Malbon (1999) tells us of the need to constantly practise skills and competencies, while Thornton (1995) refers to the need to acquire considerable amounts of 'subcultural capital' first if we are to negotiate and locate oneself in a bewildering and constantly changing maze of 'taste cultures'. As a result, isolated and rather rare moments of ecstasy seemed to be on offer, rather than prolonged periods, and a great deal of collective talk among participants afterwards seems to be required in order to 'talk them up' as moments that define the experience, rather than the hard work that goes on before and afterwards.

We also review the work of Csikszentmihalyi (1975) on 'flow' (see **pleasure**), and note that 'flow' can be generated by activity in paid employment as well as in leisure activities such as rock climbing or dancing. Any task that involves the right level of challenge, sufficient to absorb us so that we can forget ourselves, but not too challenging that it produces a sense of anxiety and failure, can generate 'flow'. Some redesign activities have apparently taken place so as to make work itself generate more 'flow' – in a way, that is also what lies behind the plea for suitably 'deep' educational tasks (Entwistle, 2003).

We are left with a complex picture of the relation between work and leisure. The two may be heading towards complete merger, as the dull compulsion of rational work penetrates even a few moments of imaginative escape there are left to us. This pessimism can be found in the works of Adorno (1991) or Ritzer (1999), both of whom urge us not to be taken in by the apparent commitment to leisure of modern societies. For Ritzer, it is really only a rather cynical business of attempting to 're-enchant' a thoroughly invasive and rational process. For Adorno, leisure is chronically likely to be subordinated to work unless the whole issue of work can be examined – in capitalism it has become alienating and its products are produced solely for the indifferent mechanism of the market. Once we can think what else work might become, the problem of leisure alternatives will disappear.

Parker (1983) is often cited but not often read carefully. The theme of work and leisure is worth tracing through the various contributions by Rojek (1989, 1993, 1995), and the recent discussion of Rojek's work by Bramham (2002) can assist. Notes on Adorno's short essay on free time is available on my website (Harris, 2003).

REFERENCES

Adorno T. (1991) 'Free Time', in T. Adorno *The Culture Industry: Selected Essays on Mass Culture* (edited and with an Introduction by J. Bernstein), London: Routledge.

Bramham, P. (2002) 'Rojek, the Sociological Imagination and Leisure', *Leisure Studies*, 21: 221–34.

Csikszentmihalyi, M. (1975) *Beyond Boredom and Anxiety*, San Francisco: Jossey-Bass.

De Certeau, M. (1984) *The Practice of Everyday Life*, Berkeley, CA: University of California Press.

Entwistle, N. (2003) 'Promoting Deep Learning through Teaching and Assessment: Conceptual Frameworks and Educational Contexts' [online] http://www.ed.ac.uk/etl/docs/entwistle2000.pdf

Haraszti, M. (1977) *A Worker in a Worker's State*, London: Pelican Books.

Harris, D. (2003) 'Dave Harris (and Colleagues): Essays, Papers and Courses' [online] http://www.arasite.org/

Hebdige, D. (1988) *Hiding in the Light*, London: Comedia/Routledge.

Hite, S. (1981) *The Hite Report on Male Sexuality*, London: MacDonald.

Malbon, B. (1999) *Clubbing: Dancing, Ecstasy and Vitality*, London: Routledge.

Parker, S. (1983) *Leisure and Work*, London: George Allen and Unwin.

Ritzer, G. (1999) *Enchanting a Disenchanted World: Revolutionizing the Means of Consumption*, Thousand Oaks, CA: Pine Forge Press.

Rojek, C. (ed.) (1989) *Leisure for Leisure*, London: Macmillan.

Rojek, C. (1993) *Ways of Escape*, London: Macmillan.

Rojek, C. (1995) *Decentring Leisure: Rethinking Leisure Theory*, London: Sage.

Stebbins, R. (1982) 'Serious Leisure: A Conceptual Statement', *Pacific Sociological Review*, 25: 251–72.

Thornton, S. (1995) *Club Cultures: Music, Media and Subcultural Capital*, Cambridge: Polity Press.

267

key concepts

> *Young people developed particularly spectacular styles of clothing and musical tastes in post-war Britain, and these were the subject of much social commentary. Early analysis was designed to show they could be read as genuine cultural activities not as deviant, pathological, or incomprehensible.*

> **Section Outline:** *Youth subcultures as symbolic politics, 'upwards', 'downwards' and 'magical' solutions. The work of the CCCS and double articulation. Criticisms: women, the media, 'normal youth', 'taste publics'. Punk as 'surrealism of the streets'. Acid House, rave and moral panics: a political challenge to Thatcherism?*

There had long been a tendency for young people to associate together in public spaces and adopt distinctive styles of clothing, their own idiomatic speech, and their own ways of life, sometimes criminal ones. However, there seemed to be a new and more widespread set of distinctive youth cultures emerging in Britain in the 1960s. The point of discussing them was to inquire about why young people engage in these activities and in particular, what they mean to them. In answering these questions, early analysts deployed a mixture of **semiotics** and marxist analysis, a feature of **gramscian** work, and developed this into a research and publication programme at the Centre for Contemporary Cultural Studies (CCCS) at the University of Birmingham in the UK.

Cohen (1972) had suggested initially that forming youth cultures could be seen as a reaction to social pressures and social problems. These problems were provided by social change and its impact upon the traditional working-class communities, including some in the East End of London, which were causing cultural dislocation to young people. Cohen suggested that their reaction might be to respond with a kind of cultural politics, the creation of a cultural alternative to the rapidly declining traditional communities. The alternatives could express different sorts of symbolic reaction to change: 'downward' options would feature an attempt to nostalgically recreate the past in cultural terms (bikers and skinheads fitted well here), and to celebrate the values and ways of life that were under threat; 'upward' options would look forward to some future social life of stability where all the old differences and problems were magically left behind in some new cultural grouping (mods and clubbers). Cohen used what looked like **functionalist** terminology to explain this reaction, with cultural solutions compensating for social change. He specifically noted the political impotence of such cultural adaptations, which offered only a 'magical' solution to real problems of social change and powerlessness.

Nevertheless, this provided a kind of breakthrough in understanding these activities, which had genuinely puzzled and alarmed cultural commentators, politicians and the police. Teddy boys, for example, seemed to be present in every city centre, in dance halls, in coffee bars and on the streets, wherever young people gathered in the 1950s. They had distinctive clothing, hairstyles, and shoes, and they were prone to fighting anyone who attempted to mock them. In the case of mods and rockers, there were several British seaside resorts which experienced fighting on the streets and beaches during public holidays in the 1960s. Cohen thinks that the press actually played a part here in listing and polarizing the differences between the two groups – mods preferred to ride the new Italian scooters instead of British motorbikes, and wore smart casual clothing (actually several variants of the mod look existed) instead of the greasy leathers and denims associated with rockers. Again, the differences seemed important enough to the participants to result in violent confrontation. Skinheads too became seen as a symbol of violent youth, with their distinctively short hair, industrial clothing, distinctive shirts and large boots ('bovver boots' – the term 'bovver' representing the Cockney pronunciation of 'bother', a euphemism for fighting). The classic location to find skinheads, apart from streets, cafés and dance halls, was the football ground, and they became associated with the increase in, and substantial public worry about, violence at football matches.

If cultural analysis did not help to control these groups, at least it offered an understanding for their existence, cohesion, and activities. Early work was done by Willis (1978) who attempted to do an **ethnographic** analysis of bikers and hippies in particular. Bikers, for example, celebrated their own skill and technical know-how in maintaining their British bikes (which were under threat from the Japanese motorcycle industry), and adopted a romantic version of themselves as outlaws, urban cowboys or pirates.

An influential collection of essays appeared to advance the new kinds

269

of cultural analysis, this time with a definite marxist inflection (Hall and Jefferson, 1976). I have discussed the actual analyses involved in Harris (1992), and there is an excellent summary in Brake (1985). Young people were seen as acting out the social tensions in their lives and forming cultural solutions to them, in the very way they dressed and behaved. The Introduction to that collection also represents one of the first attempts to theorize systematically, specifically to attempt to apply versions of marxist theory to the phenomenon of youth culture.

It is easy to argue, for example, that it was working-class youths (in fact, mostly male youths) who tended to adopt the more spectacular kinds of street culture, which led to attempts to explain their reaction in class terms as a result of powerlessness, alienation, or reification. Some of the cultural resources used were rooted in a working-class tradition of resistance to bourgeois values and power, involving stressing masculinity, mocking authority, and settling arguments with physical not symbolic violence. It was clear that there was a definite boundary associated with age as well, which led to the famous formulation of the 'double articulation' – youth subcultures offered a version of the working-class 'parent culture' specifically adapted for their own circumstances. The more youthful influences could be seen in the adoption of those values that rejected those of their parents, especially in terms of musical taste, or clothing. It is this partial adaptation to the values of mainstream working-class culture that led to these activities being seen as a result of a 'subculture', a rather controversial term that had been used in bourgeois sociological analyses of crime and deviance (see Downes, 1966).

Almost as soon as it was achieving some theoretical solidity, the CCCS analysis came under attack. Hints of the attack are found in the Hall and Jefferson (1976) collection. Hebdige, for example, was already beginning to note a certain relationship to styles associated with 'the white negro' in his analysis of mods, and this was to emerge into a full-blown insistence on the importance of 'race' as well as age and class, as we illustrate in the entry on **'race' and leisure**. McRobbie too was advancing a feminist critique that was to swell into a full-blown alternative, that came to reject not only the term 'subculture' (McRobbie, in Bennett et al., 1982), but to produce an alternative feminist analysis that also raised serious questions about the dominant **gramscian** theoretical framework that was becoming institutionalized at Birmingham (Women's Study Group, 1978). Other critiques were emerging too: Hebdige (1979) again raised serious doubts about the apparent mechanism at the heart of the formation of youth subcultures, their perception of their powerlessness and their sense of having lost a cultural tradition. As he points out, this actually presupposes considerable sociological analysis on the part of rebellious youth, and it is far more likely that they will have gained these ideas from the media.

Certainly, those themes are prominent in a number of 'British New Wave' films of the period, and they also came to feature in some popular soap operas such as *Coronation Street*. It is also likely that popular media were helping positively to form youth styles, and this leads Hebdige to reject a rather vague mechanism called 'homology'. This had been used to explain the cultural connections between, say, the black leather jackets of 1960s' bikers, and the leather jackets of London stevedores of an earlier generation: the theory was that each group was drawn to the same sort of symbolic clothing as a clear analogical expression of their views of themselves as tough and manly (like the material itself). Media programmes offered a clearer mechanism; they simply consolidated the style by depicting bikers wearing black leather jackets, and they also helped to purify the look of mods as well, via emerging youth style programmes about pop music and clothes.

The power of the media to engage with youth leisure, especially in the production of music is developed by Thornton (1995) as well, in her study of club culture. Thornton points to the creation of short-lived musical 'taste cultures' as influential in the formation of more recent cultural styles among youth, and analyses both mass and local media (including fanzines and flyers). Thornton suggests that these media supply the detailed knowledge and the defining stereotypes (especially of 'the mainstream') that provide the 'subcultural capital' that is such a feature of club life: this subcultural capital enables the fine distinctions to be drawn between groups maintaining boundaries and differences among themselves.

Classic gramscian analysis rapidly seemed to become dated as well. Spectacular youth subcultures, whose members thought membership important enough to fight those members of rival groups, seemed to disappear in favour of much looser collections and associations of young people based around musical styles particularly. 'Taste publics' are different from and now far more important than social classes and 'their' subcultures (see Rojek, 2000, for some additional implications). As a final irony, the very term 'subculture' has become a marketing device, says Thornton (1995), used to glamorize taste publics with an aura of rebellion and resistance.

Punk is thought to have been crucial in the transition. It could still be possible to analyse punk as a reaction to the rise in youth unemployment of the late 1970s, and traces of resistance to rejection might be found in the 'trash aesthetics' of wearing plastic bin-liners and torn clothes. However, punk had another creative mechanism at work as well, provided by well-educated youth, in the form of art students and suburban school students. Students deliberately incorporated artistic techniques associated with avant-garde movements, according to Hebdige (1988), acting as a 'surrealism of the streets'. Punk also rapidly evolved a number of looks, almost as quickly as popular commentary could classify them, and partly from a desire to keep ahead of such classifications. Finally, punk too came to an end, partly, according to Hebdige, because real youth politics emerged as more important, as demonstrated in the urban riots of the 1980s.

Punk was also commercialized, and a number of commercial organizations realized the potential of expanding their youth markets for clothes and music (and for drugs as well, if we include illegal organizations supplying goods for illegal leisure). Given the relentless search for novelty in commercial organizations, and their ability to market to niches, it is not surprising that youth subcultures as a way of life were replaced by a variety of options which rapidly changed. Indeed, looking back, critics began to suggest that tightly organized subcultures, demanding permanent allegiance and commitment from members were only ever the preserve of a minority. 'Normal youth' might occasionally indulge in futuristic clubbing and drug-taking at weekends, but returned to the constraints of work on Monday morning (as they do now – see the entry on **illegal leisure**). Indeed, it is likely that most youth did not even bother to flirt with the spectacular youth subcultures that they saw on the streets, or, more likely on the television screen.

With the emergence of more free-floating cultures, and the growth of leisure industries designed to manipulate them, which we discuss in the entry on **postmodernism**, youth styles became more autonomous, quite capable of generating their own momentum, using the common **semiotic** principles of elaboration, inversion and contrast. Hebdige (1988) suggests as much for punk, whose aggressive musical amateurism was a rebuke to the social isolation and posturing of earlier progressive rock with its guitar virtuosi stars, or whose female participants openly mocked and flaunted male obsessions with spectacular fetish lingerie by wearing it on the outside. I am told by my students that there simply is no dominant youth style these days, that organized 'looks' come and go, and fashions run their course (at the time of writing, many girls seem to wear bootleg cut trousers and cropped tops), but these are not symbolic forms of protest, not inducing specifically political opposition to parental values, and not a response to a declining community. They may function as a sign of adulthood and independence, as a celebration of youth, and as a distancing device, but there is no need to deploy any kind of marxist analysis to understand those. The activity of 'clubbing' also offers a serious challenge to gramscian analysis, especially in terms of the relevance of concepts like subculture; we discuss some of the work in more detail in the entry on **ecstasy**.

However, Hill's (2002) account of Acid House has a self-conscious relationship to the early CCCS work on subcultures and gramscian analysis generally. For example, he rephrases the work by Hall and Jacques (1983) on Thatcherism as a hegemonic project, articulating together a number of political themes in order to gain power, but also pursuing a definite adversarial politics, involving confrontations with various examples of 'the enemy within'. The initially hostile reaction to Acid House indicated this process quite clearly, and echoes the tradition of governments acting against disorderly forms of popular culture that we have discussed as 'rational recreation' (see **social class**). Acid House produced another characteristic reaction, the 'moral panic', involving hostile press campaigns, and an attempt to connect the practice of raving with general themes about youth degeneracy, overt sexuality, victimization of girls, and drug-taking (see also Redhead, in Redhead, 1993). However, we still encounter problems in applying the term 'subculture' to Acid House. Hill points out that participants were drawn from a range of social classes, and that they also included embryonic entrepreneurs, organizing parties and making money in an impeccable Thatcherite spirit. In the end, though, Hill decides that the ability of Acid House to generate a moral panic claims it for gramscian analysis via a more '"basic" sense that echoes earlier definitions' (2002: 91), but it is also one that retreats quite a way from gramscian politics.

The things about Acid House that upset the authorities can be categorized under several headings, each with considerable symbolic and political importance in the widest sense. The first one is the 'noise that it produced' (ibid.: 92). Excessive noise was a major reason for taking police action, but there is a long history of using noise to express social dissent, and it was this that 'did not fit with' (ibid.: 93) the Thatcherite hegemonic project. The music itself threatened social order, with its excitement and its promised '*jouissance*, an extreme experience of pleasure that induces a loss of self' (ibid.: 93) (see **pleasures**). Acid House also seem to threaten values associated with the English countryside, with its associated tranquillity and respectability; illegal parties seemed like an invasion, evoking other Thatcherite fears about urban dwellers taking over the countryside. There were also traditional 'fears of the mob' (ibid.: 96) and

273

its inherent threat to law and order, especially if the participants were consuming drink and illegal drugs. Ravers were seen as a direct challenge to police authority, and the police responded with some aggression. Again, one strand in Thatcherism concerned social discipline and order, and so raving offered a particular threat. Considerable efforts ensued to mobilize the police, to pass enabling Acts through Parliament, and to finance large-scale policing. Hill believes that the unusually large size of the reaction indicates the particular combinations of perceived threat represented by Acid House specifically, in comparison with other youth subcultures. Equally unusual was the way in which advocates of Acid House also attempted to make a political case themselves by forming a pressure group to oppose authoritarian legislation; no merely 'magical' solutions for them.

The subculture challenged bureaucratic authority and modern forms of regulation (including proposed new forms to license parties, to ensure that they met safety regulations, and so on). Safety and hygiene problems, and the traffic congestion caused, were highlighted in the political struggle. The authoritarian state gained more practice in regulating large crowds as a result: 'A revealing parallel has been drawn between the ways the police acted to limit the mobility of participants in acid house and restrictions placed upon the movements of pickets in the 1984 miners' strike' (ibid.: 102). Again, this is a classic gramscian theme on the emergence of authoritarianism in the British State, which is seen as being justified by moral panics about crime, while really being about preparation to defeat industrial and political opposition (see Hall et al., 1978).

274

FURTHER READING

Hebdige (1979, 1988) is the classic work here. McRobbie, in Bennett et al. (1982), is an excellent demonstration of the power of feminist analysis as well (and we explore her subsequent work on female youth in the entry on **gender**). Thornton (1995) has a good critique of the concept of 'subculture' and an analysis of some recent 'taste cultures'. Punk continues to attract adherents and there is a good online database on Worldwide Punk (2003), while Fast'n'Bulbous (2003) offers quite a different history of punk from the one in British accounts (arguing it was an American phenomenon, for example).

REFERENCES

Bennett, T., Boyd-Bowman, S., Mercer, C. and Woollacott, J. (eds) (1982) *Popular Television and Film*, London: BFI Publishing in association with the Open University Press.

Brake, M. (1985) *Comparative Youth Cultures*, London: Routledge and Kegan Paul.

Cohen, P. (1972) *Working Class Cultures in East London*, Working Papers in Cultural Studies No. 2, Birmingham: University of Birmingham.

Downes, D. (1966) *The Delinquent Solution: A Study in Subcultural Theory*, London: Routledge.

Fast'n'Bulbous (2003) [online] http://www.fastnbulbous.com/punk.htm

Hall, S. and Jacques, M. (eds) (1983) *The Politics of Thatcherism*, London: Lawrence and Wishart, and *Marxism Today*.

Hall, S. and Jefferson, T. (eds) (1976) *Resistance Through Rituals*, London: Hutchinson.

Hall, S. Critcher, C., Jefferson, T., Clarke, J. and Roberts, B. (1978) *Policing the Crisis: Mugging, the State, and Law and Order*, London: Macmillan.

Harris, D. (1992) *From Class Struggle to the Politics of Pleasure: The Effects of Gramscianism on Cultural Studies*, London: Routledge.

Hebdige, D. (1979) *Subcultures: The Meaning of Style*, London: Methuen and Co.

Hebdige, D. (1988) *Hiding in the Light*, London: Comedia/Routledge.

Hill, A. (2002) 'Acid House and Thatcherism: Noise, the Mob and the English Countryside', *British Journal of Sociology*, 53 (1): 89–105.

Redhead, S. (ed.) (1993) *Rave Off: Politics and Deviance in Contemporary Youth Culture*, Aldershot: Avebury Press.

Rojek, C. (2000) *Leisure and Culture*, Basingstoke: Macmillan.

Thornton, S. (1995) *Club Cultures: Music, Media and Subcultural Capital*, Cambridge: Polity Press.

Willis, P. (1978) *Profane Cultures*, London: Routledge and Kegan Paul.

Women's Study Group (1978) *Women Take Issue*, London: Hutchinson.

Worldwide Punk (2003) [online] http://www.worldwidepunk.com/

275